BLACK MIGRATION
AND POVERTY
Boston 1865–1900

This is a volume in

STUDIES IN SOCIAL DISCONTINUITY

A complete list of titles in this series appears at the end of this volume.

BLACK MIGRATION AND POVERTY

Boston 1865–1900

ELIZABETH HAFKIN PLECK

Center for Research on Women
Wellesley College
Wellesley, Massachusetts

ACADEMIC PRESS

A Subsidiary of Harcourt Brace Jovanovich, Publishers

New York   London   Toronto   Sydney   San Francisco

ACADEMIC PRESS, INC.
111 Fifth Avenue, New York, New York 10003

United Kingdom Edition published by
ACADEMIC PRESS, INC. (LONDON) LTD.
24/28 Oval Road, London NW1 7DX

Library of Congress Cataloging in Publication Data

Pleck, Elizabeth Hafkin.
    Black migration and poverty in Boston, 1865–1900.

    (Studies in social discontinuity)
    Bibliography: p.
    1. Afro–Americans––Massachusetts––Boston––Economic
conditions.   2. Afro–Americans––Massachusetts–Boston––
Social conditions.   3. Boston––Economic conditions.
4. Boston––Social conditions.   I. Title. II. Series.
F73.9.N4P55   301.45'19'6073074461   79–21063
ISBN 0–12–558650–7

PRINTED IN THE UNITED STATES OF AMERICA

79 80 81 82   9 8 7 6 5 4 3 2 1

TO MY MOTHER AND FATHER

Leah and Fred Hafkin

CONTENTS

LIST OF TABLES
AND ILLUSTRATIONS

TABLES

MAPS

ILLUSTRATIONS

PREFACE

In the quest for material success, the place where millions of farmers and former peasants shed the burdens of past heritage and began the long climb into the middle class was the city. Black migrants to northern cities are the most telling exception to this general principle; their urban history has taken a different road than the acculturation accompanied by economic advance among European immigrants. Venturing back to the time when both groups were newcomers to one northern city allows us to witness the driving of the initial socioeconomic wedge between them, the beginnings of a long-term process whose effects are still with us today. In this book, my dual aim has been to contrast racial and immigrant poverty in late nineteenth-century Boston and to examine the effects of black poverty, along with racial discrimination and city living, on black community and family life.

This book begins with the end of the Civil War, as the first group of ex-slaves began to arrive in Boston, and, through the examination of aggregate data, undertakes to highlight 35 years of urban history marked by slight economic deterioration for black Bostonians, amid urban economic growth and amelioration of the economic misery that had once been the almost universal plight of Boston's European immigrants. The city's reputation as a community providing virtually full civil rights to blacks early in the century made it suitable as one of the best possible cases to study.

Although this book is a case study of a particular and unique black community, it has implications beyond its immediate range. It permits a close examination of the impact of urbanization on blacks, and precisely because it is a case study, it allows us to revise existing generalizations. Black Boston was a small part of a major northern city and its inhabitants were in many ways better off than blacks elsewhere. No black community is exactly identical to the next; the history, population mix, and social conditions in Boston will always be unique. But the appearance of virtually similar conditions in city after city suggests the outlines of a far more general process of black urbanization.

As a selective history more concerned with long-term trends and themes than with specific events, I concentrate on ordinary experience and behavior. I devote special attention to family life, a universal human institution which is also the specific tool of a culture intent on transmitting distinctive value and opportunities from one generation to another. In this inquiry into the lives of otherwise anonymous black Bostonians who left behind no written records, I find group experience, far from unified, to be divided internally between a first post-Emancipation generation of blacks who moved directly from the South to the North and those free blacks already situated in the North. These two groups are systematically compared in an attempt to separate three confounding experiences in black history: slavery, migration to the North, and city life. I conclude that in black Boston the result of urban life was the mutual and continuing influences of racial barriers in employment, poverty, and acculturation to mainstream values. Racial discrimination in jobs helped confine black workers to jobs at low pay, and poverty-level wages placed added burdens on health, childbearing, and married life. The slave culture of black Boston's migrants from the South sheltered them from the full impact of bitterness that fell with special force on free-born blacks, whose middle-class values were ill suited to their lower-class incomes.

This case study does more than substantiate once again the generalization that racial discrimination is a major source of black poverty, which in turn shapes black community and family life. Discrimination left at its most general level covers a wide range of practices and beliefs, which it has been my goal to make far more specific and concrete. In northern cities a century ago, racial discrimination was, above all else, a question of barriers in jobs, rather than in housing or elsewhere, and even more specifically, a question of two distinct and separate barriers that hamstrung black abilities to secure and retain better-paying jobs. This conclusion suggests that the major theme in black urban history—certainly in this period of history—was less the formation of a ghetto than the formation of a racially divided labor market.

ACKNOWLEDGMENTS

I have had the benefit of the criticism and suggestions of John P. Demos, who oversaw this project in its initial stage as a dissertation. In completing the dissertation I received aid from the National Science Foundation, the Ford Foundation Ethnic Studies Program, and the Irving and Rose Crown Fellowship program at Brandeis University. A Rackham Faculty Fellowship from the University of Michigan generously granted me funds for additional research assistance, which was carried out by Elizabeth Wolf, who spent a summer in Washington, D.C. coding the information on black Bostonians to be found in the manuscript census schedules for 1900.

I am grateful to Leo and Helen Flaherty for their hospitality during the several months of my research at the Massachusetts State Archives, and to Herbert Kloza who granted permission to copy information from the vital records of Massachusetts. Herbert Gutman, whose own work taught me the value of examining neglected sources in new ways, drew my attention to the usefulness of the Civil War pension records; Theodore Hershberg kindly allowed me to make use of his unpublished data on Philadelphia blacks. Margaret Hay typed the final version of the manuscript. Friends and colleagues who have read and criticized earlier drafts of this book include Henry Binford, Nancy Cott, Stanley Engerman, Estelle Freedman, Ruth Gladstone, Peter Knights, James Horton, Lynn Hunt, Douglas Jones, Allan Kulikoff, Phyllis Vine, and Virginia Yans-McLaughlin. I remain most indebted to Joseph H. Pleck, a demanding and honest reader of my work.

Three friends and mentors who have read several drafts of the manuscript deserve my most profound thanks for offering me the example of their own high standards and committed scholarship. Louise Tilly gently urged me to reconsider some of my most cherished assumptions, in a manner that has enabled me to improve on the final product. Many of the conclusions of this study were anticipated more than a decade ago in a brief but exceedingly insightful essay by Charles Tilly, "Race and Migration to the American City." He has helped me immeasurably in clarifying and refining my arguments, and in expanding the scope of my undertaking. Stephan Thernstrom, who shares my interest in the social history of Boston, encouraged me in this project from my first year in graduate school to the final stages of preparation of this manuscript. His scholarship paved the way for my work and for that of many others, and his teaching steered my efforts in the most useful directions but still allowed me to find my own way.

CHAPTER I

INTRODUCTION

The problem of work, the problem of poverty, is today the central, baffling problem of the Northern negro.

W.E.B. DuBois, *The Black North in 1901*

Within the last 100 years former black sharecroppers and tenant farmers from the rural South have come to dwell in the major metropolitan centers of the North and West. The Black Belt used to denote a band of cotton-growing counties stretched across the middle of Alabama; by the early twentieth century it had come to mean solid blocks of South Side tenements close to Chicago's lakefront. At the end of the Civil War, ex-slave men and women drifted into southern cities, taking jobs as laborers and maids, but even as late as 1910, nine out of ten blacks still lived in the rural South. Then lynchings, followed at the turn of the century by floods and the boll weevil, began the push out of the South, which was later accompanied by the pull from the North, the recruiting of blacks for wartime industry. So great was this revolution in residence that hundreds of thousands no longer knew how to pick cotton or hunt possum but knew everything about how to get water from a fire hydrant on a hot, summer's night, or how to sneak into a movie theater without paying. With the shortage of labor in northern and midwestern cities as World War I approached, the Great Migration began (and some metropolises exploded soon thereafter, as southern migrants, intent on getting jobs and housing, collided with white competitors). The population increases in Gary, East St. Louis, Detroit, Pittsburgh, and Chicago in these years made new cities out of old; why a mud flat of shanties could be called Paradise Valley was a mystery known only to a black from Alabama making $5 a day in a factory turning out the Model T. After World War I, the urban black population grew so vast, and so ghettoized, that virtual all-black cities arose with their own businesses, professionals, and community institutions. Then the same process of wrenching and resettling, competition, and getting by recurred during World War II, as tens of thousands of potential workers climbed into their old jalopies and headed for Oakland, Los Angeles, Seattle, and other points North and West. Even after the war's end, the typical graduation present for a Mississippi black youth was a Greyhound bus ticket to Chicago. As the mechanical

---

Chapter opening photo
African Meeting House on Smith Court in the West End, c. 1890. (Courtesy of the Society for the Preservation of New England Antiquities.)

cotton reaper made handpicking redundant by the 1950s, blacks were once again pushed out, so that the black population of the rural South came to include only the old, the young, and those on a temporary visit from Cleveland or Newark.

A unique cultural and institutional life arose in these new black cities. A manner of dress and a way of walking and talking were identified with the metropolis; jazz was born in New Orleans and matured in New York City. The classic blues of the 1920s were a Chicago invention designed to sound like plantation work songs. Marcus Garvey, Father Divine, and Malcolm X appealed to the hearts of the masses, just as Richard Wright and W.E.B. DuBois addressed themselves to their minds. William Dawson channeled the votes of South Side Chicago blacks into a solid political bloc (appropriately enough for Chicago, called a submachine). Still, racial prejudice and poverty persisted and, even after a decade of unprecedented social struggle, black median income in 1975 stood at just 64% of white.

This book is about the impact of the city and racial poverty on Boston black community and family life between the Civil War and the turn of the century. It examines three fundamental features of black urban life: racial barriers in employment, poverty, and acculturation. It seeks to understand how racism contributed to black poverty, and how poverty was perpetuated. It then proceeds to show how poverty and the city shaped community norms and family life. The study concludes that, in the short run, the move from the South to the North strengthened traditional slave folkways, but that in the long run residence in the city gave blacks access to the American dream without the economic progress that was supposed to go with it. The familiar immigrant story of acculturation, then, can be found here without the familiar element of economic advance, and it was this discrepancy between aspirations and incomes that so often shaped black personal relationships and family life.

Themes such as these appear often in sociological writing about urban blacks, but they have been given less prominence in historical work. A single fact of black urbanization, the emergence of the ghetto, has attracted most of the attention. Of all America's ethnic and racial groups, blacks are today the most residentially segregated. Yet the ghetto as we know it is largely a twentieth-century phenomenon. Between 1890 and 1920, whites in many northern cities began to evacuate the urban core, so that more and more black enclaves were consolidated into black-only areas of residence. Excellent historical studies describe the origins of the black South Side, Hough, and Harlem, but most other aspects of black urban life have been seen only in relation to the process of ghettoization.[1] Moreover, the ghetto has been assumed to have been as much a disadvantage in the past as it is today. Yet many of the current hardships associated with ghetto residence now were missing a hundred years ago. Residence far from suburban employers is a relatively recent problem: In the nineteenth century, northern city blacks lived near the docks and warehouses, close to the central business district, and within walking distance of hundreds of shops, factories, and offices.

By and large, most of the research about black poverty and urbanization has been carried out by sociologists, anthropologists, and economists. In this study I have not sought to match the mathematical precision of economists' analyses of black poverty; instead, I have deliberately kept the numerical analysis simple and straightforward so as to be comprehensible to the average reader. Despite my intent to document the everyday life of the black poor a century ago, the written records I have used can never approach the detail to be found in current on-the-scene accounts. But analyses of black poverty from these disciplines have informed this work, and my hope is that an inquiry into the history of a single Gilded Age black community will help contrast urban black poverty in the past with poverty in the present.

Without too much oversimplification, it can be said that most studies about black urbanization and poverty have been written from one of two perspectives, depending on the conclusions reached about the long-run impact of the city. They form a logical succession, and the second refutes the first. In the first perspective, associated especially with the works of E. Franklin Frazier, Daniel Moynihan, Nathan Glazer, Oscar Handlin, and Edward Banfield, the city is seen as the solution to the problems of racial poverty and discrimination brought to it from elsewhere.[2] The studies written from this perspec-

1. Studies fundamentally concerned with the development of the urban ghetto include St. Clair Drake and Horace Cayton, *Black Metropolis* (New York, 1945); Karl E. Taeuber and Alma F. Taeuber, *Negroes in Cities: Residential Segregation and Neighborhood Change* (New York, 1969); Gilbert Osofsky, *Harlem: The Making of a Ghetto* (New York, 1971); Allan Spear, *Black Chicago: The Making of a Ghetto* (Chicago, 1967); Kenneth L. Kusmer, *A Ghetto Takes Shape: Black Cleveland, 1870–1930* (Urbana, 1976); Thomas J. Philpott, *The Slum and the Ghetto: Neighborhood Deterioration and Middle-Class Reform, Chicago 1880–1930* (New York, 1978); John H. Bracey, Jr., August Meier, and Elliott Rudwick, eds., *The Rise of the Ghetto* (Belmont, California, 1970); Lawrence B. De Graaf, "The City of Black Angels: Emergence of the Los Angeles Ghetto, 1890–1930," *Pacific Historical Review*, v. 39 (August 1970), pp. 328–350. Richard Ballou has almost completed a dissertation on the history of the Boston ghetto, 1900–1970, at the University of Michigan.

2. E. Franklin Frazier, *The Negro Family in the United States* (Chicago, 1939);

tive concern not only the effects of urbanization but also the effects of slavery and migration to the northern city. From this point of view, blacks are faced with a series of handicaps: rural origin, slavery, migration, and the initial shock of urban life, all of which are eventually overcome after a generation or more of city residence. In this line of thought, slavery was the first and most fundamental blow to black life because it destroyed most of West African culture and offered so little to replace it: Most slaves never learned to handle money, manage their own affairs, acquire skills, or sign contracts. Probably the most detrimental effect of slavery, it is claimed, was that family life was destroyed, and the slave father had so little power in his own home. During Reconstruction ex-slaves tried to rebuild their personal lives, but their success was brief, because, after they moved to the northern city, they were once again overwhelmed: by alienation, family breakdown, and a host of social problems that had been missing from their peasant life in the rural South. All was not bleak, however, because, after a generation or two of residence in the North, the children of migrants underwent a "rebirth": They advanced economically and reconstituted family life along middle class lines.

The role of the city, then, is to solve the problem of racial poverty brought to it from outside. Since blacks are recent arrivals in the northern city, their urban history has just begun, and it may take them as much as three generations to rise. Eventually, however, the racial gap between blacks and whites will be closed, and we will see the familiar trajectory of upward mobility, suburban resettlement, and progressive acculturation, so much a part of the immigrant encounter with the city. In this analogy with immigrant economic mobility, the problem for blacks is not so much discrimination as recency of arrival in the northern city. Edward Banfield writes, "Today the Negro's main disadvantage is . . . that he is the most recent unskilled, and hence relatively low-income migrant to reach the city from a backward rural area."[3]

Edward Banfield, *The Unheavenly City Revisited* (Boston, 1974); Daniel P. Moynihan and Nathan Glazer, *Beyond the Melting Pot: The Negroes, Puerto Ricans, Jews, Italians, and Irish of New York City* (Cambridge, 1963); Oscar Handlin, *The Uprooted* (Boston, 1951); Office of Policy Planning and Research, U.S. Department of Labor, *The Negro Family: The Case for National Action* (Washington, D.C., 1965); Clyde V. Kiser, *Sea Island to City: A Study in Harlem and Other Urban Centers* (New York, 1932; New York, 1969); Joseph J. Persky, "The North's Stake in Southern Rural Poverty," in Joseph J. Persky, ed., *Rural Poverty in the United States* (Washington, D.C., 1967), pp. 288–308.

3. Banfield, *Unheavenly City*, p. 78. The analogy can also be found in Oscar Handlin, *The Newcomers: Negroes and Puerto Ricans in a Changing Metropolis* (Cambridge, 1959); Nathan Glazer, "Blacks and Ethnic Groups: The Difference and the Political Difference It Makes," *Social Problems*, v. 8, No. 4 (Spring 1971), pp. 441–461;

In the last 15 years a substantial group of scholars have offered another perspective, which differs in almost every respect in its view of slavery, migration, and city residence. In this new research, slaves are seen as more purposeful and less the pawns of outside forces. They make a creative synthesis of West African culture and white influences in their religious, cultural, and family life, and along the way they find a few economic skills and the desire for more. During Reconstruction they try to realize the gains denied them as slaves, but face a series of racial barriers and white-sheeted terrorism which helps to confine them to debt peonage in the rural South. No longer the great uprooting, the move to the city is seen more often as an extension of the old world to the new, where traditional customs are preserved and even strengthened in the urban environment. City residence, rather than the one ray of hope in an otherwise dreary sequence of depredations, comes to be seen as the major detriment that rural birth or slavery was once considered to be.[4]

Irving Kristol, "The Negro Today Is Like the Immigrant of Yesterday," *New York Times Sunday Magazine* (September 11, 1966), pp. 50–124; Stephan Thernstrom, "Up from Slavery," *Perspectives in American History*, v. 1 (1967), pp. 434–440. The viewpoint is implicit as well in Oscar Handlin, *Boston's Immigrants, 1790–1880: A Study in Acculturation* (Cambridge, 1959).

    4. Eugene D. Genovese, *Roll, Jordan, Roll: The World the Slaves Made* (New York, 1974); Herbert G. Gutman, *The Black Family in Slavery and Freedom, 1750–1925* (New York, 1976); Robert William Fogel and Stanley L. Engerman, *Time on the Cross: The Economics of American Negro Slavery* (Boston, 1974); Lawrence W. Levine, *Black Culture and Black Consciousness: Afro-American Folk Thought from Slavery to Freedom* (New York, 1977); Josef J. Barton, *Peasants and Strangers: Italians, Rumanians, and Slovaks in an American City, 1890–1950* (Cambridge, 1975); Michael Anderson, *Family Structure in Nineteenth Century Lancashire* (London, 1971); Rudolph J. Vecoli, "Contadini in Chicago: A Critique of the Uprooted," *Journal of American History*, v. 51 (December 1964), pp. 404–417; Virginia Yans-McLaughlin, *Family and Community: Italian Immigrants in Buffalo, 1880–1930* (Ithaca, 1977); John S. MacDonald and Beatrice D. MacDonald, "Chain Migration, Ethnic Neighborhood Formation and Social Networks," *The Millbank Memorial Fund Quarterly*, v. XLII, No. 1 (January 1964), pp. 82–97; Claudia Dale Goldin, "Female Labor Force Participation: The Origin of Black and White Differences, 1870 and 1880," *Journal of Economic History*, v. XXXVII, No. 1 (March 1977), pp. 87–112; John Bodnar, "Immigration and Modernization: The Case of Slavic Peasants in Industrial America," *Journal of Social History*, v. 10, No. 1 (Fall 1976), pp. 44–71; Tamara K. Hareven, "The Laborers of Manchester, New Hampshire, 1912–1922: The Role of the Family and Ethnicity in Adjustment to Industrial Life," *Labor History*, v. 16 (1975), pp. 249–265; Elizabeth H. Pleck, "The Two-Parent Household: Black Family Structure in Late Nineteenth Century Boston," *Journal of Social History*, v. 6, No. 2 (Fall 1972), pp. 1–31; Elizabeth H. Pleck, "A Mother's Wages: Income Earning among Married Italian and Black Women, 1896–1911," in Michael Gordon, ed., *The American Family in Socio-Historical Perspective* (New York, 1978), pp. 490–510; Carol Groneman, " 'She Earns as a Child; She Pays as a Man': Women

In the vast quantity of new scholarship that belongs within this second perspective, one piece of research deserves special attention because it forms the necessary foundation for what is to follow. One of the cornerstones of the older, constructive-city point of view was the idea that, after a generation or two of city residence, blacks would move up as the immigrants before them had done. This analogy, as it is usually stated, depends on comparing the black situation today to that of immigrants a century ago ("blacks today are like the immigrants of yesterday," wrote Irving Kristol[5]). Stephan Thernstrom and I argued that the late nineteenth century was an opportune period in which to test the validity of this analogy because many of the contemporary disadvantages of urban blacks—distance from jobs in the suburbs, inferior educational opportunities, union seniority rules, and diminished demand for unskilled labor—were almost totally absent a century ago.[6] Using occupational information drawn from the federal manuscript census schedules of 1880, we compared the occupational status of blacks and Irish in Boston, divided according to generations of northern residence. We found that black Southerners were far more concentrated in menial jobs than Irish immigrants and that, far from diminishing with increased residence in the city, the racial gap in occupational status only widened in the second generation. Blacks born in the North were still largely working in menial jobs, unlike their Irish counterparts; most of the American-born sons of Irish immigrants were employed in skilled trades, clerical jobs, or factory work. We concluded that black economic progress

Workers in a Mid-Nineteenth Century New York City Community," in Milton Cantor and Bruce Laurie, eds., *Class, Sex, and the Woman Worker* (Westport, Connecticut, 1977), pp. 83–101; Thomas Kessner, *The Golden Door* (New York, 1977); John Briggs, *An Italian Passage* (New Haven, 1978); Kathleen Neils Conzens, *Immigrant Milwaukee, Accommodation and Community in a Frontier City* (Cambridge, 1976); Donna R. Gabaccia, "Houses and People: Sicilian Migrants in Sicily and New York, 1890–1930," unpublished Ph.D. dissertation, University of Michigan, 1978.

5. I. Kristol, "The Negro Today Is Like the Immigrant of Yesterday," *New York Times Sunday Magazine* (September 11, 1966), pp. 50–124.

6. Among the many refutations of the "immigrant analogy," the most useful are Otto Kerner *et al.*, *Report of the National Advisory Commission on Civil Disorders* (New York, 1968), pp. 278–282; Sam Bass Warner, Jr., and Colin Burke, "Cultural Change and the Ghetto," *Journal of Contemporary History*, v. IV, No. 4 (October 1969), pp. 173–188; Allan H. Spear, *Black Chicago*, pp. 223–229; Stanley Lieberson, *Ethnic Patterns in American Cities* (Glencoe, Illinois, 1963); and Theodore Hershberg, Alan N. Burstein, Eugene P. Ericksen, Stephanie Greenberg, and William L. Yancey, "A Tale of Three Cities: Blacks and Immigrants in Philadelphia: 1850–1880, 1930, and 1970," *Annals of the American Academy of Political and Social Science*, v. 441 (January 1979), pp. 55–81.

did not fit the model of even the most limited example of nineteenth century immigrant advance, that of Irish Bostonians.[7]

Why not? Dozens of difficulties in city life have been cited as the sources of racial inequality: dead-end jobs, inferior schools, ghetto residence, broken families, the multifaceted forms of racial discrimination. Arguments by analogy are often made—that urban blacks are similar to a pariah caste (like the untouchables of India) or a colonized group dependent on an imperial power.[8] Argument by analogy is usually stronger on emotion than logic, because it depends on proving that the comparison holds in all significant respects, and that is often problematic (apples are never oranges, although they may resemble them somewhat). It is far more useful to understand the factors behind racial inequality than to rely on catchwords like these. We must ask why blacks were a caste or a colonized group. Usually the answer is that, unlike white ethnic groups, blacks in northern cities confronted a more virulent, fundamentally different form of

7. Stephan Thernstrom and Elizabeth H. Pleck, "The Last of the Immigrants: A Comparative Analysis of Immigrant and Black Social Mobility in Late Nineteenth Century Boston," unpublished paper delivered at the annual meeting of the Organization of American Historians, April 1970; Stephan Thernstrom, *The Other Bostonians: Poverty and Progress in the American Metropolis, 1880–1970* (Cambridge, 1973), pp. 176–219.

8. The caste analogy is made by the following authors: David Manners Katzman, *Before the Ghetto: Black Detroit in the Nineteenth Century* (Urbana, 1973); David A. Gerber, *Black Ohio and the Color Line, 1860–1915* (Urbana, 1976); David A. Fowler, "Northern Attitudes toward Interracial Marriage: A Study of Legislation and Public Opinion in the Middle Atlantic States and States of the Old Northwest," unpublished Ph.D. dissertation, Yale University, 1973; W. Lloyd Warner, "American Caste and Class," *American Journal of Sociology*, v. 32 (September 1936), pp. 231–237; Gunnar Myrdal, *The American Dilemma* (New York, 1944); Gerald D. Berreman, "Caste in India and the United States," *American Journal of Sociology*, v. LXVI, No. 1 (July 1960), pp. 120–127. I would also place Drake and Cayton's *Black Metropolis* in the category of works written with the caste analogy in mind.

An equally large literature considers the residential segregation of urban blacks—or the dependence of the ghetto economy on "white colonizers"—as the domestic equivalent of colonial status. In this vein, see William K. Tabb, "Race Relations Models and Social Change," *Social Problems*, v. 18 (Spring 1971), pp. 431–444; Robert Blauner, *Racial Oppression in America* (New York, 1972); Robert Allen, *Black Awakening in Capitalist America; An Analytical History* (Garden City, New York, 1970); Stokeley Carmichael and Charles V. Hamilton, *Black Power: The Politics of Liberation in America* (New York, 1965); William K. Tabb, *The Political Economy of the Black Ghetto* (New York, 1970); Harold Cruse, "Revolutionary Nationalism and the Afro-American," in Harold Cruse, ed., *Rebellion or Revolution* (New York, 1968), pp. 74–96; Ira Katznelson, *Black Men, White Cities* (New York, 1969); Michael Hechter, *Internal Colonialism: The Celtic Fringe in British National Development, 1536–1966* (Berkeley, 1973).

discrimination. Any serious explanation for the inequalities of urban blacks eventually returns to the question of racial discrimination. The next problem is relatively straightforward: deciding which forms of racial prejudice help reduce black incomes. The list of possibilities is large: restricted access to housing, entry-level jobs, and promotions, unequal pay for equal work, denial of credit for home mortgages and businesses, differential hiring and firing (thus using blacks as cheap labor), refusal of whites to buy from black businesses, and so forth. A full understanding of urban racial poverty and its effects can only come from knowing the kind of discrimination that operated to limit black opportunity and what groups of urban blacks were most affected.

In *The Other Bostonians,* Stephan Thernstrom explored the sources of racial poverty in Boston between 1880 and 1970. He argued that Boston's blacks were more concentrated in menial jobs than the Irish because of their cultural deficiency in establishing businesses and their exclusion from many avenues of employment, from sales to factory work. A more complete summary of Thernstrom's argument and his evidence can be found in Chapter V, but my basic criticism is that, in focusing on only one of two types of racial barriers to be found in late nineteenth-century Boston, exclusion (the barrier he identifies), and overlooking another, unsuccessful competition, Thernstrom overemphasizes the cultural deficiencies of blacks in business and underemphasizes the importance of racial discrimination. The unresolved problem in Thernstrom's analysis, which the distinction between these two barriers helps to clarify, is the paradox of competition. In an economy based on the profit motive, employers are supposed to lose money if they restrict their supply of labor artificially by excluding one group. Since blacks were so confined to menial jobs, they were even more available for work at wages below the prevailing rate. In theory, the profit-minded employer could have hired blacks at lower than average wages, and thus undercut other firms. Given this inherent dynamic between racism and competition, the task is to explain why competition failed to undermine racial segregation in jobs.

Confinement to menial work was only one of the many effects of nineteenth-century urban racism, as Theodore Hershberg points out. In examining the condition of antebellum Philadelphia blacks, based on the analysis of unusually rich social surveys made by Quakers and abolitionists, Hershberg concluded that the northern city was "destructive" to black life in two respects: First, the socioeconomic position of antebellum Philadelphia blacks was declining between

1838 and 1856 and, second, blacks with the longest contact with the city, those who were free born, were actually worse off than ex-slaves.[9] It is quite correct, as he points out, that Philadelphia blacks confronted a triple dilemma: increasing frequency of racial attacks, a black population so disease-ridden that it was unable to reproduce itself, and disenfranchisement as it took form in the state constitution of 1838. It is certainly reasonable to conclude that in these three respects Philadelphia's blacks were losing ground, but Hershberg argues the point more broadly to include "destruction" in socioeconomic realms. He furnishes eight examples of black losses: rising rates of female-headed households and of residential segregation, declining rates of membership in churches and beneficial societies, school attendance, property ownership, representation in skilled trades, and literacy.[10] In only one of these, the rate of literacy, was there a precipitous decline (between 1847 and 1856); in the other seven, no statistically significant trend appeared in either a positive or a negative direction. Nor was the city especially destructive to those who knew it best, the free-born blacks. Ex-slaves differed from free-born blacks in only one of the eight social indicators, the rate of church membership, which was consistently higher among ex-slaves. We learn from reexamining the evidence in these surveys that Philadelphia blacks were at an impasse in the antebellum decades, a sobering thought in itself, but the far stronger verdict of destructiveness, based on declining socioeconomic status, seems unwarranted from the evidence at hand. Along with Frank Furstenberg and John Modell, Hershberg has also directed special attention to one particular nineteenth-century social trend, the higher proportion of female-headed households (husbandless households) among Philadelphia's blacks than among its immigrants. They claim that this family pattern resulted from the unusually high death rate among Philadelphia's black husbands.[11] I agree with their insistence on the urban

9. This argument may appear deceptively similar to that of E. Franklin Frazier. In *The Negro Family in the United States*, Frazier entitled Part 4 "In the City of Destruction," but Part 5 of the book is called "In the City of Rebirth." Frazier sees the city as destructive in the beginning, but constructive in the long run, and, for that reason, his work still fits squarely within the first perspective.

10. Theodore Hershberg, "Free Blacks in Antebellum Philadelphia: A Study of Ex-Slaves, Free-Born and Socioeconomic Decline," *Journal of Social History*, v. 5 (Winter 1971–1972), pp. 183–209, and Theodore Hershberg, "Free-Born and Slave-Born Blacks in Antebellum Philadelphia," in Stanley L. Engerman and Eugene D. Genovese, eds., *Race and Slavery in the Western Hemisphere: Quantitative Studies* (Princeton, 1975), pp. 395–426.

11. Frank Furstenberg, Jr., Theodore Hershberg, and John Modell, "The Origins of

rather than rural origins of the female-headed household, as I make clear in Chapter VI, but I disagree that its roots are primarily to be found in excessive male mortality rather than in the combined effects of poverty, sterility, and declining community regulation of family life.

Despite these differences of opinion, my study also concludes that the nineteenth-century city was destructive. It argues that black migrants were able to rebuild their lives and find new ways to insure survival amidst a life of poverty, and it finds destructiveness most of all in the nineteenth-century city's failure to solve the problem of racial poverty. Urban employers, workers, and unions helped to perpetuate it by erecting two major, distinct racial barriers, exclusion and unsuccessful competition. This study is largely distinguished from others in the same perspective by a different, and I hope more complete, accounting of the relationship between racism and black poverty, on the one hand, and changing community norms and family life on the other.

But this work also resembles other research findings in its comparisons of different groups of urban blacks, divided by their region of birth. The analytical foundation of this book is the concept of "generation" borrowed from American immigrant history, the idea that an ethnic group is fundamentally changed by its life in the New World, that the American-born children of Polish or Irish immigrants are just as American as they are Irish or Polish. This commonplace of immigrant history has begun to be applied in sociological and historical research about urban blacks, but the origin of the idea that urban blacks are not a monolithic group originates with W.E.B. DuBois. In *The Philadelphia Negro* (1899), he insisted that "the generalization that includes a North Carolina boy who has migrated to the city for work and has been here a couple of months in the same class with a descendant of several generations of Philadelphia Negroes, is apt to make serious mistakes."[12] DuBois made a number of unfavorable remarks about southern migrants, whom he regarded as a largely criminal and unrespectable element. His judgments were harsh, punitive, and I think fundamentally wrong, but time and again I have made "discoveries" only to find them anticipated by his casual observations. But *The Philadelphia Negro* still belongs in the city-as-

the Female-Headed Black Family: The Impact of the Urban Experience," *Journal of Interdisciplinary History*, v. VI, No. 2 (Fall 1975), pp. 211–233.

12. W.E.B. DuBois, *The Philadelphia Negro: A Social Study* (Philadelphia, 1899; New York, 1967), p. 74.

constructive perspective, because it clings to the notion that the northern city holds out the promise of racial equality to its black citizens and that many of the social problems to be found originate with southern migrants. Had DuBois taken his own advice, and systematically compared southern migrants with Philadelphia blacks, I think he would have reached some different conclusions.

This book returns to the period DuBois studied, beginning with emancipation and ending at the turn of the century, although some background about the history of antebellum Boston blacks is also provided. The beginning of the new century was less a momentous turning point than a convenient place to end, because the most important kind of evidence—social divisions between blacks divided by birthplace, as found in the federal manuscript census schedules—was unavailable after 1900. But the 35-year span between the Civil War and the turn of the century is also worthy of special attention as one of the great hopeful "moments" in the history of American blacks: For the first time most Afro-Americans could live their own lives, make their own decisions, legally marry, and freely migrate. Eventually the jubilation of emancipation turned into a sober reckoning with rural poverty. Recent research tells us that the roots of southern racial poverty between Reconstruction and World War I were to be found in black occupational and educational handicaps, white terrorism, indebtedness to the country merchant and the landlord, and, most important of all, entrapment within a stagnant and underdeveloped economy.[13] The black poor of Boston had left most of these problems behind. The handicaps of low occupational skills and illiteracy were mitigated by the metropolitan demand for unskilled labor and by the readiness of city employers to hire even ex-unskilled laborers in factory jobs and construction. Despite Boston's legal freedoms, absence of racial violence, and economic development, most blacks within it were poor: The study of the reasons behind racial poverty in the urban North, then, forms an important counterpoint to what is already known about it in the rural South.

At a time when the average black lived off the land, the history of a post-Civil War northern black community is exceptional, all the more so because of the selection of Boston as a case study. Throughout the period under examination, blacks never formed more than 2%

13. Jay R. Mandle, *The Roots of Black Poverty; The Southern Plantation Economy after the Civil War* (Durham, North Carolina, 1978); Roger L. Ransom and Richard Sutch, *One Kind of Freedom: The Economic Consequences of Emancipation* (Cambridge, England, 1977); Robert Higgs, *Competition and Coercion: Blacks in the American Economy, 1865–1914* (Cambridge, 1977).

of the city's inhabitants, despite their rapid rate of population increase: from 3496 in 1870 to 11,591 in 1900. Black Boston in the nineteenth century will always be noteworthy as the home of the *Liberator* and of Garrisonian abolitionism. Massachusetts blacks enjoyed more legal freedoms than most northern blacks: The disenfranchisement that befell antebellum Philadelphia's blacks bypassed Boston. In the expansion of legal rights, the atmosphere of interracial association, and the militance of the community leadership, black Boston was almost without equal. But some of the destructive factors in Philadelphia—disease and race riots—were to be found in Boston as well. It was a more segregated city than all but a few other cities in the North. It is impossible to say whether Cleveland, Detroit, Philadelphia, or Boston was the "best" city for blacks, because that judgment depends on the basis of the comparison, but, when all things are considered, it seems fair to say that Boston belonged in the first rank. In this study I have compared the social and economic life of black Bostonians with that of blacks in other northern and southern cities, noting similarities as well as differences, and finding what was more general in the instance I know best.

Black Boston in these years was still small enough for me to study all of its inhabitants. I copied information from the federal manuscript census schedules of 1870 and 1880 (3496 entries in 1870 and 5873 in 1880) and analyzed the data with the aid of a computer. Although the federal manuscript census schedules for 1890 were burned in a fire, I was able to make use of the manuscript census schedules for 1900. With the use of an alphabetical index of names for the 1900 census, all black 20-year residents of Boston in 1900 were located (a total of 1048 black Bostonians enumerated in both the 1880 and the 1900 census). In these three decades information from the census about literacy, skin color (mulatto or black), household composition, and birthplace became the basis for reaching most of the conclusions set forth in this book. While the census was by far the most complete enumeration of Boston's black population, it was sometimes useful to supplement it with other Boston documents in which blacks were listed, especially city directories and registrations of marriages and deaths.[14] Although this book concerns black poverty in late nineteenth-century Boston, most of the city's poor, indeed, most of the city's inhabitants, were Irish: In the late nineteenth century they were three out of every five Bostonians. Two samples of Boston's Irish, consisting of 2996 in 1870 and 3203 in 1880, were

14. An investigation of the reliability of the census can be found in Appendix C.

drawn from the federal manuscript census schedules to allow me to separate the purely racial disadvantages of Boston's blacks from those attributable more to poverty or recency of arrival in the city.[15]

The city had as much of an impact on black consciousness as on black incomes. But the masses being studied here left few written records, diaries, or personal memoirs. Yet their personal journeys are surely as interesting as the education of Henry Adams or the breakfast conversation of Oliver Wendell Holmes. In offering here a glimpse of the aspirations of a people for themselves and their children, I have come to rely on the Civil War pension applications of black veterans or their widows.[16] The Victorian equivalent of a mod-

15. The sample was stratified by the 25 wards of the city so that the proportion of Irish to enter the sample was equal in each and every ward of the city. For example, since 2% of Boston's Irish, according to tabulated figures in 1880, lived in Ward 1, 2% of the census sample was to be drawn from Irish residents of Ward 1. This ward representation factor was used to select a sampling interval within each ward. The number of census pages in the ward was divided by the target goal of Irish names to be selected. I chose an Irish name from every nth census page. Then when I came to the proper page of Ward 1, I copied the information about the first Irish name to be found there.

The major determinant of the reliability of my generalizations about differences between blacks and Irish was the size of the Irish sample. No absolute rule of thumb defines whether a sample size is sufficient: It must be large enough to permit generalizations within a reasonable range of error, yet small enough to fit within the researcher's limited budget. But the degree of reliability can be ascertained using statistical procedures to estimate the "standard error," the discrepancy between findings reported in a sample of a certain size and in the population from which it is drawn. In a sample of 3000, the standard error is a little less than 3%. Thus, if the representation of Boston Irish were known (for example, the actual rate of female-headed households), then the percentages in each of my samples would deviate from that figure by less than 3%.

16. In 1862 Congress granted pensions to disabled Union veterans, expanded the coverage to widows in 1864, and increased the amount of benefits in 1890. The applicant was asked to furnish certificates of discharge from the army or navy, medical proof of a war-related disability, and character affidavits from at least two witnesses. The applicant also had to attest to the accuracy of his information before a justice of the peace or an officer of the court. Widows were required to supply proof of their marriage (wedding certificate or testimony of witnesses) and two sworn affidavits as to their general character. In 1865 Congress made special provision for ex-slaves: They were only required to prove the existence of a consensual union, rather than legal marriage. The pension applications, housed at the National Archives in Washington, D.C., are divided according to whether the application was approved (the certificates) or rejected (the originals) and by the status of the applicant (survivor, widow, mother, or other dependent). The typical soldier's file was supposed to include his application, certificates of birth, marriage, and military discharge, a doctor's report, a statement of his military record supplied by the War Department, and a brief of the case prepared by an agent of the pension bureau. But governmental record-keeping was at best

ern welfare application, these pension records occasionally contained rich details about migrants and their families. Life histories, drawn from these pensions and other sources, are interspersed with numerical analysis, so that each source is seen in relation to the other. In making use of the pension records, it is difficult to distinguish the unusual from the typical, and all that can be said is that the material quoted from pensions falls well within the parameters of what might have been expected, given what is already known about the life of the black poor.

This study, then, is one excerpt from a much larger history of black urbanization. Within one black community and one period of time, the sources of black acculturation and of metropolitan poverty are examined, as well as the responses of ordinary and anonymous blacks to these dual realities. The persistence of racial inequality stands for all time as one of the fundamental contradictions in a society firmly committed to an egalitarian ethic. The black move to the city explores one important drama in this history, for it matches two antagonists of equal skill but unequal resources: the black poor and the American metropolis.

---

haphazard, and most of the pension files were missing at least some of these documents.

The applicant naturally wanted to appear deserving, respectable, and needy in order to get the pension. Since the applicant was asked to testify before an officer of the court, false testimony ran the risk of prosecution. The background check by the bureau's agents usually gave some insight as to the general accuracy of the applicant's information. The tendency to defraud is built into the system of application, but, if there is a bias here, it lies in the direction of appearing ultrarespectable. While the material is far from the whole truth, it is nonetheless one version of it, a more respectable version, which sometimes inadvertently revealed a great deal about black family and neighborhood life.

U.S. Census Office, Manuscript Census Schedules, 1890, Census Schedules Enumerating Union Civil War Veterans; Henry C. Harmon, *A Manual of the Pension Laws of the United States* (Washington, D.C., 1867); William H. Glasson, *Federal Military Pensions in the United States* (New York, 1918); Gustavus A. Weber, *The Bureau of Pensions: Its History, Acts, and Organization* (Baltimore, 1923); John William Oliver, *History of Civil War Military Pensions, 1861–1885* (Madison, 1917).

CHAPTER II

BLACK BOSTON

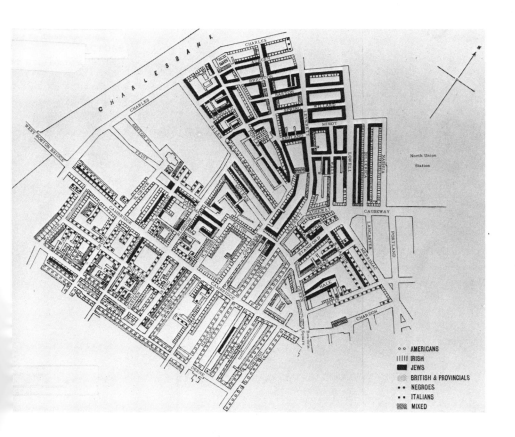

AMERICANS
IRISH
JEWS
BRITISH & PROVINCIALS
NEGROES
ITALIANS
MIXED

As cities of the Gilded Age sought to memorialize their past, Boston erected a monument to Crispus Attucks and the other martyrs of the Boston Massacre, placed statues of Wendell Phillips, William Lloyd Garrison, and Frederick Douglass in its public parks, and commissioned a bas relief of the black Civil War regiment, the Massachusetts 54th. At the ceremony dedicating the monument to Attucks in 1888, Frederick Douglass recalled the brave black soldiers who had fought in every American war since the Revolution, and John Boyle O'Reilly, the liberal editor of the Boston *Pilot*, read his poem, "Crispus Attucks": "God made mankind to be one in blood, one in spirit and thought."[1] To black Bostonians, this hallowed tradition of interracial heroism and sustained agitation made Boston a special place, "more enlightened and more Christian than other parts of the country," more "friendly, liberal and progressive than other cities," a city "where the black man is given equal justice."[2] One black resident found in Boston "liberty in the full sense of the word, liberty for the stranger within her gates, irrespective of creed, liberty and justice for all."[3] Another likened "the name Boston" to "a musical and joyous sound" because "the city was foremost in advocating the Negro's cause and vouchsafing to him the immunities of citizenship."[4]

Even a more dispassionate survey of the material conditions as well as the social atmosphere of antebellum black Boston accords the city a high mark. A certain equality of the poor prevailed among Irish immigrants and their black neighbors. Unfortunately, the coming of the Civil War helped to heighten competition for jobs and brought long-submerged racial hatreds to the surface coincident with the first

1. John R. Betts, "The Negro and the New England Conscience in the Days of John Boyle O'Reilly," *Journal of Negro History*, v. II, No. 4 (October 1966), pp. 246–261.

2. Susie King Taylor, *Reminiscences of My Life in Camp* (Boston, 1902; New York, 1968), pp. 55–57, 61; "Boston as the Paradise of the Negro," *Colored American Magazine*, v. II, No. 5 (May 1904), p. 312.

3. Susie King Taylor, *Reminiscences of My Life in Camp*, pp. 62–63.

4. Peter Randolph, *From Slave Cabin to Pulpit* (Boston, 1893), pp. 74–75.

Chapter opening photo
Ethnic groups of Boston's West End, c. 1890.

importation of ex-slaves into the city. After the war, activism declined but poverty and racial discrimination persisted; in the 30 years before the turn of the century, the small gap between blacks and Irish had expanded. As a community providing virtual civil rights to blacks early in the century, Boston's special standing still held even at the century's end. The tragedy was that the one had so little to do with the other, that the northern city could offer legal equality without giving blacks the means to achieve economic security.

LEGAL STATUS OF ANTEBELLUM BLACKS

Of all the northern states prior to the Civil War, Massachusetts was a leader in legal equality, repealing racial laws and avoiding the restrictions common elsewhere. In 1780 the Massachusetts state constitution declared all men free and equal. Although the Commonwealth never desegregated its railroads by statute, it was generally acknowledged by the 1850s that blacks could ride in first-class cars without harassment. Blacks in Worcester were probably the first northern blacks to serve on juries. Antebellum Massachusetts was extending political freedoms to blacks while other states were adding restrictions: Oregon forbade blacks from holding real estate; courts in Illinois, Ohio, Indiana, Iowa, and California refused to accept black testimony in cases where a black man was a party; Ohio required that black immigrants post $500 bond guaranteeing good behavior and produce court certificates as evidence of freedom. Decades separated the racial advance in Massachusetts from progress elsewhere. Taxpaying Massachusetts black men had the right to vote in 1783, while black men in New York, Ohio, Indiana, Illinois, Michigan, and Iowa did not enjoy the franchise on an equal basis with whites until 1870. By Massachusetts standards, blacks in Michigan were 20 years behind in gaining protection from discrimination in public accommodation, 40 years behind in securing the right to intermarry, and 57 years behind in gaining the franchise.[5]

[5] J. Jacques Vogeli, *Free but Not Equal: The Midwest and the Negro during the Civil War* (Chicago, 1967); Franklin Johnson, *The Development of State Legislation Concerning the Free Negro* (New York, 1919); Leon Litwack, *North of Slavery: The Negro in the Free States, 1790–1860* (Chicago, 1961); Louis Ruchames, "Jim Crow Railroads in Massachusetts," *American Quarterly*, v. VIII (Spring 1956), pp. 61–75; Louis Ruchames, "Race, Marriage and Abolitionism in Massachusetts," *Journal of Negro History*, v. XL (July 1955), pp. 250–273; David A. Fowler, "Northern Attitudes toward Interracial Marriage: A Study of Legislation and Public Opinion in the Middle Atlantic States and States of the Old Northwest," unpublished Ph.D. dissertation, Yale University, 1973.

Antebellum Boston blacks used these freedoms to develop a rich and varied community life. Prince Hall, a patriot of the Revolution, organized the first branch of the Masons in 1778, and several families established a society for mutual aid in 1796. A few years after Philadelphia blacks founded the first black church in North America, Boston blacks began the African Baptist church. By 1850 black Boston had four churches, several Masonic lodges, and a literary society.[6] This unusual level of community development distinguished black Boston from other antebellum black populations in the North. In black Cleveland, a community about equal in size to Boston, a black church did not appear until 1840, the first lodge was not formed in the 1860s, and a weekly newspaper did not begin publication until 1883.

The concentration of intellectuals and community leaders aided this institutional growth. Black Boston claimed its own poet (Phillis Wheatley), novelist (William Wells Brown), and historian (George W. Williams). During the abolitionist era, the preeminent leader of the community was Lewis Hayden, an ex-slave from Kentucky, who in 1859 was appointed messenger to the Massachusetts Secretary of State, a post he held for the rest of his life.[7] The abolitionist William Cooper Nell, a native Bostonian, earned his living as an accountant and collector and for a time ran the employment bureau connected with the *Liberator*'s printing office. As organizer of the 11-year campaign to integrate the Boston public schools, Nell devised the tactic of boycotting the black-only Smith School and of petitioning the state

6. Donald Jacobs, "William Lloyd Garrison's *Liberator* and Boston's Blacks, 1830–1865," *New England Quarterly*, v. XLIV, No. 2 (June 1971), pp. 259–277. For the social basis of community activism, see James Oliver Horton and Lois Horton, *Black Bostonians: Family Life and Community Struggle in the Antebellum North* (forthcoming, 1979); James Oliver Horton, "Generations of Protest: Black Families and Social Reform in Antebellum Boston," *New England Quarterly*, v. XLIX, No. 2 (June 1976), pp. 242–256; Charles H. Wesley, "The Negro's Struggle for Freedom in Its Birthplace," *Journal of Negro History*, v. XXX, No. 1 (January 1945), pp. 54–81; Jane H. and William H. Pease, *The Fugitive Slave Law and Anthony Burns: A Problem in Law Enforcement* (Philadelphia, 1975); Leonard W. Levy, "The Sims Case: The Fugitive Slave Law in Boston in 1851," *Journal of Negro History*, v. XXXV (January 1950), pp. 39–75; and George A. Levesque, "Black Boston: Negro Life in Garrison's Boston, 1800–1860," unpublished Ph.D. dissertation, State University at Stony Brook, 1976.

7. Stanley J. and Anita W. Robboy, "Lewis Hayden: From Fugitive Slave to Statesman," *New England Quarterly*, v. XLVI, No. 4 (December 1973), pp. 591–613; Wilbur H. Siebert, "The Underground Railroad in Massachusetts," *New England Quarterly*, v. IX, No. 3 (September 1936), pp. 447–467; Harold Schwartz, "Fugitive Slave Days in Boston," *New England Quarterly*, v. XXVII, No. 2 (June 1954), pp. 191–212.

legislature for desegregation, which was ultimately successful in 1855.[8]

After the enactment of the Fugitive Slave Law in 1850 providing for the return of escaped slaves to their masters, black and white Boston activists tried to aid the escape of fugitives and dramatize the human suffering such legislation had caused. Since before the Revolution, fugitives en route to Canada had hidden in the cellars and attics of black tenements in Boston's West End. Lewis and Harriet Hayden had sheltered at least 75 fugitives (legend had it that a secret tunnel connected the Hayden home with a black barbershop at the bottom of Beacon Hill). Quick-thinking abolitionists thwarted southern slave catchers from ensnaring Shadrach, William and Ellen Craft, or George Latimer, but they failed to rescue Anthony Burns, an imprisoned fugitive.

Even as the level of community activism reached its peak, the facts of mundane existence remained about the same throughout the antebellum decades. Most of Boston's poor were white, not black, the sons and daughters of Emerald Island who often lived in basement hovels, dressed in rags, and subsisted from day to day on sporadic work at the docks or in common labor. Even before the huge famine immigration of the 1840s, rioters attacked and set fire to Irish shanties. Many Irishmen would never forget the burning of the Ursuline Convent in 1834 and the subsequent acquittal of the arsonists. As late as 1842, Irish workers in South Boston were fired for refusing to work on Christmas Day. Boston's Irish were even viewed as a "race," they were believed to be "quick of impulse," "ignorant," "credulous," and "hopeless inferiors."[9] A prominent Boston economist at the turn of the century still described the typical Boston Irishman as someone

8. Carleton Mabee, "Negro Boycott to Integrate Boston Schools," *New England Quarterly*, v. XLI, No. 1 (March 1968), pp. 341–361; Leonard W. Levy and Harlan B. Phillips, "The *Roberts* Case: Source of the 'Separate But Equal' Doctrine," *American Historical Review*, v. LVI (April 1951), pp. 510–518; Donald M. Jacobs, "The Nineteenth Century Struggle over Segregated Education in the Boston Schools," *Journal of Negro Education*, v. XXXIX (Winter 1970), pp. 76–85; Leonard W. Levy and Douglas L. Jones, eds., *Jim Crow in Boston: The Origin of the Separate but Equal Doctrine* (New York, 1974); Arthur O. White, "The Black Leadership Class and Education in Antebellum Boston," *Journal of Negro Education*, v. 42 (Fall 1973), pp. 504–515; Louis Ruchames, "Race and Education in Massachusetts," *Negro History Bulletin*, v. XIII (December 1949), pp. 53–71; Stanley K. Schultz, *The Culture Factory: Boston Public Schools, 1789–1860* (New York, 1973).

9. Barbara Miller Solomon, *Ancestors and Immigrants: A Changing New England Tradition* (Chicago, 1956), p. 45.

who "lives in the present and worries comparatively little about the future. He is not extravagant in any particular way, but is wasteful in every way; it is his nature to drift when he ought to plan and economize."[10]

When both groups had so many common burdens, need we bother to point out the small distinctions between them? As a general rule, Irish and black alike were vastly over-represented among the ranks of unskilled labor, but whereas blacks went more often into sailing, the Irish more commonly remained on the shore in day labor.[11] Yet by the standards of the day, blacks in New England were doing well. Nowhere except in Providence and Boston had blacks entered the skilled trades in substantial numbers. The occupational status of blacks in six antebellum cities, as furnished in Table II-1, indicates that, in this one respect, blacks from Philadelphia, New York, Washington, D.C., and Charleston were much behind New Englanders. The special tolerance of the region, of course, was aided all the more by the small sacrifice for whites which was involved.

THE CIVIL WAR

But the Civil War demanded great sacrifices from Bostonians. The coming of the war reawakened the latent activism of black and white abolitionists. But the Irish, who refused to see the war as a great crusade, blamed local blacks. Even though the battles were being fought elsewhere, the war came home to Boston through race riots, heightened economic competition between blacks and Irish, and the first importation of ex-slaves into the city.

With the outbreak of fighting, abolitionists demanded that the state organize regiments of black troops. After several years of lobbying, they succeeded, and soon recruiters were traveling throughout the North. Headed by its Brahmin colonel, Robert Gould Shaw, a "sable army" of black recruits paraded from the Arlington Street church to the Boston Common in 1863.[12] Black enlisted men, who saw action in Virginia and South Carolina, continued to press for equal treatment in the army. They refused to accept their salaries until they

10. Frederick A. Bushee, *Ethnic Factors in the Population of Boston* (Washington, D.C., 1903), p. 93.

11. Oscar Handlin, *Boston's Immigrants: A Study in Acculturation* (Cambridge, 1941; New York, 1968), Table XIII, pp. 250–251.

12. James W. McPherson, *The Struggle for Equality: Abolitionists and the Negro in the Civil War and Reconstruction* (Princeton, 1964), pp. 202–206.

TABLE II-1
Selected Occupations of Black Male and Female Workers in Antebellum Cities, 1849–1860

City and year	Occupation						
	Sailor	Barber	Other trades	Laborer	Domestic servant	Other	N
Charleston, 1848	1	0	8	3	72	16	7355
Philadelphia, 1849	13	2	2	22	50	11	1849
Boston, 1850	25	8	4	20	8	35	575
New York City, 1855	2	2	3	15	29	49	3679
Providence, 1860	5	4	9	17	23	42	572
District of Columbia, 1860	3	2	7	55	10	23	1620

Sources: Claudia Dale Goldin, *Urban Slavery in the American South, 1820–1860: A Quantitative History* (Chicago, 1976), Table 11, p. 43; *A Statistical Inquiry into the Condition of the People of Color in the City and Districts of Philadelphia* (Philadelphia, 1849), pp. 6–19; Oscar Handlin, *Boston's Immigrants: A Study in Acculturation* (rev. ed., Cambridge, 1959), Table XIII, pp. 250–251; Robert Ernst, *Immigrant Life in New York City, 1825–1867* (New York, 1949), Table 27, pp. 214–217; Leslie H. Fishel, Jr., "The North and the Negro, 1865–1900: A Study in Race Discrimination," unpublished Ph.D. dissertation, Harvard University, 1953, Appendix, I-B, p. 9; Dorothy Provine, "The Economic Position of the Free Blacks in the District of Columbia, 1800–1860," *Journal of Negro History*, v. LXIII, No. 1 (January 1973), pp. 61–72.

received equal compensation with whites. (Congress eventually approved a retroactive compensation of equal pay for black soldiers in 1864.[13])

Boston's Irish were never committed to the war effort. Their initial opposition to the anti-slavery cause grew with the recognition that "we did not cause this war: but vast numbers of our people have perished in it. . . ."[14] Irish conservatism, prejudice against those "repulsive in hue, offensive in the odor that emanates from their person," and the large losses they sustained during the war exploded in Boston's draft riot in 1863, which, although miniscule in compari-

13. Charles W. Wesley, "The Negro's Struggle for Freedom in Its Birthplace," *Journal of Negro History*, v. XXX, No. 1 (January 1945), pp. 54–81.

14. Boston *Pilot* (April 12, 1892), as quoted in Francis R. Walsh, "The Boston *Pilot*: A Newspaper for the Irish Immigrant, 1829–1908," unpublished Ph.D. dissertation, Boston University, 1968, p. 167.

son with the clash in New York City a few days earlier, left four Irishmen but no blacks dead.[15] Toiling at the docks alongside Irish teamsters, draymen, and haulers, black day laborers arrived at work after the riot armed with clubs and knives and brawled with Irish laborers in the streets.[16] Irish leaders, who did not condone the rioting, asked that "non-leniency [be] shown those who take the law into their own hands."[17] Enlightened community leadership, however, had less to do with abatement of the tension than the victories at Gettysburg and Fort Donaldson.

The Civil War heightened racial antagonisms between blacks and immigrants. Immigrant workers demanded the firing of blacks from even menial jobs as porters, tobacco stemmers, waiters, barbers, and cooks. Evictions of blacks increased in construction work (asphalt paving, brickmaking), outdoor labor (longshore work, whitewashing), and service jobs (bootblack, waiter, shoeshining, barbering, service). In this period of flux, competitive workers held less power than employers who used the shortage of labor during the war and soon after it to import cheap black labor.[18] Racial competition for jobs increased in the first year after the war. Boston ship owners wanted caulkers to work 9 hours rather than the customary 8. The caulkers refused, but eventually the owners gained the upper hand after they brought in black caulkers from Portsmouth, Virginia, and French from Canada as strikebreakers.[19] Confrontations like these only served to strengthen resistance to the employment of black workers. Irish railroad employees in Cambridge, who stopped work when two blacks were hired, did manage to exclude black labor.[20] But, when

15. Ibid. (February 22, 1862), as quoted in Walsh, p. 166; Michael S. Hindus, "A City of Mobocrats and Tyrants: Mob Violence in Boston, 1747–1863," *Issues in Criminology*, v. 6, No. 2 (Summer 1971), pp. 55–83.

16. The *Liberator* (June 17, 1863); Ibid. (October 7, 1864).

17. Boston *Pilot* (November 28, 1863), as quoted in Francis Walsh, p. 172.

18. Herman D. Bloch, "The New York City Negro and Occupational Eviction, 1860–1910," *International Review of Social History*, v. 5 (1960), pp. 26–38; Albion P. Mann, Jr., "Labor Competition and the New York Draft Riots of 1863," *Journal of Negro History*, v. 36 (October 1951), pp. 375–405; Williston H. Lofton, "Northern Labor and the Negro during the Civil War," *Journal of Negro History*, v. 34 (July 1949), pp. 251–273; Sumner Eliot Matison, "The Labor Movement and the Negro during Reconstruction," *Journal of Negro History*, v. XXIII, No. 3 (July 1948), pp. 426–468.

19. Sterling D. Spero and Abram L. Harris, *The Black Worker* (New York, 1931; New York, 1968), p. 17.

20. Philip S. Foner, "A Labor Voice for Black Equality: The Boston *Daily Evening Voice*, 1864–1867," *Science and Society*, v. XXXVIII, No. 3 (Fall 1974), pp. 304–325.

white construction workers in Boston objected to hiring blacks, they were fired and blacks were brought in to replace them.

THE FREEDMAN'S BUREAU

The largest importation of black labor to Boston was an experiment sponsored by the Freedman's Bureau, begun in 1864 and ended in 1868. To remove the "press of population" in the Tidewater region of Virginia, the Freedman's Bureau began providing transportation for ex-slaves who wanted to come north. The Bureau sent only the "really worthy," those "who are either destitute or out of work, or liable to become dependent on the government for support."[21] They chose New England because there was "no region. . .more desirable as a home for the negro. . .where colored help is in great demand and where such sympathy is felt for their race."[22] Exactly how many black workers were brought to Boston can only be approximated. The Freedman's Bureau kept a register of those ex-slaves sent to Boston between 1866 and 1867. Other names of emigrants were found in the Bureau's correspondence. These additions to the register gave a total of 1083 ex-slaves shipped to Boston and Cambridge between 1866 and 1868, although information is incomplete for the earlier years.[23]

The origins of this program, the first large-scale immigration of ex-slaves to Boston, can be traced to one summer night in 1861 when three slaves of Confederate Colonel Charles Mallory stole into the isolated Union outpost, Fortress Monroe, at the tip of the Chesapeake Bay. When the colonel demanded the return of his property the next day, General Benjamin Butler, the commander of the fort (and later a Massachusetts governor), refused. Young men and then women and children stole away from Tidewater plantations by the dozens and

21. Record Group No. 105, Assistant Commissioner of Virginia, Fort Monroe, Register of Letters Received, 1866–1867, No. 204, Letter from General Samuel C. Armstrong to Brigadier General O. Brown, July 9, 1865; Record Group No. 105, Assistant Commissioner of Virginia, Fort Monroe, Letters Sent, No. 206, Letter from Mont S. Reed to Brigadier General O. Brown, December 31, 1866.

22. Record Group No. 105, National Archives, Bureau of Refugees, Freedmen, and Abandoned Lands, Assistant Commissioner of Virginia, Fort Monroe, Letters Sent from March 10, 1866, to July 12, 1866, No. 177, Letter Sent from General Samuel C. Armstrong to Brigadier General O. Brown, May 26, 1886.

23. Record Group No. 105, Registers of the Freedmen Sent to New England, No. 198 and District of Columbia, Assistant Commissioner, Record of Applications for Transportation, April 14, 1886–November 30, 1868.

then hundreds. In July of 1861, there were 900 ex-slaves at the fort; by March of 1862 the population had grown to 1500, 850 of whom were women and children.[24] Slave men dug ditches, women cooked and laundered, but children or the disabled could not work in return for their rations and pressed on the meager resources of the camp.

Why not remove the excess contraband to the North, suggested Lewis Tappan, abolitionist and treasurer of the American Missionary Association in New York. Tappan's suggestion went unheeded at the time, but within a year a new military commander at the fort solicited New England governors. Would they be willing to accept ex-slaves from Fortress Monroe, at least until the war was over? Governor Andrew was firmly opposed and replied that the importation of ex-slaves into Massachusetts would help create a race of "homeless wanderers."[25] But Union generals, increasingly hardpressed, sought to ship contraband women to the North in 1864, a move resisted by most of the women, despite a threatened loss of rations.[26] The generals also considered shipment to other counties in Virginia, or Florida and Texas; the ex-slaves agreed to relocate elsewhere in Virginia but refused to move to Florida or Texas. By 1866, urged by their ministers and disappointed in finding work near home, the freed people were willing to migrate.[27]

The Soldier's Memorial Society of Boston and other groups affiliated with the Freedman's Bureau solicited Boston employers of domestic servants. They met an enthusiastic response: One charity society noted that their "female domestics are becoming absorbed by the various manufacturing establishments and there is not sufficient emigration to Massachusetts to supply their places," despite the continuing demand for "well-trained servants, as a domestic comfort and necessity. . . ."[28] Moreover, they noted the "auspicious time to introduce colored servants" because "the limited supply of white female domestics" had resulted in "the increased compensation for the labor of that class of persons."[29] They hoped that black servants

24. Robert Francis Engs, "The Development of Black Culture and Community in the Emancipation Era, 1861–1870," unpublished Ph.D. dissertation, Yale University, 1972, p. 116.

25. Louis Gerteis, *From Contraband to Freedmen: Federal Policy toward Southern Blacks, 1861–1865* (Westport, Connecticut, 1973), p. 24.

26. Robert Engs, "The Development of Black Culture," p. 34.

27. Record Group No. 105, Assistant Commissioner of Virginia, Fort Monroe, Box No. 18, Letter from General Samuel C. Armstrong to Mont S. Reed, July 16, 1866.

28. *Thirty-first Annual Report of the Industrial Aid Society for the Prevention of Pauperism: October, 1866* (Boston, 1866), p. 14.

29. Ibid.

"with patience exercised towards them. . .would soon become tract-able, useful, and to say the least, as perfect in their duties as the ordinary run of whites now performing domestic duties."[30]

Boston representatives of the Bureau received applications from white New England families for "colored girl servants" and for-warded their lists of unfilled positions to the office of the Bureau in Virginia or in Washington, D.C. Most employers sought female domestics, although some requested "100–200 able-bodied men as laborers" and farm hands. The Bureau's agent in the North refused to process requests for the unemployable: women with children under 5, disabled persons, boys under 12, or invalid black women "likely to be ill more than three or four weeks."[31] In the space of a few months, the Freedman's Bureau had become an employment bureau for domestic servants.

The former black abolitionists who became the agents for the Bureau in Boston greeted the ex-slaves upon arrival. Coffin Pitts, a black clothing dealer, or Reverend Leonard Grimes, a minister from the African Baptist Church and a former activist in the Underground Railroad, met the boat carrying the refugees. They brought them to the Howard Street Industrial School in Cambridge or to a temporary home in the West End of Boston.[32] Teachers at the Cambridge school trained the freed women as house servants and tended the young children of working mothers. From 1866 to 1868, the District of Columbia Freedman's Bureau sent more than 100 mothers and their children there.[33] All that is known about the Joy Street home is that Coffin Pitts paid the rent.[34] The Freedman's Bureau in Virginia ulti-

30. Ibid.

31. Record Group No. 105, Assistant Commissioner of the District of Columbia, Letters Received from October 29, 1866, to August 17, 1867, v. 2, Letter from John Grimes, March 14, 1867; Letters from Ralph Haskins, March 28, 1867, May 8, 1867, May 14, 1867; Letter from H. L. Smith, May 28, 1867; Record Group No. 105, Assistant Commissioner of the District of Columbia, Letters Received from January 1, 1868, to September 1, 1868, v. 4, Letter from Charles A. Howard, July 28, 1868; Record Group No. 105, Assistant Commissioner of the District of Columbia, Letters Received from October 20, 1866, to August 17, 1867, Letter from H. S. Smith, April 25, 1867. See also Henry E. Swint, *Dear Ones at Home: Letters from Contraband Camps* (Nashville, 1966), pp. 87–88.

32. Record Group No. 105, Assistant Commissioner of Virginia, Fort Monroe, Letters Received from 1865 to 1868, Box 18, Letter from Mary S. Felton to General Samuel C. Armstrong, December 11, 1866.

33. Record Group No. 105, Assistant Commissioner of the District of Columbia, Letters Received from November 18, 1867, to November 4, 1868, Letter from Major O. Howard to Anna Lowell, March 15, 1868.

34. Record Group No. 105, Assistant Commissioner of the District of Columbia,

mately became disillusioned with the operations of its program in the Boston area. The head of the Bureau found that Mrs. Leonard Grimes, who had been charging $5 from each Boston employer, pocketed the fee rather than forwarding it to the Bureau.[35] He subsequently sent an acting inspector general to investigate irregularities in Boston, New York City, Providence, and Hartford.[36] The Bureau also learned in 1867 that a white matron at the Howard Street School in Cambridge, "bent on making money off freed people and [caring] . . . nothing for their welfare," was mistreating the ex-slaves and not feeding them for 24 hours after arrival.[37] In her defense, the matron accused her detractors of "ill feelings" and attributed the rumors of abuse to the "resident colored population of Boston [who] are opposed to having its numbers increased by emigration from the South."[38] The level of discontent among the immigrants is not known, but that Amanda Williams deserted her first employer, that George Banks escaped from his job at a school, and that a Virginia mother, Clarence Butler, insisted on a return ticket for herself and her 3-year-old suggest dissatisfaction.[39] Complaints and acrimony along with slackening demand for black labor, the increased transportation of blacks to other parts of Virginia, and dwindling governmental funding for the Bureau contributed ultimately to the end of this experiment. Even after its conclusion, Boston firms continued to recruit labor in Virginia. During a 2-week period in 1870, for instance, a Boston employer of cooks, housemaids, and dining room servants transported 250 ex-slaves from Richmond to Boston.[40] Black contractors also

Letters Received from August 17, 1867, to January 27, 1868, Letter from Coffin Pitts to General O. Howard, August 16, 1867.

35. Mrs. L. A. Grimes to Samuel C. Armstrong, July 5, 1866; Samuel C. Armstrong to B. L. Stearns, July 13, 1866, Samuel C. Armstrong Papers, Hampton Institute, as quoted in Robert Francis Engs, "The Development of Black Culture," p. 149.

36. Robert Francis Engs, "The Development of Black Culture," p. 55; Record Group No. 105, Assistant Commissioner of Virginia, Fort Monroe, Letters Sent from March 10, 1866, to July 12, 1866, No. 177, Letter from General Samuel C. Armstrong to Brigadier General O. Brown, May 25, 1866.

37. Record Group No. 105, Assistant Commissioner of the District of Columbia, Letters Received from October 29, 1866, to August 17, 1867, v. 2, Letter from Anna Lowell, July 15, 1867; Letter from Mrs. Casson, April 15, 1867.

38. Ibid., Letters from Mrs. M. L. Smith, April 25, 1867, and April 28, 1867.

39. Record Group No. 105, Registers of the Freedmen Sent to New England, No. 198; Record Group No. 105, Assistant Commissioner of the District of Columbia, Letters Received from January 1, 1868, to September 1, 1868, v. 4, Letter from Miss A.E. Buttrick, August 26, 1868.

40. Howard N. Rabinowitz, Race Relations in the Urban South, 1865–1900 (New York, 1977), pp. 249–250.

hired Virginia freedmen to work as servants and waiters in Boston hotels.[41]

THE GROWTH OF RACIAL DISADVANTAGE

These ex-slaves were moving to a city where the equality of poverty between black and Irish no longer prevailed, not so much because the status of blacks altered but because Irish immigrants experienced considerable social amelioration. Time stood still for Boston blacks, and, as a result, the social gap widened.

Still, the distinctiveness of abolitionist Boston, the legal advance of Massachusetts blacks, continued during Reconstruction. After blacks charged discrimination at Boston's Brigham Restaurant and Globe Theater, the state legislature passed a law in 1865 forbidding racial discrimination in licensed inns and other places of public accommodation and strengthened the provisions of the law the next year. Because of complaints about discrimination at skating rinks, the legislature in 1885 broadened the anti-discrimination law to include unlicensed places of business. Refusal of Cambridge barbers to cut the hair of a black law student led to expanded coverage of the statute in 1893 and to stiffer penalties for its violation in 1895.[42] No other northern state passed as many civil rights laws or was as inclusive in its coverage of discriminatory acts as Massachusetts.

Immediately after the Union victory, the Massachusetts State House, as the actual and symbolic home of Radical Republicans, expanded the role of blacks. Civil War veterans from Massachusetts were appointed to federal jobs at the post office and the customs house. Two black men were elected to the State House of Representatives in 1866, and, until the end of the century, one or two black men a year were elected to the state legislature. Each ward in the city of Boston elected three representatives to the City Council. Between 1876 and 1895 at least one black from the West End (Ward 9, where black voters were concentrated) served on the City Council.[43] The first

41. Alrutheus Ambrush Taylor, *The Negro in the Reconstruction of Virginia* (Washington, D.C., 1926), p. 92.

42. John Daniels, *In Freedom's Birthplace: A Study of the Boston Negroes* (Boston, 1914), pp. 94–96.

43. Between 1870 and 1890 they had significant numerical strength in the West End (where the percentage of blacks in the ward rose from 15% in 1870 to 20% in 1890). After redistricting and the movement of blacks to the South End, black numerical strength was diluted: They were reduced from 20% of the population in the West End

black judge in the North (George L. Ruffin of Boston) was appointed to the Charlestown District Court in 1883.

Even southern cities could claim many black elected officials during Reconstruction, but, after that, black officeholding dwindled. In Boston black political representation stood as a reminder of Boston's unwillingness to succumb to the national retreat from Reconstruction. But slowly the national trend toward segregation and scientific racism, couched in the language of Social Darwinism, appeared in even the most liberal of American cities. In response to pressure from its southern students, the New England Conservatory of Music, a venerated Boston institution, tried in 1885 to segregate black students in its dormitories.[44] That same year the nursing school connected with the Massachusetts General Hospital denied the application of a black woman.[45] A black refused admission to a Nantasket skating rink during his August vacation concluded that "here in the so-called 'cradle of liberty' and 'anti-slavery Massachusetts', yes, almost under the shadow of the 'Athens of America', you are ejected on account of your color."[46] In 1898 the *New England Magazine* carried a pulp romance, "Miss Theodora," about a middle-aged Brahmin spinster who lived alone except for her black maid of 30 years, Diantha. Miss Theodora regularly brought baskets of food to the poor black families in the West End and visited the Home for Aged Colored Women. She finally agreed to visit her Harvard-educated nephew in Colorado, and met there the sweetheart of her youth, now a wealthy widower. They married and Miss Theodora left Boston forever. No mention is made of any friendly visitations to the poor in Colorado, and the loyal retainer, Diantha, disappeared from the story.[47] To be sure, "Miss Theodora" was a poor imitation of *The Bostonians*, but it did underline the point that paternalism toward poor blacks was considered a thing of the past. It was sadly true that Boston had not isolated itself from the national spirit, but, at the same time, it had not totally rejected its traditions. Blacks in other cities were forced onto Jim Crow streetcars, segregated in public parks, and pushed out of public office, but never in Boston. In the 1890s black men were lynched in Michigan, Illinois, Ohio, and Pennsylvania, but not in

---

to 10%, and, in the South End, the other neighborhood of considerable black concentration, blacks were just 10% of the population.

44. Boston *Advocate* (July 25, 1885).

45. Ibid. (September 5, 1885).

46. The *Hub* (August 8, 1886).

47. Helen Leah Reed, "Miss Theodora: A West-End Story," *New England Magazine*, v. XIII, Nos. 1–5 (September 1895–February 1896), pp. 21–32, 264–278, 273–288.

Massachusetts. Everywhere a retreat had occurred, but at least in Boston it was a dignified withdrawal.

Victorian Boston was a divided metropolis, an old walking city of blacks and immigrants close to the docks, and an all-white modern city of three-deckers and single family homes in Boston's streetcar suburbs. Blacks were largely confined to one and excluded from the other, while Boston's Irish could be found "in large numbers in every tenement district of the city."[48] Thousands of recent arrivals from Ireland lived in shanties near South Cove or on Fort Hill, but many others settled on the edge of the city and in the surrounding towns near the factories where they worked. Most of Boston's blacks in the nineteenth century lived on "Nigger Hill," which developed as servant quarters for blacks employed by wealthy Beacon Hill families. It grew to be the largest area of black residence because of its proximity to the food markets near Fanueil Hall—"where black workers carried quarters and halves of meat on their backs"[49]—and to the docks where blacks were laborers and teamsters. Behind the wooden block fronts were black-only courts and alleys, and around the corner neighborhoods of Irish, British immigrants, and Yankees.

A single quantitative measure, the index of dissimilarity, permits a comparison of immigrant and black residential segregation. The index records the divergence between concentrations of any two groups by ward, in this case, blacks and Boston's Yankees (native whites of native parentage). It varies between 0 and 100, with a higher index indicating a higher level of residential segregation.[50] In the Yankee seaport of Revolutionary Boston, residential segregation was minimal (an index of just 10 in 1790) because the city was compact and blacks were equally divided between the dock district and the West End servant quarters on "Nigger Hill." By 1850 the index had climbed to 62, while that for Irish was only 21 and for Germans 31.[51] A decade later the index for blacks was about the same:

48. Frederick A. Bushee, *Ethnic Factors in the Population of Boston*, p. 25.

49. Robert A. Woods, ed., *Americans in Process: A Settlement Study by Residents and Associates of the South End House* (Boston and New York, 1902), p. 123.

50. There is no standard for judging a low from a high index, although some regard 30 and below as low and 70 and above as high. In theory, the index of dissimilarity can compare the level of segregation in any two groups. In the figures cited here, blacks, Irish, and Germans have been contrasted with a baseline population, native whites of native parentage. For a more detailed explanation of the index and its biases, consult Karl E. and Alma F. Taeuber, *Negroes in Cities: Residential Segregation and Neighborhood Change* (Chicago, 1965), Appendix A, pp. 203–204, 223–238.

51. Allan Kulikoff, "The Progress of Inequality in Revolutionary Boston," *William and Mary Quarterly*, v. XXXVIII, No. 3 (July 1971), Table VIII, p. 399; Stanley Lieber-

60 for blacks, 31 for first-generation Irish, and 46 for second-generation Irish. By 1880 racial residential segregation had declined somewhat, but the difference remained: an index of 50 for blacks, 27 for first-generation Irish, and 31 for the second generation.

This extreme concentration of blacks was unusual for its day. In 1850, Boston was the most segregated city in the North and second only to Portland, Maine, in 1860. In the late nineteenth century only two other cities, Utica, New York, and Chicago, were as segregated as Boston.[52] Most southern cities in these years had extremely low levels of segregation: Urban blacks lived in alleys and courts near wealthy whites, and the white elite had not yet evacuated the center for the suburbs. In his study of 29 New England, Mid-Atlantic, and Midwestern cities between 1870 and 1930, Kenneth Kusmer has shown that the index of segregation averaged about 40, almost 20 points lower than the index in Boston.[53] It seems doubtful that landlords in Utica, Chicago, Boston, or Portland were more prejudiced than their counterparts in other cities. To be sure, segregation increased in late nineteenth century Boston, but even in the antebellum decades Boston's level of segregation was unusually high. Each of these cities had one or two unusually large black enclaves, where most of the black

---

son, *Ethnic Patterns in American Cities* (New York, 1963), p. 76. A somewhat different estimate can be found in Leo F. Schnore and Peter R. Knights, "Residence and Social Structure: Boston in the Ante-Bellum Period," in Stephan Thernstrom and Richard Sennett, eds., *Nineteenth-Century Cities: Essays in the New Urban History* (New Haven, 1969), Table 4, p. 252. An earlier view, emphasizing the high degree of residential segregation among the Irish, was presented in Oscar Handlin's *Boston's Immigrants*, pp. 88–100, but challenged by David Ward in "Nineteenth Century Boston: A Study in the Spatial Aspects of Urban Growth," unpublished Ph.D. dissertation, University of Wisconsin, 1973, p. 66. The general pattern of increasing residential segregation is outlined by Nathan Kantrowitz in "Racial and Ethnic Residential Segregation in Boston, 1830–1970," *Annals of the American Academy of Political and Social Science*, v. 441 (January 1979), pp. 41–54.

52. Nathan Kantrowitz, "The Index of Dissimilarity: A Measurement of Residential Segregation for Historical Analysis," *Historical Methods Newsletter*, v. 7 (1974), pp. 285–293; Theodore Hershberg, "The Philadelphia Social History Project: A Methodological History," unpublished Ph.D. dissertation, Stanford University, 1972, Table 24, p. 306; Karl E. and Alma Taeuber, *Negroes in Cities*, pp. 32–33, 37–41, 47, 50; Frederick Anthony Hodes, "The Urbanization of St. Louis: A Study in Urban Residential Patterns in the Nineteenth Century," unpublished Ph.D. dissertation, St. Louis University, 1973, Table 6, p. 40, Table 12, p. 60; John Walker Briggs, "Italians in Italy and America: A Study of Change within Continuity for Immigrants to Three American Cities, 1890–1930," unpublished Ph.D. dissertation, University of Minnesota, 1972, Table XI, p. 131.

53. Kenneth L. Kusmer, "The Origins of Black Ghettoes in the North, 1870–1930: A Study in Comparative History," unpublished paper, 1976.

population lived. It appears that geographic features of Chicago and Boston helped account for the high level of residential segregation at this time; not enough is known about the development of black neighborhoods in Portland or Utica to reach any conclusions. Blacks in Chicago and Boston were hemmed in: the Chicago Black Belt by the Lake, the Loop and wealthy whites on Prairie Avenue, Boston's "Nigger Hill" by Beacon Hill, the Charles River, and the large number of public buildings in the West End. These geographic barriers helped to concentrate the population in a small area, which continued to grow because of its location near major employers of black labor. Other enclaves developed for middle-class blacks, but outside the city limits (Evanston or Robbins for Chicago's blacks, Cambridge and Chelsea for black Bostonians).

Most black Bostonians were virtually shut out of the market for single family homes. Examination of the statistics of home ownership among Boston's blacks—6% of black families in 1890 and 4% in 1890[54]—entirely supports the observation of a black newspaper, the Boston *Advocate*, that "comparatively few of the colored men of Boston are the owners of the houses in which they live; and as a natural result, after long years of toil, and the expenditure of thousands of dollars for house rent, we are not better off in old age than when we commenced to pay tribute to a hungry horde of property owners."[55] Even first-generation immigrant groups were more likely to be homeowners than blacks. In 1890 Irish immigrants were three times more likely to be homeowners than were blacks; in 1900 they were four times as likely to be homeowners.

Poverty and racial discrimination contributed to this difference, yet even blacks who could afford homes encountered barriers: It was virtually impossible for a wealthy black to purchase a home in Brookline or the Back Bay. Real estate agents, who claimed they were respecting the wishes of their clients, argued: "Plant one colored family on Commonwealth Avenue and there would be an exodus of whites for three blocks each way and a fall of thousands in the value of real estate."[56] Consequently, some blacks paid excessive amounts for a home, and others, more ingenious, discovered that the "only

54. U.S. Bureau of the Census, *Report on Farms and Homes: 1890* (Washington, D.C., 1896), Table 146, p. 581; U.S. Bureau of the Census, *Population*, Part II (Washington, D.C., 1902), Table III, p. 736.

55. Boston *Advocate* (May 5, 1885).

56. "The Race Problem in Boston, Mass.," *Zion's Herald*, reprinted in *Liberia Bulletin*, No. 8 (November, 1896), pp. 7–16.

way for a colored man to buy desirable property in Boston is through a third party."[57] Toward the end of the century, discrimination in housing increased as more real estate agents received instructions: "Under no consideration to be sold to darkies."[58]

The price of homes was high everywhere in the Northeast, and homeownership was as uncommon among blacks in Philadelphia or New York as in Boston. It was not that prejudice against black homebuyers was lower elsewhere or that eastern bankers were less willing to extend home loans, but that the cheaper price of houses outside New England directly contributed to higher rates of black homeownership. Black home purchase, then, was moderately high in some cities of the South (New Orleans, for example), quite common in midwestern cities (Cleveland, Detroit, Chicago, and Indianapolis, where single family homes predominated), and extremely common in Los Angeles, where one third of black families in 1900 were home-owners.[59]

Segregated housing patterns in Boston inevitably contributed to racially divided schools. In all fairness, we are not describing the *de jure* segregation of the South or even of such northern cities as New York, Newark, or Philadelphia.[60] In most other northern cities, such as Chicago, Detroit, or Boston, the problem was *de facto* segregation, where school attendance areas were drawn according to neighbor-hood. As a result, grammar schools in East Boston, Charlestown, Roxbury, and Dorchester had no black students, while over a third of the city's black students were enrolled in two West End grammar schools. The teaching staff in the public schools was almost com-pletely white. One black state Normal School graduate who applied for a position was told, "Go down South among your own people."[61] Throughout the nineteenth century the Boston School Committee hired one full-time black teacher, the daughter of a prominent black abolitionist, one black substitute teacher, and three black instructors for the adult evening school.

Black neighborhoods were also cesspools of disease for those living in such dense areas. Families drew their water from outside pumps, which were located near outdoor water closets. Fecal matter often contaminated the water supply and helped to spread disease.

57. Ibid., p. 9.
58. *Woman's Era* (December 1894).
59. U.S. Bureau of the Census, *Report on Farms and Homes: 1890*, Table 146, p. 581; U.S. Bureau of the Census, *Population: 1900*, Part II, Table III, p. 736.
60. John W. Blassingame, *Black New Orleans*, p. 121.
61. "The Race Problem in Boston," p. 13.

While black health conditions improved in this period, the city's vital statistics in 1890 reveal a ratio of 31 deaths to every 1000 among black Bostonians compared with 24 deaths for every 1000 white residents. Although by 1900 the racial gap remained as large, the mortality rate had dropped, but it was still 7 per 1000 greater for blacks than whites.[62] The most appalling differences, however, were not in these overall rates alone but in black infant mortality. Among Boston black babies born in 1880, 392 out of every 1000 did not live out the year, compared with 274 out of every 1000 white infants.[63] By 1900, infant mortality had fallen as a result of changes in the city's sanitation and the improved standard of living among its poor; but the health of white people improved at a faster rate and, consequently, the gap in health, by race, was somewhat larger. In 1900 the black infant mortality rate was still extremely high: 220 out of every 1000 live births compared with 189 per 1000 live births among the whites.[64] Cholera was the major cause of death among black infants, followed by debility and atrophy, bronchitis, and, to a lesser extent, consumption, convulsion, and pneumonia.[65] Even compared with Irish immigrants, whose death rate was higher than that of other white Bostonians, there was a difference of 7 deaths per 1000 between the two groups. In terms of the rate of child death (children under age 15), the largest disparities appeared: The child mortality rate was almost twice as high for blacks as for Irish immigrants.

The poor health of Boston blacks was even more glaringly deficient in a city with such excellent hospitals.[66] The black population in the West End lived within walking distance of six hospitals and the South End community was next to four hospitals, yet there were no black infants born in the Lying-In Hospital for Women between 1865 and 1900 and very few patients used Massachusetts General Hospital or New England Hospital for Women.[67] Of course, black mothers probably preferred black midwives in giving birth, but there were still enough miscarriages and emergencies to expect higher figures than these. A missionary home caring for blacks that opened in the West End in 1877 received cases "owing to the Chronic

62. New York *Freeman* (January 16, 1886).

63. Computed from data in U.S. Department of the Interior, *Report on Mortality and Vital Statistics of the United States*, Part II (Washington, D.C., 1886), Table XXII, p. 442.

64. Ibid.

65. U.S. Bureau of the Census, *Negro Population, 1790–1915*, Table 34, p. 333.

66. U.S. Census Office, *Vital Statistics of Boston and Philadelphia, Covering a Period of Six Years Ending May 31, 1890* (Washington, D.C., 1895), Table 15, p. 12.

67. Ibid.

state of the disease, which were not eligible for admission to the major hospitals."[68] Of the 39 cases the missionaries handled in the next few months, only 3, they claimed, would have been admitted to the city's hospitals. The only other alternative facility was the state hospital at Tewksbury, of which white missionaries said, "and there we do not always care to send our friends."[69]

The death rate for Boston was still lower than for blacks in major cities. In 1900 Boston's death rate for blacks was on a par with the majority of northern cities, but somewhat below that for blacks in New York, Philadelphia, or Cincinnati, and far below the disastrous health conditions for blacks in southern cities. The survival rate for black infants was higher in Detroit, Chicago, and Cincinnati than in Boston, for example, perhaps because of the lower density of the housing. But among the crowded cities of the East, Boston actually had a lower rate of infant mortality than New York and Philadelphia and stood far below the southern cities where black poverty and the absence of any sanitary reforms combined to work against the survival of black children.[70]

The unsanitary housing and poor health of so many black Bostonians might suggest malnourishment as well. No information is available about the diet of Boston blacks, but Philadelphia settlement house workers in 1892 and 1893 collected the weekly diets of very poor blacks in a nearby neighborhood. These Philadelphia families enjoyed a far better diet than the "hog and hominy" fare of rural southern blacks. During the course of one week, the survey indicated, they had some pork (bacon, smoked shoulder, sausage, and ham steak), beef (round steak, veal, and porterhouse), mutton, and chicken. While the diet was very heavy in starch (turnips, oatmeal, Irish and sweet potatoes, hominy, and bread), the families were getting adequate protein from their consumption of chicken and fish (cod, mackerel, whitefish, and smelts). The daily intake of protein for the average Philadelphia black was adequate, 100 grams a day, and, as the study suggested, the equivalent of the protein in the diets of white mechanics, farmers, and professionals in New England or New York.[71] The major deficiency in the diet was the shortfall in

68. For a general survey of Boston's medical facilities, see Morris J. Vogel, "Boston's Hospitals: 1870–1930," unpublished Ph.D. dissertation, University of Chicago, 1974.

69. New York *Freeman* (September 17, 1887).

70. Ibid.

71. U.S. Bureau of the Census, *Negro Population, 1790–1915*, Table 34, pp. 331–335, Table 29, p. 320.

calories—only 2952 per day—about 500 calories below the suggested requirements for a manual laborer employed at moderate work. To purchase this diet, these Philadelphia blacks spent an average of $1.09 per person per week, or $56.68 per year. Given that black per capita income in Boston was higher than in Philadelphia, black Bostonians could afford to spend somewhat more income on food and increase their caloric intake. Even without the actual information about the diet of black Bostonians, then, it is plausible to conclude that most Boston blacks were not severely malnourished.

The poverty of most black Bostonians was a problem of inequality rather than abject misery. The measure of a just reward has always been a comparative one. By the standard of blacks in the rural South, those in Boston enjoyed a good life. But by the standard of comparable groups in Boston, how did local blacks fare? The economist, scanning contemporary wage and salary data, can easily measure the extent of racial inequality. But the historian must rely on several different kinds of information that provide a less precise answer.

First of all, the federal census in 1870 inquired about the extent of real estate and property ownership. While it is reasonable to expect that Bostonians were wealthier than they were willing to admit, the desire to conceal was probably as widespread among blacks as among the Irish. The per capita wealth of adult black Bostonians, in 1870, as Table II-2 shows, was only 40% of that of Boston's Irish immigrants. If the large propertyless class among both groups was excluded, then black wealth fell to a mere 16% of Irish. Still, among the urban blacks that have been studied, Table II-2 also demonstrates that black Bostonians were especially unacquisitive. In terms of per capita wealth in 1870, they ranked above New Orleans blacks, but below Philadelphia or Cleveland blacks.

Another piece of data, the average yearly income for blacks (see Table II-3), provides a second measure of economic inequality.[72] In 1896 per capita income for Cambridge blacks was $178. As a result of the economic depression that year, this figure may have been lower than usual. Even so, Cambridge blacks probably earned more than black Bostonians. We know, for example, that among the 98 Cambridge black families surveyed, 72% of the household heads were employed in menial jobs, whereas 77% of black Bostonians held such

72. Ellen H. Richards and Amelia Shapleigh, "Dietary Studies in Philadelphia and Chicago, 1892–1893," *Bulletin of the U.S. Department of Agriculture* (Washington, D.C., 1903), pp. 40–44.

TABLE II-2
Per Capita Wealth of Boston Blacks and Irish and Blacks in Other Cities, 1870[a]

Group	Per capita wealth, males and females over 15 ($)	N	Per capita wealth, for those with any wealth (males and females) ($)	N
Boston blacks	107.76	1,763	821.25	359
Boston Irish	265.06	1,174	5030.00	85
New Orleans blacks	77.67	n.a.	1363.16	1,021
Cleveland blacks	251.76	971	2350.49	101
Philadelphia blacks	161.40	14,607	2334.45	1,700

Sources: Sample of Irish men and women from the U.S. Manuscript Census Schedules, Boston, 1870; all Boston blacks from the U.S. Manuscript Census Schedules, Boston, 1870; John Blassingame, "A Social and Economic Study of the Negro in New Orleans, 1860–1880," unpublished Ph.D. dissertation, Yale University, 1971, Table XVII, no page; Thomas J. Goliber, "Cuyahoga Blacks: A Social and Demographic Study, 1850–1880," unpublished master's thesis, Kent State University, 1972, Table 48, p. 105; Theodore Hershberg, "Mulattoes and Blacks: Intra-Group Color Differences and Social Stratification in Nineteenth-Century Philadelphia," unpublished paper delivered at the annual meeting of the Organization of American Historians, 1974, Table 29.1, 29.2, no page.
    [a] Ownership of real or personal property.

jobs in 1900. Despite their relatively privileged occupational position, Cambridge blacks earned less than Massachusetts working-class whites. It is true that their per capita income was $25 more than that of Massachusetts white mill workers (whose incomes were reported in 1891). However, a more comprehensive survey in 1901 showed that Massachusetts white craftsmen, laborers, as well as factory operatives earned on the average $15 more than Cambridge blacks.[73]

A third indicator of black economic inequality was the percentage of men and women employed in the lowest paying of Boston jobs, menial work. (A list of the jobs that belonged in this classification can be found in Appendix B.) Unlike the other two economic measures, this one is available for a 50-year period, thus permitting an inquiry into long-term trends in economic inequality. In Table II-4 first generation Irish workers in Boston were compared with the city's black first generation (southern migrants) and an Irish second generation was measured against a black second generation (northern-born blacks). During the second half of the nineteenth century, the occupa-

73. It might seem paradoxical that black Bostonians made such a poor showing in terms of per capita property ownership in 1870 but such a good showing in terms of per capita income in 1896. Of course, the 1896 figures apply to Cambridge, rather than Boston. But these differences can be easily reconciled: It seems quite likely that throughout this period black Boston had a small propertied class but a relatively large and well-paid laboring class.

TABLE II-3
Black and White Working-Class Per Capita Income, 1891–1903

	Per capita income ($)	Number of persons
Massachusetts cotton and woolen textile mill workers, 1891[a]	152.93	2300
Massachusetts working-class whites, 1901[a]	193.83	803
Cambridge, Massachusetts, blacks, 1896[a]	178.98	366
Philadelphia blacks, 1896[a]	103.61	9083
Xenia, Ohio, blacks, 1896	105.71	1698
Sandy Spring, Maryland, blacks, 1899	45.69	881
Whealton and Liwalton, Virginia, blacks, 1901	56.12	729
Farmville, Virginia, blacks, 1896	65.31	1213
Nashville blacks, 1896[a]	102.60	246
Atlanta blacks, 1896[a]	109.21	1292

Sources: U.S. Commissioner of Labor, *Annual Report* (Washington, D.C., 1891), pp. 876–883, 954–961, 1239, 1275; *Thirty-second Annual Report of the Bureau of Statistics of Labor: March 1902* (Boston, 1902), pp. 257–285; "Condition of the Negro in Various Cities," *Bulletin of the Department of Labor*, No. 10 (May 1892), pp. 304–318; W.E.B. DuBois, *The Philadelphia Negro* (Philadelphia, 1899; New York, 1967), p. 170; Richard R. Wright, Jr., "The Negroes of Xenia, Ohio," *Bulletin of the Department of Labor*, No. 48 (January 1903), p. 1035; William Taylor Thom, "The Negroes of Sandy Spring, Maryland: A Social Study," *Bulletin of the Department of Labor*, No. 32 (January 1901), p. 92; William Taylor Thom, "The Negroes of Liwalton, Virginia: A Social History of the 'Oyster Negro'," *Bulletin of the Department of Labor*, No. 7 (November 1901), p. 1162; W.E. Burghardt DuBois, "The Negroes of Farmville, Virginia: A Social Study," *Bulletin of the Department of Labor*, No. 14 (January 1898), p. 27.

[a] Lodgers were considered as family members.

tional gap among working women was narrowing, while among the men it was widening. The antebellum equality in occupational standing among first generation workingmen had been eroded by 1870: Irish immigrants had turned an eight percentage point disadvantage in 1850 into a 27 percentage point advantage by 1900. Similarly, the occupational gap was increasing among second generation workingmen: American-born Irish expanded a 28 percentage point lead in 1850 into a 41 point one by 1900.

CONCLUSION

In the 30 years prior to the Civil War, Boston blacks championed desegregation of public institutions in the North and abolition of slavery in the South. They won national respect for their unusual representation in the skilled trades, and for their activism, intellect, and manifold community institutions. Decades after the end of the

TABLE II-4

Menial Male and Female Workers as a Percentage of All Employed Irish and Blacks, by Migrant Generation, 1850–1900

	Percentage of menial workers							
	1850	*N*	*1870*	*N*	*1880*	*N*	*1900*	*N*
Males								
First-generation blacks	45	140	84	744	84	1337	82	847
First-generation Irish	53	6,644	68	548	68	946	55	58,122
Second-generation blacks[a]	45	228	77	545	82	812	77	3,613
Second-generation Irish[b]	17	9,209	50	129	50	592	36	47,732
Females								
First-generation blacks	n.a.		92	286	97	574	92	384
First-generation Irish			49	129	85	225	55	26,757
Second-generation blacks[a]	n.a.		90	288	92	449	69	1,754
Second-generation Irish[b]			28	72	52	135	46	22,078

Sources: Janet Riblett Wilkie, "Social Status, Acculturation, and School Attendance in 1850 Boston," *Journal of Social History*, v. 11, No. 2 (Winter 1977), p. 186; U.S. Manuscript Census Schedules, Boston, 1870 and 1880, and *Social and Industrial Condition of the Negro in Massachusetts* (Boston, 1903), pp. 249–251. The figures for 1900 include blacks in Boston and in seven other cities. The data for Irish derive from the 1870 and 1880 manuscript census schedules. Data for Irish in 1900 were computed from the U.S. Bureau of the Census, *Special Report, Occupations at the Twelfth Census* (Washington, D.C., 1904), Table 43, pp. 494–499.

[a] Second generation applies only to Massachusetts-born blacks. Migrants from Canada or other northern states were in roughly the same position as southern migrants.

[b] Applies to all children of immigrants, not just to the Irish.

war, they continued to elect blacks to state and local posts and to press for civil rights legislation. Still, Boston's high level of residential segregation for its day suggests that blacks were being excluded from the modern metropolis of bank clerks, indoor plumbing, and single family homes and confined to small enclaves within the older part of the city.

Even after the end of the war, black Boston was still a privileged black community. Compared with blacks in other cities, blacks in Boston continued to enjoy unparalleled social freedoms, an unusual range of civil rights, continued political representation, good health conditions, and excellent educational opportunities. Boston in the Gilded Age could never return to its glorious days in the struggle for equality, but it ranked close to Cleveland, Philadelphia, or Detroit as one of the best locales for blacks at the time.

Black poverty in late nineteenth-century Boston was less a question of starvation than of nagging and almost inexplicable inequalities. Once blacks had stood, side by side, in the same kind of poverty as the Irish (although blacks had always been more segregated), but, by the turn of the century, the distance between the groups had widened: a growing disadvantage in health and inequality in property ownership, income, and occupational status. The Irish, once the most downtrodden group in Boston, had climbed the social ladder by the turn of the century, whereas black Bostonians remained at its bottom rung.

CHAPTER III

SOUTHERN MIGRANTS

We have seen that there is in Philadelphia a large population of Negroes, largely unmarried folks. . . . The question now arises, whence came these people? How far are they native Philadelphians, and how far immigrants, and if the latter, how long have they been here? Much depends on the answers to these questions; no conclusions as to the effects of long, close contact with modern culture, as to the general question of social and economic survival on the part of this race, can be intelligently answered until we know how long these people have been under the influence of given conditions, and how they were trained before they came.

W.E.B. DuBois
The Philadelphia Negro

Immediately after the Civil War, the Freedman's Bureau sent excess contraband to Boston and several thousand more southern blacks arrived in the next 30 years. Was the lack of black advance in post-Civil War Boston due, in some part, to the arrival of these southern migrants? Had their extreme poverty simply masked the substantial progress made by the rest of Boston black society? An abundant literature, as outlined in the introduction, points to such a conclusion. Black migrants from the South, it is claimed, arrived in the city ill-educated and unprepared for city life. They came to escape from poverty and racial discrimination, but they were soon overwhelmed by the complexity of city life. Their experience in slavery had left them with limited skills or personal resources, which were diminished even more by the shock of removal from the simple community life of the South. Southern migrants to Boston, it has been predicted, grew embittered, and developed limited horizons, which helped to trap them in what has been subsequently termed "a culture of poverty." W.E.B. DuBois advanced such a view in *The Philadelphia Negro*: "Emancipation and pauperism must go hand in hand: when a group of persons have been for generations prohibited from self-support, and self-initiative in any line, there is bound to be a large number of them who, when thrown upon their own resources, will be found incapable of competing in the race of life."[1]

Before reaching such a bleak conclusion, it is necessary to fully assess the process of cultural change among southern migrants who settled in the northern city. In *A Century of Negro Migration*, published in 1918, Carter G. Woodson suggested that many of these southern migrants were highly skilled artisans and professionals, a conclusion he derived from only a few examples.[2] As the foundation

1. W.E.B. DuBois, *The Philadelphia Negro* (Philadelphia, 1899; New York, 1967), p. 269.
2. It has often been claimed that southern migrants prior to World War I were elite blacks. The classic study of southern migration to the city remains Carter G.

Chapter opening photo
Peter Randolph (1825–1893) and St. Andrews Presbyterian Church in 1868, later to become Ebenezer Baptist Church. (Photo of St. Andrews Presbyterian Church courtesy of the Boston Public Library.)

for a much larger movement in the early twentieth century, the previous historical record is almost a blank. Southern migrants actually faced several choices, whether to abandon their past way of living, desperately hold on to it, or fashion some halfway compromise. This chapter will make clear that the process of cultural adaptation to Boston life was just such a halfway compromise. Elements of change were slowly absorbed into a highly traditional southern black culture. This slow process of acculturation did not resemble the dire predictions of observers such as DuBois. The dual reasons behind this favorable outcome were the renewed importance of the family in the process of migration and the continuing cooperation between migrants even after they became settled in the city.

SOUTHERN NEWCOMERS

The majority of Boston's southern migrants were born in Virginia (Table III-1). The predominance of Virginia migrants increased after the Civil War: The proportion of black Virginians rose from 13% in 1860 to 30% in the next decade. From 1870 to 1900, black Virginians continued to form about a third of the entire Boston black population. These figures included children, most of whom were born in Massachusetts, and thus a much larger part of the adult black

---

Woodson's *A Century of Negro Migration*, published in 1918, which described the migration from the end of the Civil War to World War I. Most of his generalizations concerned the decade prior to 1910. In the earlier decades, he identified three groups of southern migrants to the North: black politicians ejected from office (most of whom accepted federal appointments in Washington, D.C.), the children of southern businessmen attending northern schools, and his largest and most amorphous group, "the intelligent laboring class."

Without any systematic examination of published census figures, subsequent studies, using Woodson as their source, have characterized late nineteenth-century black movement as the Migration of the Talented Tenth. John Daniels, a Harvard-educated social worker who described the Boston black community around 1914, portrayed southern migrants to Boston after the Civil War as an elite who "had trades or could do work above the common grade . . . and [who] were therefore in a position to earn better wages and live better." Fifty years later the authors of a report published by a Boston housing agency, probably basing their account on Daniels, found that the black community in Boston prior to World War I "was becoming further diversified by the entry of increasing numbers of persons from the South, many of whom on the basis of greater education and ambition were assuming positions of leadership." Carter G. Woodson, *A Century of Negro Migration* (Washington, D.C., 1918), p. 163; John Daniels, *In Freedom's Birthplace: A Study of the Boston Negroes* (Boston, 1914), p. 166; Rheable M. Edwards and Laura B. Morris, *The Negro in Boston* (Boston, 1964), p. 7.

TABLE III-1
Proportion of Boston's Native Black Population Born in Selected States, 1870–1900

	1870	1880	1890	1900
Northern born				
Massachusetts	32.2	34.5	32.9	28.2
New York	4.3	3.0	2.8	2.9
Pennsylvania	4.3	3.1	2.5	2.8
Connecticut	1.8	1.4	n.a.	2.5
New Jersey	1.0	.9	n.a.	1.1
Maine	2.3	1.3	1.5	.9
Rhode Island	1.2	.9	n.a.	.9
Southern born				
Virginia	29.8	33.0	29.9	27.6
North Carolina	4.0	4.9	7.4	11.5
Maryland	8.0	5.3	4.5	4.7
Georgia	1.0	2.1	2.5	3.8
District of Columbia	1.8	2.0	2.7	2.9
South Carolina	2.5	2.7	2.6	2.9
Total	3,118	5,074	6,971	10,409

Sources: U.S. Census, 1870 and 1880 manuscript schedules; for 1890 and 1900 figures, John Daniels, *In Freedom's Birthplace: A Study of the Boston Negroes* (Boston, 1914), p. 468.

population was southern. Most of the other southern migrants were born in Maryland, North or South Carolina, or the District of Columbia. Between 1870 and 1900 the proportion of newcomers from South Carolina remained about the same, but the fraction of black residents of Boston born in Maryland fell (from 8 to 5%), and the percentage of North Carolina black migrants tripled (from 4 to 12%).

Applicants for a marriage certificate in Boston were required to furnish their county or town as well as state of birth.[3] These cer-

___

3. It is possible that the marriage records overrepresented migrants from certain states, in contrast to the population enumerated in the census. The fact that such a large proportion of the population was born in Massachusetts would distort any comparison of the census with the marriage records. Since most of the Massachusetts-born were children, their inclusion would tend to overrepresent Massachusetts natives in the census as compared with the marriage records, and therefore a fair comparison must exclude Massachusetts-born blacks. The census frequencies of birthplaces for Boston blacks in 1870 were compared with the frequencies of birthplaces for blacks married in Boston between 1870 and 1879 to determine if the distributions were the same. The

tificates thus supply a more detailed geographical record than the federal census, which enumerated only the individual's state of birth. Tabulations based on birthplaces of all blacks marrying in Boston between 1870 and 1879 (1153) were used in making Map III-A. Similarly, Map III-B was drawn according to a list of all the birthplaces for blacks marrying in Boston between 1890 and 1899 (3453). Both maps show that black migration to Boston was concentrated in Baltimore, Washington, D.C., and the North Carolina coastal towns of Wilmington and Newbern and, most important of all, in the seaports and towns along the James River in Virginia.

It is no accident that southern black migration began here. A weekly steamer sailed from Norfolk, Richmond, and Baltimore to Boston, but these seaports were also connected with Boston through the flow of information. In the first years after emancipation, many ex-slaves knew little about the outside world; some did not even learn of their emancipation until several years after Lincoln's death, but the relatively cosmopolitan black inhabitants of these coastal areas had heard about northern cities from employers, from unloading ships at the docks, or from mingling with sailors.

evidence below indicates that the distributions in the two types of sources correspond almost exactly:

Place of origin	Boston marriage records, 1870–1879	Manuscript census schedules, Boston, 1870
Canada (not Maritimes)	.022	.012
Nova Scotia	.063	.074
New Brunswick	.032	.030
New England states	.060	.059
Pennsylvania	.048	.054
New York	.047	.061
New Jersey	.012	.015
Midwest states	.017	.012
Virginia	.384	.350
Maryland	.063	.110
District of Columbia	.035	.018
North Carolina	.058	.046
South Carolina	.032	.038
Other southern states	.065	.054
West Indies	.033	.032
Other foreign countries	.021	.026
Total	1153	3496

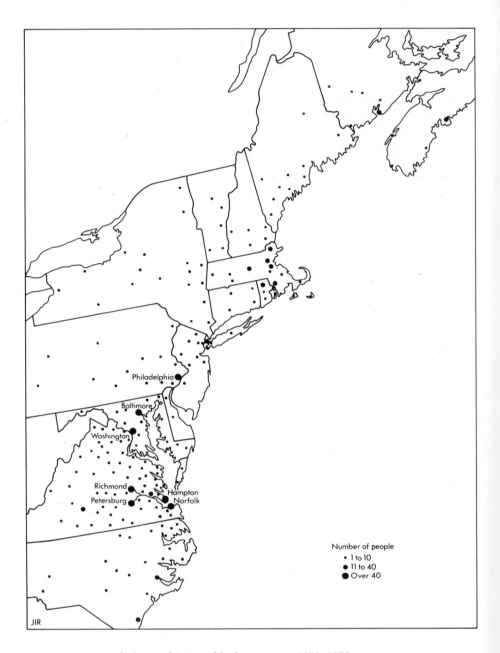

Map III-A. Birthplaces of Boston black migrants, 1870–1879.

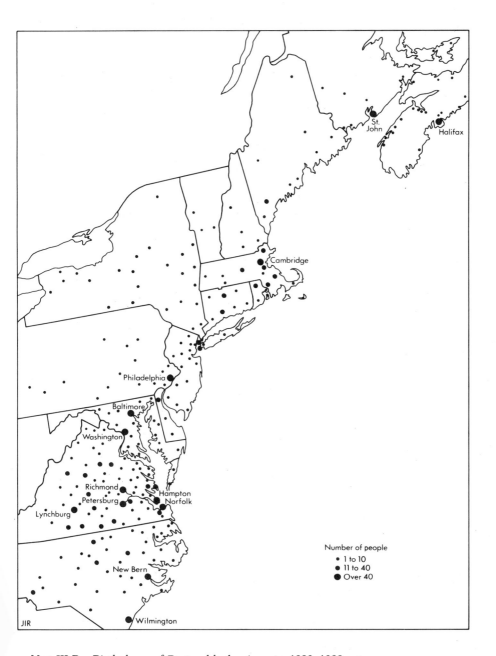

Map III-B. Birthplaces of Boston black migrants, 1890–1899.

49

It might be thought that by the turn of the century black migration would have rippled outward from its original coastal concentration. Instead, Map III-B was virtually identical to Map III-A. North of Virginia, most of the southern blacks arriving in Boston continued to be natives of Baltimore or Washington, D.C. The largest number of ex-Virginians were still from the Tidewater, although a few now left the southwest part of the state, either the tobacco-growing region around Albemarle County, or Lynchburg, a tobacco market town. The migration from North Carolina had expanded into the hinterland, although the seaports of Wilmington and Newbern remained the major places of origin.

SELECTIVITY OF SOUTHERN MIGRATION

At a time when most southern blacks wanted only to buy some land near their former plantations, these Southerners were leaving the South for a city 500 miles to the north. The simple fact of migration to a distant northern city made them different from other southern blacks. It is customary to think that southern black migrants were rural and ill-educated and to attribute many of their problems to those facts. Knowing how Boston's southern blacks "were trained before they came" is necessary for understanding their subsequent adaptation to Boston life.

First of all, many southern blacks had been prepared for northern urban life by their residence in a southern city. Among the birthplaces furnished by black migrants on their Boston marriage applications between 1870 and 1880, one third were born in towns—that is, they knew Petersburg, Norfolk, Hampton, or Richmond. The Richmond of their youth was something less than a metropolis; it had gas lights but no paved streets and numbered just 28,000 inhabitants in 1860. Norfolk that year, according to a keen northern observer, Frederick Law Olmsted, was a small town:

> It has all the immoral and disagreeable characteristics of a large seaport, with very few of the advantages that we should expect to find as relief to them. No lyceum or public libraries, no public gardens, no galleries of art, and though there are two "bethels," no "home" for its seamen; no public resorts of healthful and refining amusement, no place better than a slight tobacco-impregnated barroom or licentious dance-cellar. . . .[4]

4. Frederick Law Olmsted, *A Journey in the Seaboard Slave States, with Remarks on Their Economy* (New York, 1856; New York, 1904), p. 151.

Nevertheless, these places were still medium-sized labor markets, containing a relatively heterogeneous population. The rest of black Virginians were from the neighboring James River plantations, which were not as isolated as they might seem, a subject to be considered a little later in more detail.

Boston's black Virginians were increasingly urban in background by the turn of the century: Among those marrying in Boston in the decade after 1890, the largest group (about a third) was from Richmond, followed by another third from smaller cities in the state, and the rest from rural counties. The migrants from elsewhere in the South were even more knowledgeable about city life than black Virginians. The proportion of southern urbanites among Boston blacks between 1870 and 1879 varied from half of those from Maryland to two thirds of the migrants born in North and South Carolina. The Carolinians were from Charleston, Wilmington, and Newbern. At the turn of the century, more migrants from these other states were from urban backgrounds. North Carolina black migrants, increasingly rural in origin, were the single exception.

The typical black resident of a former Confederate state lived and died within the South. Black Southerners in Boston had departed from this expected course by deciding to move north. Shortly after Emancipation they had arrived in Boston, while most black Southerners refused to be uprooted. In what ways did these two groups differ?

First of all, black Southerners in Boston were more likely to be city-bred. It is true that only a third of Boston's black Virginians were urbanized, yet as a group their knowledge of city life extended far beyond that of other Virginia blacks. Table III-2 provides the rural and urban distributions of blacks throughout Virginia in 1850 and 1870. Data above these figures indicate the population size of the towns or cities where two successive cohorts of Boston's black Virginians were born, a first cohort born around 1850, and a second born about two decades later. Both cohorts, as Table III-2 shows, were much more likely to be urban born than other black Virginians, but the second cohort was even more unrepresentative of black Virginians than the first.

In comparison with other Southerners, those living in Boston had an unusually high rate of literacy. According to the Boston manuscript census schedules for 1870, two thirds of Virginia-born men and two fifths of the women were literate (Table III-3). The extent of their education, of course, can be doubted: Most probably knew little beyond how to sign their names or read a few words. Nonetheless,

TABLE III-2
Level of Urbanization for Virginia Blacks in Boston, 1870–1879 and 1890–1899

	Population size of Virginia towns				
Group	Rural	2500–9999	10,000–49,999	50,000+	N
Black Virginians in Boston born around 1850	63%[a]	6%[a]	31%[a]	0	634
All black Virginians, 1850	91%	2%	9%	0	831,617
Black Virginians in Boston born around 1870	51%[a]	11%[a]	25%[a]	13%[a]	1,004
All black Virginians, 1870	88%	3%	5%	4%	1,225,163

Sources: Boston Marriage Records, 1870–1879 and 1890–1899; J. B. D. DeBow, *Statistical View of the United States Census* (Washington, D.C., 1854), pp. 338–393; U.S. Census, *Population*, v. 1, pp. 278–283.
[a] Differences with stable population statistically significant.

this level of accomplishment distinguished them from most Virginia blacks in 1870, who were wholly illiterate. To be sure, many antebellum slaves in Tidewater towns acquired some education. During the war white missionaries quickly established schools there. But more accurate regional figures would doubtless show that black migrants to Boston were far more literate than other blacks from the Tidewater region.

Had these migrants come to Boston to take advantage of its excellent public schools? Ex-slaves all over the South wanted desperately to learn how to read the Scriptures and write their names. These migrants may have learned that Boston's schools were desegregated; perhaps some of them even hoped to send their children to a Boston-area college. This kind of speculation might be given additional support if it was learned that Boston's Southerners had a rate of literacy higher than that of black migrants elsewhere. But it can be seen in Table III-3 that southern migrants in Philadelphia in 1870 were as literate and perhaps even more so than those in Boston. Even if these migrants came north to further their educations, it was nonetheless the case that Boston held for them no unique attraction.

Among those who made the journey to Boston were a large number of mulattoes. Federal census enumerators were instructed "to note those quadroons, octoroons, and all persons having any

TABLE III-3
Selectivity of the Migration: Literacy and Skin Color

Birthplace	Residence	Males	N	Females	N
(A) *Rate of Illiteracy among Black Adults, by Migration Status, 1870[a]*					
Virginia	Virginia	99%	73,725	92%	304,376
Virginia[b]	Philadelphia	35%[c]	953	38%[c]	958
Virginia	Boston	32%[c]	441	56%[c]	367
(B) *Mulattoes as a Percentage of the Total Afro-American Population, by Migration Status, 1870*					
Virginia	Virginia	13%	248,228	8%	479,358
Virginia[b]	Philadelphia[a]	77%[b]	953	28%[b]	958
Virginia	Boston	28%[b]	495	29%[b]	427

Sources: U.S. Census, *Population*, v. 1 (Washington, D.C., 1872) p. 608; U.S. Census, Manuscript Census Schedules, 1870, Boston; Theodore Hershberg, "Mulattoes and Blacks: Intra-Group Color Differences and Social Stratification in Nineteenth-Century Philadelphia," unpublished paper delivered at the annual meeting of the Organization of American Historians, April 1974, no page.
[a] Among black adults, 21 and over.
[b] Includes migrants born in the District of Columbia.
[c] Difference with the stable group statistically significant.

perceptible trace of African blood."[5] In 1870 they determined that a little more than one quarter of Afro-Americans in Boston were mulattoes: The comparable figure for the state of Virginia was 1 in 10. Although Boston drew more than its share of light-skinned southern blacks, it was not the only city to do so: An even larger proportion of southern mulattoes migrated to Philadelphia, as Table III-3 indicates. Theodore Hershberg has observed that an unusually large number of mulattoes arrived there between 1850 and 1860, perhaps in response to growing restrictions in the Upper South, and that the proportion actually fell after that.[6] Nonetheless, even during Reconstruction, southern migration to Philadelphia as well as to Boston still vastly overrepresented the light-skinned.

Unlike most black Southerners, those in Boston were disproportionately urban, mulatto, literate, and from the Upper South. These were also the attributes of the South's free blacks. The logical conclusion is that most black Southerners in Boston had been free even before the Civil War. Certainly the migrants reaching Boston

5. Carroll D. Wright, *The History and Growth of the United States Census* (Washington, D.C., 1900), p. 171.
6. Theodore Hershberg, "Mulattoes and Blacks: Intra-Group Color Differences and Social Stratification in Nineteenth-Century Philadelphia," unpublished paper delivered at the annual meeting of the Organization of American Historians, April 1974, no page.

around 1900, most of whom were under 35, had been born in freedom. Inferences can be made about those who had arrived earlier. In 1850, 90% of Baltimore's blacks and 80% of those in Washington, D.C. were free. If random selection had operated, then virtually all black Bostonians from Maryland or the District of Columbia were free born. It is also known that in 1850, 9 out of 10 Virginia blacks were slaves.[7] Based on simple probabilities, most black Virginians in Boston were born into slavery. But it has already been established that black Virginians in Boston did not resemble other blacks from their home state and thus in this case, a better method of proof is necessary.

More direct evidence about the slave origins of Boston's Southerners is difficult to find, especially since Boston's black Southerners were never surveyed about their pre-war heritage. Another method for determining slave background, tracing antebellum slaves to their postbellum Boston residences, was prohibited because the federal census in the South did not enumerate the last names of the slaves. The one direct source about the slave past of Boston's Southerners was a register of names kept by the Freedman's Bureau, which was supplemented with additional names culled from their correspondence. These rosters were compared with a list of Virginia-born blacks from the 1870 federal manuscript census schedules. In this manner, 56 names out of 922 black Virginians in the Boston census of 1870 were linked, thus showing that 7% were ex-slaves.[8]

Although it is difficult to determine reliably whether a black Bostonian was a slave, there is a way to determine if that individual was free. The antebellum federal census enumerated the first and last names of free blacks. Thus free blacks, as listed in the census, could be traced to Boston records. Richmond was selected as the test case because it was the most common birthplace of black Virginians who married in late nineteenth-century Boston (more than a third of all black Virginians were born there). Indeed, among the birthplaces of black Southerners appearing in the Boston marriage records, Richmond was the most frequent place of birth. A list of all 3590 of Richmond's free blacks, compiled from the manuscript census

7. J.D.B. DeBow, *Statistical View of the United States Census* (Washington, D.C., 1854), pp. 338–393.

8. Massachusetts Vital Statistics, Suffolk County, Boston Marriage Records, 1865–1870; Manuscript Census Schedules, Boston, 1870; Record Group No. 105, Registers of the Freedmen Sent to New England, No. 198 and District of Columbia, Assistant Commissioner, Record of Applications for Transportation, April 14, 1866–November 30, 1868.

schedules for 1860, was matched against the names of Virginia-born blacks from the federal manuscript census schedules for 1870 and from the Boston marriage records (1865 to 1870) to determine whether any names were the same.[9] None of Richmond's free blacks could be located in these Boston records. Therefore, no direct proof was found that Boston's Southerners came from free backgrounds. But excellent evidence established that a small group of Boston's black Southerners were ex-slaves. The only sensible conclusion is that, intuition to the contrary, most of the black Southerners in late nineteenth-century Boston had once been slaves.

THE ECONOMICS OF BLACK MIGRATION

A self-selected group of ex-slaves moved to Boston in the late nineteenth century. With some hindsight, it is clear that a brighter future awaited them in the cities of the industrial North than on the farms of the rural South. If the move to the northern city was the best available alternative, why did so few take it?

The usual explanation for black migration to the North is a recitation of push and pull factors: shortages of labor in the North during World Wars I and II, the curtailment of foreign immigration to northern cities around the time of World War I, the devastation of the cotton plants by boll weevils and floods, the widespread adoption of mechanical cotton pickers, and the terror of the lynch mob. Only a few of these reasons for migration occurred prior to World War I. The boll weevil epidemic, which began around 1890, spurred migration from the cotton-growing regions of the Lower South, but had no impact on black movement from the wheat, corn, and tobacco regions of the Upper South. It is true that lynch mobs murdered more blacks in the 1890s than in any other decade, but they ran rampant more in the Lower than in the Upper South. Therefore, none of the traditional explanations account for black migration from the Upper South prior to World War I.

For this earlier period, the most dramatic instance of black northward movement was the Kansas Exodus of 1879. Within a few short months, wagon trains carrying more than 6000 ex-slaves from Louisiana, Mississippi, and Texas entered Kansas.[10] The migrants

9. Manuscript Census Schedules, Boston, 1870; Manuscript Census Schedules, Richmond, 1860; Boston Marriage Records, 1865–1870.
10. Nell Irvin Painter, *Exodusters: Black Migration to Kansas after Reconstruction* (New York, 1977).

traced their discontent to the crop lien system, mortgages on their farms, and the deprivation of schooling for their children. Many of them witnessed robberies, plunder, and murder by white night riders and even feared a return to slavery. Amidst this uneasiness, black leaders, especially the charismatic Pap Singleton, urged black farmers to occupy free land in Kansas. The migrants approached their emigration in millenarian terms: as a flight out of bondage into a land of freedom.

But the reasons for the Kansas Exodus did not govern black migration from the Upper South. Blacks from Virginia and Maryland could send their children to schools, although such schools were segregated. Some of the migrants may have been discontented with their failure to buy land or a heavy burden of debt, but many of Boston's black newcomers were town and city dwellers, who cared nothing about the state of southern agriculture. The people of the Kansas Exodus were transferring old peasant dreams of land to a new context; black migrants to the North were urbanized blacks moving to a larger and more liberal city. The Kansas blacks were religiously motivated; the more economically calculative migrants to Boston were less inclined to believe they were entering the promised land. The Kansas migrants were illiterate, probably dark-skinned ex-slaves who had endured the worst form of slavery; the black migrants to the North were more likely to be light-skinned and literate, reared in an older, milder, and more paternalistic slave regime.

It might be claimed that both the Kansas Exodus and the Boston migration were ripples in a placid sea. The reason more ex-slaves did not move *to Boston* was that, after the brief period of migration following emancipation, freed men and women were largely immobile, trapped in debt peonage, and ill-informed about economic opportunities in the South. Two economists who favor this point of view, Roger Ransom and Richard Sutch, believe that "it required a series of shocks from without" during the wartime shortages of World War I to reawaken the dormant migratory impulse in southern blacks.[11] The best evidence for their conclusion is the simple fact that in 1910 the center of black population remained about what it had been in 1860.

The population concentration did indeed remain the same, but southern blacks moved constantly. The greatest loss of black population began in the war-devastated, overpopulated regions of the Upper

---

11. Roger L. Ransom and Richard Sutch, *One Kind of Freedom: The Economic Consequences of Emancipation* (London, 1977), p. 196.

South. Even after taking into account the high fertility of the black population and the small stream of out-of-state blacks who settled in Virginia, the black population of Virginia continued to register a net loss: from 48,000 between 1870 and 1880 to 74,000 two decades later.[12] Of all the southern states, Virginia showed the largest drop in black population throughout the late nineteenth century. The movement, as A.A. Taylor explained, emanated from the Tidewater, "a highly exhausted, somewhat densely populated region, where economic stress was acute. . . ."[13] Upper South agriculture did not quickly recover after the war; those farms in operation paid low wages to hired laborers. Black migration flowed from those southern states offering the lowest wages for farm labor (Virginia, North and South Carolina) to those with the highest wages (Mississippi, Louisiana, Arkansas, Tennessee, and Florida).[14]

Some southern blacks permanently left the countryside for the city, others moved to small towns, and even more simply moved about—as seasonal laborers. Black farmers left after the harvest at the end of November or early December and returned to prepare for the first planting in the middle of January. They moved again after the July harvest and returned in September to pick the crops and bring them to market.[15] A smaller group of migrants appeared to move in the opposite direction, becoming farm laborers during the slack periods in factory work. Floyd Thornhill's movements within Virginia in the two decades after his emancipation conformed to both patterns:

> The first work that I did after emancipation was for the man I belonged to. I stayed with him about a year. Then I came to Lynchburg, and tended a garden for a gentleman that now lives in Danville. I worked in Lynchburg at that about a year. I was going on to about seventeen years of age then, and he gave me $5 a month and board. After that summer I went out on the Manassas Railroad, and worked there from Mount Jackson to Harrisonburg. Then after that I

12. Hope T. Eldridge and Dorothy Swaine Thomas, *Population Redistribution and Economic Growth, United States, 1870–1950. III. Demographic Analyses and Interrelations* (Philadelphia, 1964), Table A1.20, p. 260.

13. Alrutheus Ambrush Taylor, *The Negro in the Reconstruction of Virginia* (New York, 1926), p. 93.

14. Robert Higgs, *Competition and Coercion: Blacks in the American Economy, 1865–1914* (London, 1977), pp. 44–45, and Stanley Lebergott, *Manpower in Economic Growth: The American Record Since 1800* (New York, 1964), pp. 91–94.

15. An excellent discussion of seasonal migration among black sharecroppers can be found in Peter Gottlieb, "Making Their Own Way: Southern Blacks' Migration to Pittsburgh," unpublished Ph.D. dissertation, University of Pittsburgh, 1977, pp. 52–71.

went down to _____ deposit, and worked there about nine months. Then I came back to Lynchburg, and went into the tobacco factory . . . it was run up to about October; then the tobacco business was dull and there could be nothing done for three months or better, in the year, and I would go out on the railroad to work and come back to the factory in the Spring.[16]

If illiterate railroad construction workers, migrant laborers, and Exodusters were willing to travel hundreds of miles, why did so few of them move to Boston? It is true that most ex-slaves between 1865 and 1880 moved within the South, but out-migration from Virginia had begun to head north by 1880. Even then, most black Virginians went to New York, Pennsylvania, or New Jersey, and not to Massachusetts.[17] Among the states selected for settlement by Virginia lifetime migrants, Massachusetts ranked seventeenth in 1880, eighteenth in 1890, and fourteenth in 1900.[18]

The best evidence about the choice of *city* destinations is only available for 1870, a decade prior to the redirection of Virginia migration toward the North. Still, the same trends evident later had appeared by then. These lifetime southern out-migrants still confined their moves to nearby southern cities (Baltimore or Washington, D.C.), although a sizable number went to New Orleans. Of the northern city destinations, Philadelphia topped the list, and New York was second. As the destination for southern migrants, Boston lagged behind: As Table A-1 in Appendix A shows, Boston was the sixth choice for District of Columbia black migrants, seventh for Maryland-born blacks, and ninth for black Virginians.

Why did fewer Virginia migrants move to Boston than to New York City or Philadelphia? A cursory examination of at least some of the economic differences between the three cities, as presented in Table III-4, does not suggest any distinctive shortcoming to Boston resettlement or any singular benefit from residence in these other cities. If Virginia migrants had wanted to select the city with the largest labor market, they should have chosen New York rather than Philadelphia. If they sought the city with the highest wage differen-

16. U.S. Senate, *Report of the Committee upon the Relations between Labor and Capital*, v. 4 (Washington, D.C., 1885), p. 3.
17. Hope T. Eldridge and Dorothy Swaine Thomas, *Population Redistribution and Economic Growth*, Table 1.20, p. 260.
18. U.S. Census Office, *Statistics of the Population of the United States* (Washington, D.C., 1883), Table XII, pp. 488–491; U.S. Census, *Population*, v. 1 (Washington, D.C., 1890), Table 28, pp. 576–579, and U.S. Census, *Population*, Part I (Washington, D.C., 1901), Table 29, pp. 702–705.

TABLE III-4

Relationship of Interregional Migration from Virginia to Boston, Philadelphia, and New York, 1870

City	Interregional migration rate[a]	Wage differential[b]	Percentage of foreign born	Number of foreign born	Number of immigrants arriving at the port, 1860–1869	Population of the city
Boston	.18	+66¢	35	87,986	103,527	250,526
New York City	.26	+87¢	45	419,094	1,671,248	942,292
Philadelphia	.37	+55¢	27	183,624	23,732	694,022

Sources: "Comparative Position of Boston Wages, 1870–1898," *Massachusetts Labor Bulletin*, No. 9 (January 1899), pp. 1–3, and figures from the published federal census.

[a] The rate of migrants moving from Virginia to one of the three cities. It is computed by the formula $[A/(B + C)] \times 100$, where A is the number of Virginia migrants to a particular city, B is the number of black Virginians resident within the state, and C is the number of black Virginians who moved outside the state to any one of 49 cities.

[b] Difference between the wage for teamsters in Richmond versus Boston, Philadelphia, or New York City.

tial (that is, the greatest wage increase above their earnings in Richmond), then New York should have been first and Boston second. Or, if they had wanted to avoid competition with foreign-born workers, then Philadelphia, with the smallest percentage of foreign born, was the best city, but Boston deserved second place. The "theory of intervening opportunities," proposed by demographers, explains Boston's disadvantage. Between Richmond and Boston lay two great cities, each offering some distinct attractions. The labor markets of Philadelphia and New York thus acted to siphon off potential migrants who might have headed to Boston.[19]

Still, even as a destination somewhat off the beaten track, the black community of Boston was growing very rapidly, especially in the decade just after the Civil War and again in the middle of the 1880s. It has been demonstrated that sound economic wisdom favored relocating in New York or Philadelphia. Does it follow that those who came to Boston were unmoved by economic consideration, simple wanderers and, at the worst as DuBois claimed, "the off-scourings of country districts, sharpened and prepared for crime by the slums of many cities through which they have passed"?[20]

If black migration to Boston had been based on material gain, then we might expect to uncover its underlying economic sources. Inhabitants of low-wage regions tend to leave for high-wage ones, which was the case in the move from the Tidewater to New England. The common street laborer made anywhere from 17 to 82 cents more in Boston than in Richmond (Table III-5). Even if the lower cost of living in Richmond was taken into account (no information was available to make this estimate), the move to Boston was still in the laborer's economic interest. Black migration, according to classical economic theory, should vary directly in response to fluctuations in the wage differential: the higher the differential, the larger the volume of in-migration. But black migration failed to operate according to plan: In fact, precisely when the wage differential between the cities reached its peak, black in-migration came almost to a halt.

19. Samuel A. Stouffer, "Intervening Opportunities: A Theory Relating Mobility and Distance," *American Sociological Review*, v. 5 (1940), pp. 845–867; Samuel A. Stouffer, "Intervening Opportunities and Competing Migrants," *Journal of Regional Science*, v. 2 (1960), pp. 1–26; O. R. Galle and Karl E. Taeuber, "Metropolitan Migration and Intervening Opportunities," *American Sociological Review*, v. 31 (1966), pp. 5–13; M. B. Levy and W. J. Wadycki, "What Is the Opportunity Cost of Moving? Reconsideration of the Effects of Distance on Migration," *Economic Development and Cultural Change*, v. 22 (1974), pp. 198–214.

20. W.E.B. DuBois, *The Philadelphia Negro*, pp. 77–78.

However, higher wages do not always correlate with increased rates of in-migration, as even current economic studies show. A hidden feature of the economy, it is said, intervenes to suppress the effect of the wage differential. The presence of so many European immigrants in Boston constituted such a feature. They took most of the jobs in unskilled labor, leaving few jobs for blacks. Indeed, across the North in this period, the sheer size of immigrant populations placed a ceiling on black migration.[21] Even so, we still need to account for the rapid fluctuation in the rate of black in-migration to Boston.

It is often thought that a sharp decrease in the volume of European immigration leads to an increase in the rate of black migration. The best example of this was during World War I, when the supply of European immigrants to northern industry was curtailed, and black southern migrants were brought in as replacements. But, at least in the late nineteenth century, black migration to Boston responded to another rhythm. The rate of black and European immigration to Boston between 1865 and 1901 is reproduced in Table III-5. The upswings and downturns in the rate of in-migration for both groups coincided with booms and busts in the Boston economy, falling during each of the three major depressions and climbing during each recovery. The one exception was the decade of the 1870s, when the volume of black in-migration remained steady through the early years of the depression, then fell, and failed to immediately respond to economic recovery. In that decade, it appears that European immigrants rather than blacks were more attuned to Boston's economic trends. However, as a rule, both groups were highly sensitive to changing economic opportunities in Boston. Despite the fact that blacks and European immigrants were often arriving at precisely the same time, they were largely confined to separate labor markets and rarely competed for jobs, a subject to be explored more fully in Chapter V.

CHAIN MIGRATION

Southern migrants were much more pulled to Boston than pushed out of the South. They came because they had heard that jobs

21. Caroline Golab, *Immigrant Destinations* (Philadelphia, 1977), pp. 11–42. A methodologically sophisticated study of black migration found that the best predictors of black northward migration between 1900 and 1960 were two characteristics of the receiving region, its income advantage, and the rate of growth in the labor market. William Edward Vickery, "The Economics of the Negro Migration, 1900–1960," unpublished Ph.D. dissertation, University of Chicago, 1969.

TABLE III-5
Business Conditions, Foreign Immigration, and the Rate of Black Population Increase, 1865–1901

Year	Wage differential Richmond vs. Boston[a]	Percentage of rate of unemployment		Number of foreign-born passengers arriving at the port of Boston	Five-year rate of growth in the black population[b]	Percentage of population increase, adjusted for mortality[c]
		Male	Female			
1865	n.a.			10,007		
1866	n.a.			4,534		
1867	n.a.			11,483		
1868	n.a.			12,529		
1869	n.a.			23,294		
1870	51¢			33,028	49	55
1871	65¢			27,024		
1872	64¢			26,909		
1873	65¢			31,676		
1874	68¢			24,225		
1875	38¢			17,645	42	46
1876	34¢			9,711		
1877	17¢			7,887		
1878	25¢			8,756		
1879	25¢			10,364		
1880	49¢			34,062	18	19
1881	60¢			41,018		
1882	66¢			58,816		

Year	Wage[a]			Population[b]		
1883	82¢			48,188		
1884	82¢			35,036		
1885	76¢	18		25,660	3	9
1886	53¢	11		25,046		
1887	51¢			36,209		
1888	51¢			44,873		
1889	52¢			35,198		
1890	51¢	14		29,813	34	40
1891	52¢	11		30,951		
1892	52¢			32,343		
1893	52¢		21[d]	29,583		
1894	51¢			17,558		
1895	51¢			20,472	10	
1896	51¢			21,846		
1897	50¢			13,333		
1898	50¢			12,271		
1899	n.a.			19,227		
1900	n.a.	18	16	15,754	22	
1901	n.a.			25,616		

Sources: Report of the Committee on Immigration on the Problem of Immigration in Massachusetts (Boston, 1914), Table IV, p. 267; "Comparative Position of Boston Wages, 1870–1898," Massachusetts Labor Bulletin, No. 9 (January 1899), pp. 1–3; U.S. Department of Interior, Census Office, Vital Statistics of Boston and Philadelphia (Washington, D.C., 1895), Table 80, p. 126; Carlos C. Closson, Jr., "The Unemployed in American Cities," The Quarterly Journal of Economics, v. III (1894), pp. 168–257. Population figures and other rates of unemployment were found in the state census of Massachusetts and published federal census reports.

[a] The wage for a street laborer.

[b] The rate of increase is a conservative estimate of black population growth. There was no natural increase in the black population during this period, and all of the increase was due to in-migration.

[c] Adjusted to account for the excess of deaths over births.

[d] For males and females.

were plentiful, and they chose Boston because family or friends lived there. The move to Boston formed part of the history of the black family, insofar as family and friends, rather than recruiting agents, made it possible. Kinfolk were the invisible links that extended from the Tidewater to Wheeler Street, substantially the same kind of chains as those that connected Sicily with Little Italy or the Azores with Toronto. Although some blacks have relocated without the aid of relatives, and others have been directly recruited by employers, for the most part, the black move to the northern city, in the past or the present, has depended on kin. Black islanders from St. Helena, South Carolina, who reached Harlem in the 1930s, tended to stay with relatives before finding an apartment; they often married blacks from the islands or other parts of South Carolina or Georgia, and, during the depression, they often aided unemployed relatives. Most migrants returned to the island every year and often funerals were delayed until sons or daughters living in the North could return home. Some near-universal characteristics of chain migration can be specified: "Prospective migrants learn of opportunities, are provided transportation and have initial means of accommodation and employment arranged by means of primary social relationships with previous migrants."[22] Chain migration usually spans long distances and often begins with young men, some of whom return home and, as the movement continues, adds young women, and then whole families.

Chain migration from the South began with black men in their twenties, traveling by themselves or in twos. Gabriel Johnson and James Ross, two friends from Gloucester County, Virginia, "came from the South together in 1861" and continued to live near one another for the next 20 years.[23] According to tabulations from the

22. Clyde V. Kiser, *Sea Island to City: A Study of St. Helena Islanders in Harlem and Other Urban Centers* (New York, 1932), pp. 83–84, 210; John S. McDonald and Leatrice D. McDonald, "Chain Migration, Ethnic Neighborhood Formation and Social Networks," *The Milbank Memorial Fund Quarterly*, v. XLII, No. 1 (January 1964), pp. 82–97. Other analyses of chain migration include Robert E. Bieder, "Kinship as a Factor in Migration," *Journal of Marriage and the Family*, v. 35 (1973), pp. 429–439; James S. Brown, Harry K. Schwarzweller, and J. J. Mangalam, "Kentucky Mountain Migration and the Stem Family," *Rural Sociology*, v. 28 (1963), pp. 48–69. Studies concerned with the use of kin in black migration include Harvey M. Choldin, "Kinship Networks in the Migration Process," *International Migration Review*, v. 7 (1973), pp. 163–175; Daniel O. Price, "Rural to Urban Migration of Mexican-Americans, Negroes, and Anglos," *International Migration Review*, v. 5 (1971), pp. 281–291; and Charles Tilly and C. Harold Brown, "On Uprooting, Kinship, and the Auspices of Migration," *International Journal of Comparative Sociology*, v. 8 (1968), pp. 139–164.

23. Record Group No. 15, Records of the Veterans Administration in the National Archives, Civil War Pension of Gabriel Johnson, S.C. 509103.

manuscript census schedules for 1870, there were 100 southern-born men in Boston for every 92 southern-born women. For a brief period during Reconstruction, whole families began to move to Boston, a conclusion suggested by the fact that a majority of the oldest children of southern-born parents listed in the 1870 census were born in the South. Whether this family migration was related to the reunion of so many slave families after emancipation cannot be known. However, the older pattern reappeared by 1880: An examination of the census showed that most of the first children of Southerners were born after their parents had settled in the North. One of these migrant couples was the Burrells, Spotswood and Josephine. These Virginia ex-slaves had married in Warwick County in January of 1873, moved to Boston in April of that year, and had their first child in October.[24] In other families, a wife and children followed the husband to Boston, like the Allstons of Edenton, North Carolina. Phillip Allston recalled, "I was left in the care of my mother when only a few years old, my father hastily leaving for the North, and I did not see him for eight years. I came to Boston, July, 1871, where my mother joined my father."[25]

Even migration assisted by employers rather than kin could result in the beginnings of a chain. This was true for Ella Beam, the first migrant from the South Carolina sea island of St. Helena to reach Boston. She attended the Penn School in St. Helena, an all-black institution begun by Yankee schoolteachers at the end of the Civil War. A New England teacher at the school secured her a position as a domestic in Milton, Massachusetts. She went there in the summer of 1876, but returned home in the winter. After her second summer in Milton, she decided to stay. She soon found a place in service for a girlfriend. After 10 years there, she settled in Boston and learned dressmaking. "To tell the truth," she recalled years later, "I was so much alone there that breeds dissatisfaction."[26] Years later, after her mother died, she invited her two young sisters north to live with her.[27]

A few migrants, like the seasonal farm laborers who followed the crop harvests, did not move directly from the South to the North. William Gibson, a fugitive slave from Rappahanock County, Virginia, took odd jobs in Boston for a few months and then became a farm laborer in Paxton, Massachusetts. He worked for three Paxton farm-

24. Civil War Pension of Spotswood Burrell, W.C. 849037.

25. John Daniels, *In Freedom's Birthplace: A Study of the Boston Negroes* (Boston, 1914), p. 358.

26. Clyde Vernon Kiser, *Sea Island to City*, p. 97.

27. Ibid., p. 170.

ers and another in nearby Colebrook and then returned to Boston.[28] Some migrants moved between friends and kin spread across the North. David Brown left Elkton, Maryland, and stayed with friends in Norristown, Pennsylvania, relocated near relatives in Worcester, and then came to live with friends in Boston.

Often chain migration also involved some return to the place of origin. Similar patterns have been observed among Italian or Greek emigrants to the United States, who earned just enough money to return to their homeland, or crossed the ocean several times. Gradually, of course, some settled permanently in America, although a significant number were only temporary residents. Patience Avery was the daughter of a black domestic and a white master. Sometime during the 1870s she moved to Boston and worked as a domestic for an abolitionist family. Then she returned to Petersburg and married an ex-slave she had known from childhood.[29] Around 1875, Matilda Carter went to New York City but decided to go back to her family in Virginia. She simply alluded to the reason for her return: "I went to New York an' stayed a long time. Finally I got tired an' come home."[30] It is difficult to estimate the extent of return migration among the southern blacks in Boston. In Philadelphia, far closer to Maryland and the Upper South, DuBois noted a seasonal movement: "Every spring the tide of immigration sets in, consisting of brickmakers, teamsters, asphalt workers, common laborers, etc., who work during the summer in the city and return to the cheaper living of Virginia and Maryland for the winter."[31] He found that many of these sojourners left "their families in the South with grandmothers" and lived "in lodgings here."[32] Boston was farther from the South than Philadelphia, and the cost of transportation was somewhat higher. Still, return migration appears to have been common. A limited estimate about its extent can be made by examining the destinations of southern black Civil War veterans who identified their whereabouts in a Civil War pension application. These out-migrants from Boston went to the suburbs (11), moved to Detroit (1), and returned to the South (6). Even when southern migrants stayed in Boston, most maintained some contact with their families back home. Newcomers

28. Civil War Pension of William Gibson, S.C. 342076; Civil War Pension of David Brown, W.C. 314199.

29. Charles L. Perdue, Jr., Thomas E. Barden, and Robert K. Phillips, *Weevils in the Wheat: Interviews with Virginia Ex-Slaves* (Charlottesville, 1976), p. 17.

30. Ibid., p. 70.

31. W.E.B. DuBois, *The Philadelphia Negro*, p. 135.

32. Ibid.

carried news of families in the South and visited their relatives in Boston. Cora Washington, a migrant from Virginia, heard about her family from other migrants. She explained, "Annie Mays [of Everett] goes down to Richmond every summer and then sees my folks and tells me about them."[33]

SLAVE CULTURE

These former town slaves from the antebellum Upper South were far better informed about Boston than illiterate field hands from rural plantations. At the same time, they had been shaped by bondage and by the distinctive slave culture of the Upper South. Whether the move to Boston was a brittle uncoupling with the past or a smooth transition depends not only on understanding their special attributes and their reasons for choosing Boston but also on taking the full measure of that slave culture, its unique privileges and considerable burdens.

Opportunities for learning through religious instruction, reading newspapers, and contact with free blacks contributed to the unusual level of literacy among blacks in Richmond and Petersburg. At least in Virginia, the law against teaching the slaves to read and write had not been strictly enforced. The white minister of a Richmond black congregation was seemingly unperturbed by this law. His church even bought hymn books for the slave choir! This minister believed that reading was perfectly compatible with slavery "because literate slaves will make more useful servants, if in a state of bondage, and more safe and reliable residents, if free . . ."[34] Immediately after the end of the war Lucy and Sarah Chase, two Quaker school mistresses from Worcester, noted that "in spite of the rigid law against teaching the Negroes, nearly every colored family in Richmond has one or more members who can read."[35] Sometimes slave owners educated their chattel, like Robert Francis of Richmond, who hired a slave from an owner in Goochland County and wrote to the owner: "Sir, you will let me know how long I can keep him Beverly—he is a good boy and I would like to keep him for five years and I will learn him to read and write and I'll teach him the barber trades and I will make

33. Civil War Pension of George Washington, W.C. 890909.
34. John Thomas O'Brien, Jr., "From Bondage to Citizenship: The Richmond Black Community, 1865–1867," unpublished Ph.D. dissertation, University of Rochester, 1975, p. 21.
35. Ibid., pp. 139–140.

him a good man—if you ever call down to Richmond to see me."[36] In other cases, exceptional slave parents taught their children, or enterprising children found their own means to an education, such as those who employed "little systems of bribery exchanging with white children a nut or an apple for a letter . . ."[37]

Slaves in the cities of Virginia, and in Baltimore and Washington, D.C., enjoyed better housing, superior diet and clothing, and improved general health compared with their kin in the countryside. Frederick Douglass, a plantation slave sold to a man in Baltimore, immediately noticed the differences:

> Instead of the cold, damp floor of my master's kitchen, I found myself on carpets, for the corn bag in winter, I now had a good straw bed, well furnished with covers; for the coarse corn-meal in the morning, I now had good bread and mush occasionally; for my poor tow-linen shirt, reaching to my knees, I had good linen clothes. I was really well off.[38]

Despite the higher standard of living—or perhaps because of it—the Upper South bred more than its share of discontent. Runaways from their masters hid in the forests or mingled with free blacks. Fears of insurrection, whether warranted or not, plagued Richmond's whites in the 1850s. Even some of the trusted servants on Tidewater plantations were known, during the master's absence, to burn the mansion to the ground. On the plantation, Frederick Douglass had thought about escape but his residence in Baltimore gave him the opportunity. Several fugitives, like Douglass, hid on board vessels that sailed to New Bedford and Boston.[39]

Slaves in this region were also able to develop semi-independent religious styles. By 1860 Richmond had four black churches, all with white ministers. At Richmond's largest antebellum black church, the First African, the white minister, Reverend Robert Ryland, delivered the sermons but called upon black preachers, sitting at their benches,

36. Luther Porter Jackson, *Free Negro Labor and Property Holding in Virginia, 1830–1860* (New York, 1942), p. 177.

37. John Thomas O'Brien, Jr., "From Bondage to Citizenship," pp. 139–140.

38. As quoted in Richard Wade, *Slavery in the Cities* (New York, 1964), pp. 173–177.

39. Frederick Douglass, *My Bondage and My Freedom* (New York, 1855; Chicago, 1970), pp. 248–268; Jane H. Pease and William H. Pease, *The Fugitive Slave Law and Anthony Burns: A Problem in Law Enforcement* (Philadelphia, 1975), p. 29; William H. Siebert, "The Underground Railroad in Massachusetts," *New England Quarterly*, v. IX, No. 3 (September 1936), pp. 441–467.

"to pray, several times at each religious service."[40] Such men, who Ryland admitted were "ministers of respectable gifts," often officiated at the most important ritual of slave life, the funeral, casually supervised at a distance by white overseers. The style of worship at Richmond churches, one observer claimed, "was very much like that of a white congregation, except that the hymns were sung with unusual fervour, and when the last was given out the people began to grasp each others hands, singing all the time, and beginning to drift slowly out, much of the handshaking and singing going on after the people had got into the open air." White visitors praised the singing of European hymns by the church choir, but, after Reverend Ryland left the room, an English visitor noted that "a few old people got very much excited, swinging their feet, and shaking hands frantically with everybody near them, myself among the rest."[41]

At The First African Baptist, 11 black deacons, slaves as well as free men, participated actively in church affairs with Ryland's encouragement. They even vetoed his decisions on occasion. Each month they met to discuss complaints from congregants about the moral conduct of church members: allegations of wife abuse, excessive discipline of children, desertion, and bigamy. They did not allow remarriage when spouses were alive, except in cases of sale, and ejected from the church adulterers. Given the prevailing notion that slavery encouraged only informal unions, it is remarkable to note that these Richmond deacons insisted that cohabiting couples marry and excluded from the congregation those living in "unlawful wedlock."[42]

Even in bondage, blacks in the Upper South had made the transition from feudalism to quasi-wage labor. The growth of industrial

40. John Thomas O'Brien, Jr., "From Bondage to Citizenship," p. 55. The development of Christianity among Virginia's slaves was described by Luther Porter Jackson in "Religious Development of the Negro in Virginia from 1760–1860," *Journal of Negro History*, v. XVI (April 1931), pp. 168–239, and by Milton C. Sernett in *Black Religion and American Evangelicalism: White Protestants, Plantation Missions, and the Flowering of Negro Christianity, 1787–1865* (Metuchen, New Jersey, 1975). Luther P. Jackson presented the history of the slave and free blacks who formed the congregation of Petersburg's black churches in "Free Negroes of Petersburg, Virginia," *Journal of Negro History*, v. XII, No. 3 (July 1927), p. 384. The most famous of the slave preachers continued to hold revivals in Richmond after the Civil War. See William Hatcher, *John Jasper, the Unmatched Negro Philosopher and Preacher* (New York, 1908).

41. Marianne Finch, *Englishwoman's Experience*, as quoted in Dena J. Epstein, *Sinful Tunes and Spirituals: Black Folk Music to the Civil War* (Urbana, 1977), p. 207; Alrutheus Ambrush Taylor, *The Negro in the Reconstruction of Virginia*, p. 198.

42. John Thomas O'Brien, Jr., "From Bondage to Citizenship," pp. 24, 44, 49.

manufacturing in southern cities and the large supply of slave labor created a slave proletariat as well as a large group of slave (as well as free black) skilled workers. In 1860 Virginia ranked fifth in the number of manufacturing establishments, just behind Massachusetts.[43] The South had few of the North's dark satanic mills: Most of Virginia's factories processed tobacco (52 plants in Richmond, 47 in Lynchburg just before the war) or other agricultural products. Richmond also milled flour and forged iron; Norfolk had a flour mill, iron foundry, and plow and furniture factories. All of these plants hired slave labor or a combination of slave and free workers. Richmond factories employed 5767 slaves in 1850 and about 1000 more a decade later. In all, about one third of Richmond's adult male slaves worked in the tobacco and iron factories.[44]

The abundant supply of slave labor as well as the growing demand for unskilled workers led to new patterns of slave employment. In southern cities large slave populations tended to diminish the number of unskilled white workers; in fact, employers often preferred slave or free black labor to whites. The absence of a large white artisan class opened some skilled occupations to slaves; slave carpenters and blacksmiths even trained their own apprentices. Since the

43. Luther Porter Jackson, *Free Negro Labor*, pp. 44–45, 55. The origin of the slave industrial labor force was analyzed by Ronald Lewis in two articles, "Slavery on Chesapeake Iron Plantations before the American Revolution," *Journal of Negro History*, v. LIX (1974), pp. 242–254, and "The Use and Extent of Slave Labor in the Chesapeake Iron Industry: The Colonial Era," *Labor History*, v. XVII (1976), pp. 388–412. Robert Starobin raised the issue of coercion as the mechanism for disciplining slave workers in *Industrial Slavery in the Old South* (New York, 1970); "The Economics of Industrial Slavery in the Old South," *Business History Review*, v. XLIV (Summer 1970), pp. 131–174; and in "Disciplining Industrial Slaves in the Old South," *Journal of Negro History*, v. LIII (April 1968), pp. 111–128. See also Charles B. Dew, "Disciplining Slave Iron Workers in the Antebellum South: Coercion, Conciliation, and Accommodation," *American Historical Review*, v. LXXIX (1974), pp. 393–418, and "Black Ironworkers and the Slave Insurrection Panic of 1856," *Journal of Southern History*, v. XLI (1975), pp. 321–338. Some additional studies with useful information concerning slave factory workers include Kathleen Bruce, *Virginia Iron Manufacture in the Slave Era* (New York, 1931); Charles B. Dew, *Ironmaker to the Confederacy: Joseph R. Anderson and the Tredegar Iron Works* (New Haven, 1966); Joseph Clarke Robert, *The Tobacco Kingdom: Plantation Market, and Factory in Virginia and North Carolina, 1800–1860* (Durham, N.C., 1938); Kathleen Bruce, "Slave Labor in the Virginia Iron Industry," *William and Mary Quarterly*, v. VII, 2nd series (January 1927), pp. 21–31; and Sydney Bradford, "The Negro Ironworker in Antebellum Virginia," *Journal of Southern History*, v. XXV (May 1959), pp. 194–206.

44. Luther Porter Jackson, *Free Negro Labor*, p. 55, and Claudia Dale Goldin, *Urban Slavery in the American South, 1820–1860: A Quantitative History* (Chicago, 1976), p. 27.

federal census never accurately enumerated slave occupations, it is impossible to learn exactly the size of the skilled slave work force. However, in a special city census for Charleston in 1848, 17% of the slaves were skilled, and, in the mortality schedule for Norfolk in 1850 (those slaves who died in the previous year), 20 out of 22 adult male slaves had a skill.[45] Even if the Charleston figure was nearer the mark than Norfolk's, either one represents a substantial proportion of skilled slave workers.

Because of the availability of slave labor in the cities and on the nearby plantations, factory owners, as well as other urban employers, "hired" slaves: They rented labor on a contract basis for a day, a month, or a year, although the typical contract covered a year. Urban employers employed the excess labor from the Tidewater plantations, and, as a result, two thirds of slave men in Richmond and one third of the women in 1860 were hired out.[46] Masters liked this profitable arrangement because they were relieved of excess labor between planting seasons. Every year at Christmastime a Tidewater planter sent some of his slaves to agents. In a diary entry in 1859, this owner noted, "I've sent him [the slave, Edmund] as usual to Richmond" and another entry in the diary notes that "ben was sent to Petersburg under the care of an agent there."[47] Eighteen agents in Richmond hired, transported, and supervised the laborers.[48] One Christmas in 1856, for instance, Frederick Law Olmsted observed a large group of black men and boys, led by a white agent, carrying coarse white blankets drawn together at the corners to hold some articles for clothing. Olmsted noted that they "had been sent into the town to be hired out as servants or factory hands."[49] The next year the *Richmond Daily Dispatch* remarked that the streets of the city were "filled with negroes brought in from the country for hire."[50]

The hiring-out contract specified the price, the nature of the work, and the conditions of treatment. Some slaves found employers by inquiring for work or visiting special hiring halls, such as those in Richmond. The *Richmond Daily Dispatch* was amused by the story of

45. Claudia Dale Goldin, *Urban Slavery*, pp. 42–45.

46. Ibid., Table 8, p. 36. See also Clement Eaton, "Slave Hiring in the Upper South: A Step toward Freedom," *Mississippi Valley Historical Review*, v. XLVI (1960), pp. 663–670.

47. Luther Porter Jackson, *Free Negro Labor*, p. 177.

48. Ibid., p. 176.

49. Frederick Law Olmsted, *A Journey in the Seaboard Slave States*, pp. 33–34.

50. *Richmond Daily Dispatch* (January 3, 1854), as quoted in John Thomas O'Brien, Jr., "From Bondage to Citizenship," p. 14.

a slave who, in bargaining to work for a Judge Lomax, needed some time to "inquire into the standing and character of the Judge."[51] Some skilled craftsmen were even leased to themselves: Slave carpenters, barbers, and draymen operated their own shops, handled customers, and received their own wages.[52] Slaves who paid for their own lodgings with the master's "board money" often lived with free blacks; the rest set up a wooden shack in an alley or lived with their master or temporary owner. One Virginia slave owner, questioned by Olmsted, admitted the potential danger in all of these arrangements: "They earned money, by over work and got a habit of roaming about and taking care of themselves."[53]

As a rule, masters maintained their property better than those who rented slave labor. Tidewater aristocrats usually fed slaves properly, clothed them adequately, and met their medical needs. The man who hired slave property treated his work force with far less care. He often relied on the whip to discipline workers, although not to the point of causing them to run away. The only restraint on irresponsible treatment was the owner; if his slaves were severely maltreated, he was reluctant to hire them out again. Still, most slaves, when offered the choice, wanted to be hired, even though they traded a considerable degree of material well-being for some greater freedoms.

But perhaps the greatest hardship for these relatively privileged slaves was the threat of sale. Some were sold to masters on neighboring plantations, but most feared was the sale to a harsh taskmaster in the lower South. On the days of slave sales three red flags hung from the doors of Richmond's auction houses. Virginia's slaves had managed to avoid sale to the lower South, but they could not escape resentment at such a cruel system and fear for themselves and their families. Slavery in this region, then, was a netherworld of freedoms amidst limitations. Some slaves learned to read and write, handle money, acquire a trade, or make decisions for the community. But they operated within a coercive system, which could crush their liberties whenever it was expedient to do so.

CULTURAL TRANSFER

Within their lifetimes the southern migrants in Boston had made two significant transitions: from slavery to freedom, and from the

51. Ibid.
52. Luther Porter Jackson, *Free Negro Labor*, pp. 178–179.
53. Frederick Law Olmsted, *A Journey in the Seaboard Slave States*, p. 31.

semi-cosmopolitan southern town to the decidedly sophisticated northern city. It would have been understandable had they desired to obliterate any trace of the slave past from their new life. Many of the light-skinned and literate perhaps sought to pass as white or as dark natives of New England. DuBois hinted that southern migrants to Philadelphia had these motives in mind: "Strong social considerations lead many Negroes to give their birthplace to Philadelphia when, as a matter of fact, it may be elsewhere."[54] On the other hand, these southern blacks might have wanted to preserve what was theirs, the life they made as slaves—in fact, to hold fast to it as they began anew in an alien and even hostile world.

In the first phase of their adjustment to Boston, these southern newcomers depended on friends and family for food, a place to sleep, and a job. Residence with a relative was, for most, a brief stay, lasting only about a week. In 1870 and 1880, relatives were living in only about 1 in 10 southern-born households. Nevertheless, even after the first few weeks of adjustment, most Southerners continued to live in a southern world. In over half of the southern families taking in boarders in 1870 or 1880, both tenant and landlord were from the same home state.[55]

An initial pattern of dependence tended to develop into a long-term relationship based on mutual aid. Friends and relatives from the South were more than a housing agency: They were present at every family event and at every personal crisis—as godparents at baptisms, midwives at births, and mourners at funerals. Male friends, colleagues, and neighbors met at neighborhood taverns. (In roughly a five-block area from the Charles Street jail to Bowdoin Square there were more than 10 saloons in 1877 and 88 in the entire West End area by 1902.[56]) Barbershops were an informal thronging

---

54. W.E.B. DuBois, *The Philadelphia Negro*, p. 80.

55. For a similar contemporary pattern, see Charles Tilly, "Race and Migration to the American City," in James Q. Wilson, ed., *The Metropolitan Enigma* (Cambridge, 1968), p. 136. Even black migration to modern cities works this way, as one can see from the life histories of black migrants to Washington, D.C., in the 1960s:

> When Tonk and Pearl got married and took an apartment near the Carryout, Pearl's brother, Boley, moved in with them. Later, Pearl's nephew, J.R., came up from their hometown in North Carolina and he, too, moved in with them. J.R. joined Tonk and Boley on the street corner and when Earl told Tonk of some job openings where he worked, Tonk took J.R. with him. These three, then, were kinsmen, shared the same residence, hung out together on the street corner, and two of them—for a time at least—were co-workers [Elliot Liebow, *Tally's Corner* (Boston, 1967), p. 165].

56. *A Schedule of the Buildings and Their Occupancy on the Principal Streets and*

social center; in fact, barbers complained about the loss of "many bars of toilet soap" on the "deadweights" who frequented their establishments.[57] They also gave advice, introduced neighbors, and peddled information. At the pool hall, men placed bets with numbers runners and spent hours waiting between jobs. They met at neighborhood gymnasiums and attended boxing matches together. Women friends cared for pregnant mothers, supervised children when mothers worked, provided an extra cot in an emergency, offered food, and gave small loans. They shared information about available apartments, jobs in domestic service, experienced midwives, unfaithful husbands, delinquent children, and remedies and cures for common ailments: They talked across the laundry line, at the market, and at the water pump. Very close friends usually belonged to the same church. Fannie Simmons said about her friend Jeannette Goodwin, "We are both members of the same church for over 20 years—the African Methodist Episcopal church on Charles Street here in Boston. We have been like sisters over all the years."[58]

These Southerners, who lacked warm clothing and adequate coal for the winter, turned to friends when they became ill. Henry James, a freedman from Fairfax County, Virginia, who rented rooms at the boardinghouse of Frances Douglass, became very sick. Douglass nursed him for 8 or 9 months and, in return, he promised to repay her when he recovered.[59] During one of his frequent illnesses, George Banks asked Charles Brown to give him a place to stay. As Brown explained, "I took him in my room [he] was laid up about three or four weeks . . . his rent mounted up to about three dollars. I charged him 50 cents a week."[60] Both men continued to live in Boston and remained close friends for over 20 years. George W. Turner, a neighbor of George Banks for 17 years, had once brought Banks through a bout with pneumonia.[61] After Mary Williamson, a live-in domestic in Newton, took sick, she telegraphed her friend, Mary Jones. Mrs. Jones's daughter brought Williamson to her mother's apartment in Boston.[62] Rachel Brown was nursed by her friend, Anna Burwell, for 3 weeks until she was taken to the insane asylum in Worcester.[63]

Wharves of the City of Boston (Boston, 1877), pp. 29–31; Robert A. Woods, *Americans in Process: A Settlement Study by Residents and Associates of the South End House* (Boston and New York, 1902), p. 291.

57. The *Hub* (September 15, 1883); ibid. (October 13, 1883).
58. Civil War Pension of James W. Simmons, C.W. 074105.
59. Civil War Pension of Henry James, C.W. 842789.
60. Civil War Pension of George Banks, W.C. 773756.
61. Ibid.
62. Civil War Pension of William Williamson, C.W. 902002.
63. Civil War Pension of John S. Brown, C.W. 895570.

The constant presence of death and dying required aid from friends. Spencer Williams comforted Mills Moore, who lay dying of consumption in a Boston room.[64] At the bedside of her chronically ill husband, Isabella Shepard was consoled by her friend Mary Nichols.[65] When Charlotte Brown's husband died, Augusta Stafford gave her some money to help pay burial expenses. Some southern migrants died at the homes of their relatives.[66] Stephen Wallace, a migrant from Petersburg, died of consumption at his sister's home in Dedham.[67] Attendance at the funeral often proved the final act of friendship. Edward Ditmus performed the burial ritual for his old wartime companion, Elias Hall, and gave money to Hall's widow.[68]

As southern migrants turned to each other for assistance, they met other newcomers, and, thus, in selecting a husband or wife, they tended to choose someone from the South, a partner at a dance, a neighbor, or a stranger introduced to them by a friend, relative, or minister. According to the manuscript census schedules for Boston in 1870 as well as 1880, five out of six southern men in late nineteenth-century Boston married southern-born women. This figure includes couples married in Boston as well as those who married prior to the move. Even among those migrants who married only after they had settled in Boston, the preference for another Southerner persisted. Tidewater migrants, for example, tended to select mates from the same region. In the Boston marriage records for 1870 to 1880, for example, about half of the black women from Tidewater cities (Richmond, Norfolk, Petersburg, or Hampton) chose a partner born in one of those four cities. Many of these Tidewater couples were married by a Virginia-born black minister.

TENSIONS WITHIN BLACK SOCIETY

Southern migrants who actively sought the companionship of other Southerners were often shunned by other blacks. Since Southerners were so isolated from the rest of society, they may have insulated themselves from experiencing some of these slights, but their dialect, colorful dress, distinctive walk, and superstitions set them apart as black Southerners, recent arrivals from "Southside," and easy marks for pickpockets, con artists, and unscrupulous landlords.

64. Civil War Pension of Charles M. Moore, C.W. 564774.
65. Ibid.
66. Civil War Pension of George Banks, W.C. 773756.
67. The *Hub* (July 5, 1884).
68. Civil War Pension of Elias Hall, W.C. 634126.

In New York City hostility toward southern migrants and a heightened pride in northern heritage led to the founding of the Sons of New York in 1884.[69] No similar group of Massachusetts-born blacks was formed in Boston, but, nonetheless, a certain prejudice toward southern migrants existed, as the reaction to a sensational newspaper report illustrates.

A white reporter investigated the existence of voodoo in Boston. After several unsuccessful inquiries, he was led to the fifth floor of a South End tenement where he found 20 blacks from the West Indies, Virginia, and Maryland, between the ages of 10 and 60, and a voodoo priest and priestess. He attended two different ceremonies and on his third visit, he asked the priest, an ex-slave who had lived in New Orleans, to give him some herb medicine for his sore knee.

At one gathering the priestess, encircled by her guests, stood in the center of the room, adorned with "herbs, a piece of old iron, a handful of horsehair which she raised above her head as she uttered her prayer."[70] She took a dead snake out of a bottle, raised it above her right hand, and sang a song. Then she and the priest sat silently on a throne, a sturdy plank suspended between two chairs, while the group, seated in a circle, prayed, "O thou God Voodoo, take all evil away. O thou God Voodoo, keep us from all charms and spells."[71] After this prayer each of the participants explained why spells had been cast on them. Accompanied by Uncle Joe on the fiddle, the participants danced and removed one article of clothing at a time. Spirited dancing continued late in the evening—the shocked reporter withdrew at one in the morning.

It might be thought that the practice of voodoo was alien to the slaves in the Upper South. It is true that this religious ritual began in New Orleans and spread to other regions of Louisiana, but less orthodox forms, "hoodoo" or conjuration, reading signs, brewing remedies and cures, were known throughout the South. Even in the Upper South elderly Africans and slaves imported from the West Indies had introduced voodoo to the plantation.[72] There is no way of knowing whether this South End group was practicing Dahomeyan serpent worship or simple hoodoo, and the authenticity of their observance is unimportant. What matters is that the reporter's interest

69. Seth M. Scheiner, *Negro Mecca: A History of the Negro in New York City, 1865–1920* (New York, 1965), p. 117.

70. Boston *Sunday Herald* (July 14, 1889).

71. Ibid.

72. Charles L. Perdue, Jr., Thomas E. Barden, and Robert K. Phillips, *Weevils in the Wheat*, p. 267.

in the exotic had revealed yet another instance of the cultural transfer between the Tidewater and New England.

At the same time, nothing better illustrated the division between the migrants and cosmopolitan blacks than the explosive reaction to the *Herald* articles. At first black leaders, who charged white newspapers with fabrication, denied that voodoo existed, but later the National League of Boston, a black civil rights organization, was forced to admit the existence of voodoo but tried to minimize its scope. An investigative committee appointed by the League reported that they found "something approaching this practice . . . in a house on Primus Avenue in the West End. . . ."[73] Even though they claimed that the newspapers overestimated the extent of the practice, the League still passed a series of resolutions condemning voodoo as a "degrading and disreputable" superstition and chastised its adherents as "foolish," "low," and "ignorant persons."[74] The incident can be limited to the National League's opinions on voodoo, but it actually expresses widespread embarrassment about the practices of these newcomers.

SEPARATE NEIGHBORHOODS

The needs of newcomers for housing near their jobs as well as this hostility from other blacks and from whites led to separate southern black neighborhoods in Boston. Black areas of residence dominated by Southerners could be found throughout the North. Virginia migrants in Detroit tended to settle near the docks and the downtown commercial district. In New York City, most of the migrants from Maryland, the District of Columbia, Virginia, and the Carolinas were living on San Juan Hill.[75] The one area of Boston disproportionately inhabited by Southerners was the six black neighborhoods within the South End. Ex-slaves began moving there immediately after the Civil War: By 1880 two thirds of all southern black adults lived in the five wards of the South End, but less than a quarter of blacks from elsewhere resided there.

Lodgings in the South End were convenient to the hotels and railroads where blacks worked. A good number of men in this area

73. New York *Age* (July 20, 1889).
74. Ibid.
75. Mary White Ovington, *Half a Man: The Status of the Negro in New York* (New York, 1911; New York, 1969), p. 35; David Manners Katzman, *Before the Ghetto: Black Detroit in the Nineteenth Century* (Urbana, 1973), p. 30.

Children on Wheeler Street, South End, c. 1890.

were employed in the large hotels of Copley Square and the Back Bay "into whose service they are drawn when there is exceptional need . . . ."[76] The residents of one boarding house in the South End were all southern-born black waiters. After black strikebreakers were used at the Boston and Albany Railroad yards, most of the laborers hired were blacks.[77] Three black neighborhoods in the South End probably originated because of the proximity to these yards.

76. Robert A. Woods, ed., *The City Wilderness: A Settlement Study by Residents and Associates of South End House* (Boston, 1898), p. 94.
77. New York *Freeman* (February 19, 1887).

To the social workers who were developing charity homes in the South End, the streets on which blacks lived were the slums, some of the worst in the South End, if not in the whole city. The sorriest cases of destitution were found there, such as the 11-year-old black child "in a third story of a house on a back street, alone, without food or fire, in an advanced state of consumption."[78] In many courts and alleys with inadequate sanitation, uncollected refuse accumulated and the surface water ran "into vacant lots and [remained] until evaporated."[79] The tenements were overcrowded three- and four-story wooden and brick buildings, housing eight families in what had been a comfortable dwelling for one. Black marias from the nearby police station often patrolled these areas: In the black neighborhoods in the South End lower class whites mingled with blacks in the gambling rooms, saloons, and at the Rialto on Pleasant Street. From the social worker's point of view, these black neighborhoods were centers of vice, "of licentiousness," prostitution, and policymaking.[80]

The black South End consisted of six islands amidst a sea of Irish. Three of the neighborhoods, with a population centered around Kirkland Street, were contiguous to the Boston and Albany rail yards. This section was cut off from the other two by the rail yards and solid blocks of lodging houses for Irish and British men. The center of the area around Kirkland Street was only four blocks long, while to the north between Tremont Street and Columbus Avenue was another neighborhood of about twelve blocks; the third area to the west between Tremont and Shawmut was only two blocks across. Aside from lodging houses, most of the families in these neighborhoods lived in tenements "crowded into dark and unwholesome rooms, where they miss the elevating influence of bright and cheerful surroundings."[81] On most blocks they lived near Germans, Irish, British, Jews, and a few Italians. A few streets were entirely black. Many black worshippers attended the closest religious institution, the Morgan Chapel, developed by white Methodist missionaries.

The three additional black neighborhoods in the South End were

78. *Seventeenth Annual Report of the Associated Charities of Boston: November, 1896* (Boston, 1896), p. 34.

79. Robert Woods, *City Wilderness*, p. 68; Horace G. Wadlin, *A Tenement House of Boston* (twenty-third annual report of the Bureau of Statistics of Labor) (Boston, 1893), p. 103.

80. Frederick A. Bushee, *Ethnic Factors in the Population of Boston* (New York, 1903), p. 115; Robert Woods, *City Wilderness*, p. 94.

81. *Nineteenth Annual Report of the Associated Charities of Boston: November, 1898* (Boston, 1898), p. 39.

separated from this Kirkland Street area. The Bradford Street district, a lodging house area of dubious reputation, was the "scene of robbery and sometimes of murder."[82] Only blacks lived on some of these streets, although around the corner were English-born neighbors. To the west was a small rectangular twelve-block area between West Brookline and Upton Streets, a tenement and lodging house area, where blacks lived on the same streets with Irish and British. Another area in the South End to which the black population increasingly came from the West End was just across the street from the Chickering Piano Factory at Tremont and Camden Streets. By 1900 this became an important South End center. A small black business area developed. Three black churches could be found within a five-block area—St. Paul's Baptist and the Columbus A.M.E. Zion Church, both of which left the West End for this new area of black settlement, and, on West Springfield Street, a congregation of ex-slaves: the Ebenezer Baptist.

Its pastor was Peter Randolph. Born a slave in 1825 at Upper Brandon, a tobacco plantation in Virginia's Tidewater, Randolph, his wife, and children, along with 63 other manumitted slaves, arrived in Boston in 1847. At his death, Carter Edloe manumitted these slaves and provided $50 per head for their transportation out of state. Somehow the ex-slaves, who were not directly told of their owner's bequest, learned of the news and found a sympathetic owner who acted as their lawyer. Finally, 3 years after the master's death, the will was honored and these freed men and women left the plantation for Boston. When they arrived at Long Wharf, they were met by the city's prominent abolitionists, including William Lloyd Garrison and Wendell Phillips, who helped them to find jobs. Of the 66 from Upper Brandon, Peter Randolph was the most politically prominent. He became an abolitionist, frequently joining political meetings at the African Baptist Church in the West End. To earn his living, he scrubbed floors, worked as a servant, ran a small newspaper business, and, after training as a minister, served black congregations in Connecticut, New York, Massachusetts, and Canada. During the war he took charge of a black congregation in Richmond, but at the end of this work he returned to become the minister at Ebenezer Baptist.

Jefferson Ruffin from Upper Brandon along with other ex-slaves from neighboring counties in Virginia founded the Ebenezer Baptist Church. All of the founders of the church were born in Virginia with the exception of one North Carolinian. Most of them worked in ser-

82. Robert Woods, *City Wilderness*, p. 168.

vice and menial jobs: porters, laborers, waiters, and janitors. There were no women officers of the church although there were a few females among the founders. None of the women founders, according to the census, held jobs outside the home. Ebenezer Baptist originated from a prayer meeting in 1868 held in the kitchen of Martha Jones, a South End resident of Ottawa Court. She converted one of the court's apartments into a chapel for services three nights a week. Later another room was added for the regular meetings of the evening school. One member described their worship this way: "We come together to sing the praises to the Lord, and to Jesus Christ, his son, who came to do us good and to save us, and then we feel so thankful, that we sing the tunes pretty loud, and the 'glory to God' comes out very full and strong."[83] The songs and shouts came out so loud that urbanized blacks, considerably offended, referred to the church as "the Jay Bird Tabernacle."[84]

The migrants established a formal church in the fall of 1871. Reverend George Lorimer, pastor of a white Baptist church, helped them to find larger quarters in the South End. When the congregation again outgrew its building, they made a down payment of $5000 on the purchase of a large brick edifice, St. Andrews Presbyterian Church, in the South End. Ebenezer Baptist had developed in a few years from a prayer meeting into a major South End religious institution.[85]

As Ebenezer Baptist grew in membership and in prosperity, changes occurred in church practice. The pastorate of this church was an opportunity for Peter Randolph to modify emotional black religion: "The meeting carried on till a late hour, the groaning and shouting, the getting happy, and falling over benches."[86] One incident illustrated his difficulties: Since Randolph's church lacked baptismal facilities, he borrowed part of the back hall in a white Baptist church for a Saturday morning. He appeared at the church with 21 candidates, all of whom he cautioned "to be as careful and calm as possible" in front of the white congregation. His congregants, however, grew more excited "till some got happy in the water,"[87] and the embarrassed white congregation and its minister withdrew. Randolph, who had been trying to impress the white minister, repudiated

83. Massachusetts, Report of the Bureau of Statistics of Labor, *First Annual Report* (Boston, 1870), pp. 180–181.

84. Ibid.

85. New York *Freeman* (September 17, 1887).

86. Peter Randolph, *From Slave Cabin to Pulpit*, p. 107.

87. Ibid., p. 113.

the "peculiar ways of his congregants that [they] had learned . . . in the house of bondage." He admitted later, "I was so ashamed of the action of my people that I never went there to baptize again."[88]

Ebenezer Baptist was the only entirely migrant black church. Most southern migrants joined already established black churches. No doubt they found the religious ritual somewhat subdued, but the majority of them appear to have accepted northern-style black religion. Their rate of church membership is uncertain, since for most black churches during this period, no membership lists have survived. By compiling the names of church officers and members from black newspapers for the period, and adding their birthplaces, as indicated in the federal manuscript census, a list of the more prominent church members was created. Even at the churches of the black elite, such as the Charles St. A.M.E. Methodist and the Twelfth Baptist, blacks born in the South formed the majority of the membership (Table III-6). The fact that southern blacks figured so large in the rosters of the church notables suggests considerable integration in black religious life. Moreover, complete membership lists have survived for one black church, the North Russell St. A.M.E. Zion in 1903, which show that fully one half of the members were born in the South.

Those migrants who settled in Boston also joined black lodges, the Odd Fellows, Masons, Daughters of Zion, and so forth. Black lodges first began in Boston, when Prince Hall established the first organization of black Masons in 1787. In their votes on new members, it seems plausible that some latent prejudice against southern blacks would have surfaced. Many of the black elite, who might have felt this way, belonged to white lodges with few black members. Moreover, in order to offer sickness and death benefits, every black lodge actively recruited new members. It is not surprising to learn, then, that among those lodge members whose birthplaces could be determined, 6 out of 10 were born in the South (Table III-6).

It might at first be considered that, of all the deficits of a background in the Upper South, the greatest was apathy about political participation. Black politicians frequently complained about under-registration and the lack of sophistication among black voters, willing to exchange their votes for liquor and a sandwich on election day. Despite this stereotype, a special survey of blacks in eight Massachusetts cities, including Boston, by the Massachusetts Bureau of Labor Statistics in 1903 found that 81% of black men over the age of 20 were

88. Ibid.

TABLE III-6
Active Organizational Membership among Blacks in Boston, 1870–1900

		Members in menial jobs[c]				
	Percentage of all members who were southern born[b]	Males		Females		
Organization[a]		%	N	%	N	Total
Veterans organizations	38	63	19	0	2	21
Social clubs	39	43	21	0	7	28
Women's clubs	44	0	0	18	61	61
Music clubs	45	9	0	0	2	11
Protest organizations	50	14	28	0	2	30
Lodges	57	33	70	0	0	70
Literary associations	58	32	25	0	13	38
Churches	61	46	74	30	44	118
Charles St. A.M.E.	52	47	19	25	4	23
Twelfth Baptist	57	50	16	0	12	28
North Russell St. A.M.E. Zion	52	52	23	48	21	44
Ebenezer Baptist	91	63	16	29	7	23
Political clubs	73	45	33	0	0	33

[a] Active members of black organizations were club members identified in black newspapers (published in Boston or a weekly column about Boston in the New York *Age*) between 1870 and 1900.

[b] Place of birth information was derived from newspapers and the federal manuscript census schedules for Boston. Persons with unknown places of birth were omitted.

[c] When the individual held several jobs over a lifetime, the occupation highest in social standing was chosen. Politicians were the one exception. Their job just prior to government employ was noted.

registered to vote.[89] Even in the occupational categories where southern workingmen were concentrated, such as personal service or unskilled labor, the rate of voter registration reached almost that level.

The political concerns of southern migrants extended even to backroom politics, for most of black Boston's elected officials and

89. Thirty-fourth Annual Report of the Massachusetts Bureau of Statistics of Labor, *Social and Industrial Condition of the Negro in Massachusetts* (Boston, 1903), p. 222.

ward officers were ex-Southerners. Twelve out of twenty elected city
councilmen and state legislators were born in the South, most of
them in Virginia. In all, 73% of the members of ward caucuses,
political clubs, and elected officials were first-generation migrants.
More than in any other sphere of black community life, Southerners
dominated here. They had worked as porters, janitors, and barbers
before taking government posts, and several studied law in the evening while working as menial laborers during the day.

Few traces of southern background appeared in the concerns of
most of these politicians. The black political leadership concentrated
on protest against Jim Crow segregation and racial massacres in the
South, passage of civil rights legislation in Massachusetts, and the
commemoration of Boston's abolitionist heritage; economic concerns
or the specific problems of Boston's southern migrants were notably
absent from the list of issues. Ex-Southerners elected to office had
lived in Boston most of their adult lives and even recent arrivals from
the South tended to echo the concerns of the elite.

Probably the most active politician was Julius C. Chappelle, who
combined his interests in civil rights legislation and protest against
Jim Crow in the South with concern for economic reform. Born in
South Carolina, he migrated to Boston as a teenager in 1870, began
work as a barber, and went to school at night to earn his high school
diploma. He was elected to the Republican State Central Committee,
the Boston City Council, and the state legislature. Chappelle urged
the Boston branch of the National League to establish an employment bureau for black women. As a state legislator he introduced
dozens of bills striking at the economic disabilities faced by Massachusetts blacks. He sponsored bills providing free textbooks in the
public schools, ending the poll tax for voters, regulating child and
female labor, funding free evening high schools in major Massachusetts cities, providing standard quantities for coal sold in baskets,
and regulating pawn brokers.[90]

Thus, in the initial stages of chain migration, migrants simply
relied on friends and relatives and on informal patterns of visiting in
neighborhoods. After a few years businesses were established (pool
halls, gyms, taverns, even brothels) that served a migrant clientele.
The migrants founded a church and affiliated with already established black churches and lodges, a halfway solution that was some-

90. Henry M. Field, *Bright Skies and Dark Shadows* (New York, 1890), p. 146; New
York *Freeman* (June 19, 1886).

thing less than a complete institutional life. The capacity for active organizational life among black Southerners was probably far less than for some immigrant groups; they had no equivalent of the German beer halls or the Irish fire house gang: Their culture was based on the trinity of kin, community, and church, a way of life they continued in Boston.

The formation of a separate church and life in a separate neighborhood were as much a cause of social segregation as its result. Sociologist Raymond Breton refers to the extent of "institutional completeness" among migrants, that is, the degree to which migrant needs for social life were met within the group.[91] He discovered a principle at the base of social relations: the greater the social organization within the ethnic community, the sharper the social segregation from the rest of society. Because black migrants from the South created a separate institutional life as well as an informal network of association, they were less likely to have white friends, to belong to white organizations, or to intermarry. For the same reasons, their contacts with blacks born outside the South were limited.

PETER RANDOLPH AND THE CREATION OF ETHNICITY

Most of those who migrated to Boston from the South cannot be traced in the written records. The opinions of a migrant like Peter Randolph, who published his autobiography in 1893, were his alone, but he was a prominent minister and a perceptive leader of his people, who tried to guide his congregation in new paths. His views on work, religion, and racial prejudice reveal how he tried to achieve a delicate balance between the southern past and the Boston future.

Randolph tried to mold the behavior of the southern migrants according to a work ethic that combined the tenets of the industrial era and the black Baptist tradition. He could have been at home in Calvinist Geneva, so strongly did he abhor the sin of idleness and extol disciplined hard labor as the only salvation. He attributed "much of the success he had in life to being on time for his appointments," and he held that punctuality was a virtue and laziness a vice.

91. Raymond Breton, "Institutional Completeness of Ethnic Communities and the Personal Relations of the Immigrants," *American Journal of Sociology*, v. 70, No. 1 (July 1964), pp. 193–205.

He preached against "the misery and folly of idleness" and exhorted his congregation to remember "how important it was for them to stick to work as the path to prosperity."[92]

Of all the virtues, he believed honesty was the most important. Like many Baptist preachers, he illustrated this simple morality with reference to a story from his own life. He once found a pocketbook in a Boston post office containing $5000 and the owner's name. He took the purse to a relative of the owner in an attempt to return it. Randolph was finally located by the owner and received a $5 reward. He considered this just compensation, but his friends, who had learned of the good deed, decided to present him with more adequate compensation, a purse with $200 inside. The moral of the story, according to Randolph, was that "honesty is always the best policy and brings its own reward."[93] His honesty also brought him extra remuneration, a subtle point he carefully added to his account.

Randolph tried to acquire learning from his first attempt to teach himself to read the Bible on the plantation to the lectures he attended at Yale while preaching in New Haven. He sought out educated companionship to improve his mind and to help him "through the conversation and discussion of important subjects."[94] He valued education for its own sake, but he also equated learning with personal advance. What blacks wanted, Randolph once told a Virginia audience of whites, "was money and education, so that we could own railroads and steamboats,"[95] a speech entirely suited to this age of great fortunes. He reassured whites that when blacks "came in possession of these we would have the white people ride beside us not behind us."[96]

Randolph's efforts to uplift his people led him to dampen emotionalism in black religion and he alternated between defending black religion against the coldness of whites and berating the "emotional element in the Negro."[97] He preached reform: Keep the sympathetic, passionate qualities but eliminate the embarrassing excesses. "Now, what must be done with this nature, destroy it?" said Randolph rhetorically. "No," he answered, "cultivate, refine and polish it, and you will have that which maketh you not ashamed, but

92. Peter Randolph, *From Slave Cabin to Pulpit*, p. 38.
93. Ibid., p. 130.
94. Ibid., p. 84.
95. Ibid.
96. Ibid.
97. Ibid

desirable, adding strength and beauty in the great temple of progress."[98]

Such were Randolph's attitudes in 1893, 46 years after his emancipation. His belief that northern life changed him emerges on his
return to Virginia at the end of the war. His account was based on his
reactions more than 20 years after the event. Randolph was no longer
a Southerner in dress, speech, or attitude; he was the successful
"Americanized" immigrant returning home. He visited a black
domestic in the kitchen of her mistress and entered into a debate with
her white employer who asserted that the Yankees were "mean and
stingy" and Southerners kind and generous. He defended his new
home and the Yankees who "had to work hard for their money and
they were careful how they used it."[99] He defined himself as a North-
erner, and, until he told his listener otherwise, it was assumed he was
another "nigger Yankee" who knew nothing of the South.[100]

As a minister in a Richmond black church, Randolph's years in
the North influenced him to change church practices that dated back
to slavery, despite resistance from his congregation. He admitted
openly that his ideas about church policy had "all been received in
the North and not from the South."[101] In one of his reforms, he gave
women a vote in church meetings, and, finding that men and women
sat separately in church, he condemned the custom as a relic of
slavery and insisted that the sexes sit together.[102] Even after he returned to his congregation in Boston, he played the reformer, trying
to reconcile the conflicting church customs of his congregants. He
noticed that "those who came from Virginia had their ideas as to how
a church should be conducted, and likewise those who came from
North Carolina, Alabama, Georgia, or Florida, had theirs also. Each
different set wanted their kind of a preacher, and the majority usually
carried the day. . . . The remedy for this babel state of affairs will
come through the intelligent, educated ministry, which shall en-
lighten the people, and bring them up to the correct standard, and
not appeal to their ignorant ethods inherited from slavery."[103]

Randolph seems to have felt only pity for the former white masters, now reduced to penury. The militance of the Reconstruction era

98. Ibid.
99. Ibid., p. 99.
100. Ibid., p. 100.
101. Ibid.
102. Ibid., p. 89.
103. Ibid., p. 114.

and his Boston experiences were responsible for his race consciousness. A series of incidents in Virginia immediately after Reconstruction demonstrated that even freedmen who never left the South had
become militant. When a mob of whites shot into a group of black
marchers during a Freedmen's Day parade in Norfolk, armed blacks
returned their fire and killed four.[104] Blacks in the Tidewater took
action against Federal soldiers who raped black women. A black
crowd retaliated when Union soldiers caused trouble in a freedman's
store.[105] Randolph urged that Richmond blacks call a meeting to
discuss these abuses.

In Boston, Southerners learned that gentlemen addressed each
other as sir. When Randolph tried his northern manners on a white
Richmond barkeeper, he was taken aback. Entering a white
Richmond hotel to meet a friend, he made inquiries from the barkeeper who, astounded by the black Yankee, refused to respond. He
related the rest of the incident:

> Finally, he [the barkeeper] said, "If you take off your hat I'll answer
> you." I had just returned from Boston and had on a new Beaver hat.
> "Why sir" said I, a little indignant at his gruff remark, "take off my
> hat in a bar-room. The other gentlemen have on their hats, and they
> do not look half as good as mine." His blunt reply was "but niggers
> take off theirs." "I am a gentleman sir," said I.[106]

Though slavery had taught him to fear and distrust whites,
friendships with William Lloyd Garrison and Wendell Phillips moved
him to say that "all white people are not alike."[107] However, he
understood that race prejudice was present in the North as well as in
the South. He had experienced racial slurs and insults where he least
expected them. When he visited Canada, Randolph was pelted with
rocks by white youths who called him a "negger." He concluded as a
result: "I had always cherished the idea that when I stood on British
soil, I should leave behind me the miserable race prejudice and hate.
But to my surprise I found this state of things as bad in Canada, as in
the States, and it may have appeared to me worse, because I was not
looking for it."[108] To combat racial prejudice he urged blacks to avoid

104. Robert Francis Engs, "The Development of Black Culture and Community in
the Emancipation Era, 1865–1870," unpublished Ph.D. dissertation, Yale University,
1972, p. 100.
105. Ibid., p. 104.
106. Peter Randolph, *From Slave Cabin to Pulpit*, p. 72.
107. Ibid., p. 101.
108. Ibid., p. 44.

stereotyped behaviors and sought to set an example in his actions. One white religious bigot who proclaimed "that he did not care to hear the negger preach" was "happily disappointed" after hearing Randolph's sermon.[109] In another city, a group of white youths had come to hear the black preacher expostulating on the great day of judgment. When the congregation failed to "jump up" or "fall over the benches," but instead prayed quietly, the white youths slipped away.[110]

Peter Randolph was a middleman who helped to manufacture a new hyphenated identity: the southern-black Bostonian. This amalgam represented a combination of slave culture, black religious style, and the Protestant ethic. Randolph passed between the world of sympathetic New England whites and unacculturated ex-slaves, explaining each to the other. He moved carefully across this cultural precipice, urging his congregants and listeners to reform their lives without eradicating their past. He was helping to forge a new regional identity, taking those from Lynchburg as well as Richmond, Baltimore along with Newbern, and calling them all Southerners, a group with common regional origins and a common heritage.

A CLANNISH CULTURE

Boston's southern migrants were better prepared for northern life than most black Southerners. They were a highly selective group: more likely to be urbanized, literate, and light in color than other ex-slaves. It is true that they had been their master's chattel, treated according to his whims. Yet they were also his valuable property, made more so by the Upper South's need for labor. The urban and industrial development of that region had led to the system of slave hiring and to a form of quasi-free labor for slave industrial workers. Many slaves took advantage of small liberties to acquire savings, live on their own, learn to read the Bible, and develop a separate religious life. Between the end of the Civil War and the turn of the century, these former town slaves and their children moved to Boston. They had not run from the South—in fact, many of them planned to return there. They simply followed friends and relatives to Boston and timed their arrival to coincide with an expanding economy.

The common heritage of these southern migrants had more than

109. Ibid., p. 46.
110. Ibid., p. 122.

its share of bitter memories. The freedom and anonymity of Boston
gave them a chance to escape that past—by merging with northern
blacks or mingling with poor white immigrants who, as recent arrivals, had not yet acquired American prejudices. Why preserve a way
of life that could have been shed so easily? The process of chain
migration strengthened bonds between kin and friends from the
South. When migrants first arrived in Boston, their friends and relatives helped them. Even after the newcomers had found a place to live
and a job, they continued to turn to kin for assistance. In giving as
well as returning favors, they helped to create a vast reserve of social
indebtedness. These patterns of mutual aid, along with hostility from
other blacks, led to a segregated social life, and that separate life
tended to take on an existence of its own.

After a few years of residence in Boston, subtle changes, encouraged by leaders like Peter Randolph, appeared in the migrants'
speech, manners, and religious practice. Many of them voted in Boston elections and joined black churches and lodges. Still, they had
acquired some of the superficial cultural gloss of black Yankees but
persisted to hold fast to southern black culture in their choice of
marriage partners and in their times of hardship. Therefore, life in
the city, far from breaking apart simple slave customs, had actually
reinforced and strengthened attachment to them.

CHAPTER IV

CHILDREN OF THE NORTH

To New England, therefore, we may look for information that cannot be had anywhere else, as to what would be the condition of the African throughout the Union today, more than a quarter of a century after his emancipation, had he been under conditions equally favorable with those of New England. If those who have spent the last twenty or thirty years under these conditions have improved in proportion to the advantages and opportunities offered by these conditions or surroundings, as a rule, then we would reasonably conclude that the same rule would obtain elsewhere.

REVEREND R. F. HURLEY
"The African in New England," *The A.M.E. Church Review* (1892)

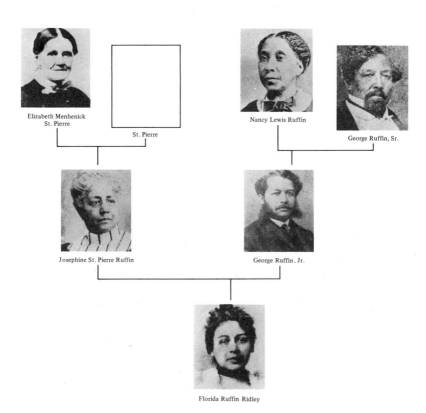

Elizabeth Menhenick
St. Pierre

St. Pierre

Nancy Lewis Ruffin

George Ruffin, Sr.

Josephine St. Pierre Ruffin

George Ruffin, Jr.

Florida Ruffin Ridley

When W.E.B. DuBois examined the condition of blacks in the North in 1901, he wrote of "two classes of people, the descendants of the northern free Negroes and the freed immigrants from the South." He believed that the "gravest social problems" were to be found among the latter, whereas the future of the race belonged to the former. We have already observed that, even after permanent settlement in Boston, southern migrants inhabited an almost self-contained community and devised a halfway compromise that helped preserve much of their traditional culture. Blacks born in the North or Canada, having intermingled with whites as a tiny minority, were aliens in this traditional world. Any observer at the time could see that northern blacks differed from southern migrants in "dress and carriage, in their demeanor toward whites, and their general air of self-reliance."[1] Free blacks of the North, like the children of European immigrants, were undergoing an almost inevitable process of "Americanization" in cultural values and in social status. Exactly what path their Americanization took, and whether it helped to perpetuate or alleviate the strains of black poverty, is the subject of the inquiry to follow.

The largest group of Northern blacks were Massachusetts natives. They were Boston born, for the most part, or from the surrounding towns in the eastern part of the state. The rest were from New York and Pennsylvania, the Maritime Provinces of Canada, or other New England states.[2] Less than a hundred black Bostonians were born in Barbados, St. Thomas, Jamaica, or other nearby Caribbean islands. Most of the West Indians were homeless sailors who lived in the boarding houses of the North End. Because their impact on the black community was quite limited, subsequent analysis will be

1. W.E.B. DuBois, *The Philadelphia Negro* (Philadelphia, 1899; New York, 1967), p. 80; W.E. Burghardt DuBois, *The Black North in 1901* (New York, 1969), pp. 20, 39.
2. The proportions of native-born blacks from these states can be found in Table III-1.

Chapter opening photo
The lineage of Josephine St. Pierre Ruffin, clubwoman and suffragist (1842–1924) and George L. Ruffin, Jr., the first black judge in the North (1834–1886).

confined to the much larger and more permanent population of
blacks from Massachusetts, other Northern states, or Canada.[3] Although the needs of these migrants for jobs, housing, food, and companionship were much the same as those of the Southerners, their
moral outlook was considerably different.[4]

One segment of Boston's black population exerted considerable
social power, a small group of 20 or so highly educated families. Most

3. Prior to the American Revolution blacks in Nova Scotia and New Brunswick
were the slaves of French and English masters. Soon thereafter about a thousand
ex-slaves of Loyalist masters, many of them from Maryland and Virginia, arrived with
their masters. Other ex-slaves, who fled behind British lines, were transported to the
Maritimes by the British. These blacks indentured themselves to English farmers in
order to pay off their debts. A small group of rebels from Jamaica also arrived in Nova
Scotia, but they soon became discontented with the climate and the failure of the
British to offer them promised farm land and sailed for Sierra Leone. More ex-slaves
came after the War of 1812, and a few arrived via the underground railroad. Most of
these blacks found that the land was rocky and infertile and soon abandoned farming
small plots for jobs in towns, where they lived in small black settlements. The men
became migrant laborers, caulkers, and sailors, and the women worked as domestics
and laundresses.

It is often thought that Canada was the place of freedom for American blacks, but
the British government imposed many racial restrictions. Black settlers received
smaller parcels of land than whites. Black men were excluded from voting until 1840.
In the antebellum decades, blacks in St. Johns were not permitted to vote, practice a
trade, sell goods within city limits, or fish off the coastal banks. Black children
attended school for only a few months a year. Missionary societies and the Anglican
church, pressed by black parents, made some provision for schooling, but the schools
remained closed for several years. In the 1850s black parents demanded the reopening
of the schools and the government established permanent institutions, which remained segregated until early in the twentieth century.

Robin W. Winks, "Negroes in the Maritimes: An Introductory Survey," *Dalhousie
Review*, v. 48, No. 4 (Winter 1968–1969), pp. 453–471; Wilbur H. Siebert, "The Under-
ground Railroad," *New England Quarterly*, v. IX, No. 3 (September 1936), p. 461;
Benjamin Quarles, "Lord Dunmore as Liberator," *William and Mary Quarterly*, third
series, v. XV (1958), pp. 494–507; Mary Beth Norton, "The Fate of Some Black
Loyalists of the American Revolution," *Journal of Negro History*, v. LVIII (1973), pp.
402–426; James W. St. Walker, *The Black Loyalists: The Search for a Promised Land in
Nova Scotia and Sierra Leone, 1783–1870* (London, 1975); Donald H. Clairmont and
Dennis William Magill, *Africville: The Life and Death of a Canadian Black Community*
(Toronto, 1974); Robin W. Winks, "Negro School Segregation in Ontario and Nova
Scotia," *Canadian Historical Review*, v. 1, No. 2 (June 1969), pp. 164–191; Frances
Henry, *Forgotten Canadians: The Blacks of Nova Scotia* (Don Mills, Ontario, 1973), pp.
18–37; W. A. Spray, *The Blacks in New Brunswick* (Fredericton, New Brunswick, 1972);
William Renwick Riddell, "Slavery in Canada," *Journal of Negro History*, v. V, No. 3
(July 1920), pp. 261–377.

4. From census figures in 1870 and 1880, it is clear that the rate of school attendance, whether in grammar school or high school, was just as high among the children
of southern migrants as among the children of Massachusetts-born blacks.

of this social set was light in color, so light that many of them could have passed for white. The social leaders included Harriet Peake Lewis, the wife of a wealthy businessman, whose "skin is very fair and delicate in texture," and another mulatto, Josephine St. Pierre Ruffin, a suffragist and the wife of a judge.[5] The fair-skinned daughters of black society selected wealthy husbands. The Ruffins' daughter married a prosperous tailor; Georgine Pindell, the blue-eyed, fair-skinned daughter of a Boston lawyer, was the bride of a Harvard graduate, William Monroe Trotter. One socialite readily admitted that her group never accepted "any West Indians or Portuguese and no dark people."[6]

The black Brahmins copied their style of life from white society. They spent Friday afternoons at the Symphony, vacationed at Newport or on Cape Cod, and lived in Beacon Hill apartments or in South End brick homes "filled with books, potted palms, dull colored plants near the window and antique furniture."[7] Their children learned the social graces at Mr. Papanti's dancing school and studied for degrees at Wellesley or Harvard. A few black families even had white servants (one member of the elite recalled her French governess and "a white coachman, Barnard"[8]). In fact, white tutors and servants were preferred because many in the elite believed that "more gentility and culture would come from exposure to whites."[9]

5. The heroine of Dorothy West's *The Living Is Easy* (Boston, 1948), a melodrama set in Boston around World War I, is a young, light-skinned woman married to a middle-aged businessman (the "Black Banana King"), who constantly meddles in the affairs of her friends and relatives. Her husband eventually goes bankrupt and must leave her to start another business in New York City. The minor characters in the book were thinly disguised sketches of black Brahmins. Mr. Binney, a wealthy tailor who dressed as a gentleman and never went out without his hat, stick, and gloves, was easily recognizable as J, H. Lewis. His son, Simeon, the Harvard graduate who publishes the militant newspaper, *The Clarion*, is obviously meant to be William Monroe Trotter. The Brahmins seem uncomfortable with the poor of their race. One of them resettles in Cambridge after other black families move into his Hyde Park neighborhood. Some of the Brahmins had married Irish women of humble origins, but they refused to mention the wife's former social status. The elite, mostly Episcopalians, were embarrassed by shouting Baptists. Aside from these brief glimpses into Brahmin snobbishness, West's major point is that each of these Brahmin families suffers some fatal tragedy because their expensive tastes outrun their meager incomes.

6. Unidentified Informant, Adelaide Cromwell Hill, "The Negro Upper Class in Boston—Its Development and Present Social Structure," unpublished Ph.D. dissertation, Harvard University, 1952, pp. 101–102.

7. Boston Sunday *Globe* (July 22, 1894).

8. Unidentified Informant, Adelaide Hill, "The Negro Upper Class," pp. 101–102.

9. Ibid.

Below the top 20 families was a group of perhaps several hundred who belonged to clubs and organizations of the black community. Very few porters, laborers, or janitors or the wives of these men joined musical societies, protest organizations, or social clubs. Most of these organizations were willing to accept black Southerners of high social standing, although some organizations, such as the women's clubs, drew most of their membership from well-to-do northern black families.[10] One elite organization was the Woman's Era Club, established in 1892. Most of its more than 100 members lived in fashionable neighborhoods of Boston or in suburban towns.[11] The few employed members were opera singers, dressmakers, and nurses. The club movement among cultured white women sponsored charitable activities and lectures and eventually became active in the fight for women's suffrage; these were the endeavors of the Woman's Era Club, an affiliate of the General Women's Clubs of Massachusetts.

When W.E.B. DuBois spoke, he sounded like a New Englander. It seems highly likely that other black Yankees also used the characteristic accent of their region. Linguistic studies of Chicago blacks in the 1960s found that higher levels of education and prolonged residence in the city contributed to the demise of black dialect.[12] Even without any direct evidence about speech patterns in black Boston, it seems reasonable to think that many blacks had lost any trace of the South in their speech. A visitor to a Philadelphia black church in 1839 was astounded to hear the service read and the sermon "delivered in pure good English, equal to that of any of the other clergymen of the city."[13] In antebellum Boston black parents were complaining that their children were learning "little more about the grammar of their language than a horse does about handling a musket."[14] The spoken English of black Bostonians is conveyed in Pauline Hopkins' novel about black Boston life around the turn of the century, *Contending Forces: A Romance Illustrative of Negro Life North and South*. Hopkins, a native black Bostonian and a magazine writer, distinguished be-

10. The detailed membership figures can be found in Table III-7.

11. The Woman's Era Club, *Constitution* (Boston, 189?); Letter from Mrs. Josephine St. Pierre Ruffin to National Association of Colored Women, August 14–16, 1899, Mary Church Terrell Papers, Library of Congress, Box 1.

12. Les A. Pederson, "Some Structural Differences in the Speech of Chicago Negroes," in Roger W. Shuy, Alva L. Davis, and Robert F. Hogan, eds., *Social Dialects and Language Learning* (Champaign, Illinois, 1964), pp. 28–51.

13. Edward Raymond Turner, *The Negro in Pennsylvania* (Washington, D.C., 1911), p. 136.

14. Arthur O. White, "The Black Leadership Class and Education in Antebellum Boston," *Journal of Negro Education*, v. XLII, No. 4 (Fall 1973), p. 511.

tween two types of black speech. The black characters born in the North and well-educated Southerners use standard English, while black Southerners speak in dialect. The Boston-born daughter of a boardinghousekeeper, Dora Smith, refers to her mother as "ma" and "mummy dear" and her brother Will, hopelessly in love with a beautiful but secretive mulatto from New Orleans, utters an occasional "pshaw" and fondly quotes Whittier. The southern-born characters, aware of black dialect, resort to it only for emphasis. In trying to ease an uncomfortable situation, Will lapses into the speech pattern of a southern-born family friend: "In the words of Doctor Peters, 'I do mos' anythin' in the wurl, honey, to git an hones' livin' without stealin' it.' "[15] His imitation of Doctor Peters suggests some of the familiar elements in southern black dialect: nonstandard verb forms ("I do mos' anythin' ") and loss of the final consonant ("hones' livin' "). It is true that the ex-slave Doctor Peter likes to use fancy talk (he asks a ship's captain, "how's yer corporosity seem to segashiate?"), but his life in Boston, we are told, has changed him: " 'You see, Miss Sappho, I've knocked 'bout the worl' some consider'ble,' he said one night, in his soft Southern tones and quaint Northernized dialect."[16]

The North had also led to changes in black clothing styles and eating habits. In the novel, southern aunties usually dress in bright-colored long smocks, covered with white aprons, and save their money to buy light-colored silk dresses and patent leather shoes. In their Prince Albert coats, white shirts and ties, southern-born men appear ludicrous to native Bostonians, who favor dark colors and calico cloth, and seek to avoid all lavish display. Massachusetts-born blacks take afternoon tea, where bonbons are offered, and serve their evening guests cake, sandwiches, Boston cream pie, sherbet, and ice cream. For her booth at a fair held to raise funds for a West End black church, "Ma" Smith, Dora's mother, plans to serve ice cream, oysters, salad, and temperance drinks. Her southern-born rival secretly arranges to have a live possum sent directly from Virginia. Unfortunately for "Ma" Smith, her potential customers prefer to buy her rival's roast possum, "corn dodgers," and boiled cabbage.

In economic terms the black elite was far behind Boston's wealthy whites, but in their desire for culture and their knowledge of literature and the arts they followed the fashion of their day. As a

15. Pauline Hopkins, *Contending Forces: A Romance Illustrative of Negro Life North and South* (Boston, 1900), p. 172.

16. Ibid., pp. 131, 137.

college student at Harvard, the youth from Great Barrington, W.E.B. DuBois, participated in this culture, performing "The Birds" by Aristophanes as part of his effort to "take culture out into the colored community."[17] He even developed a complete program of community improvement, to consist of libraries, lectures, Chautauqua circles, literary societies, and churches that stood for "education and morality."[18] With some condescension, white Bostonians acknowledged that "the best of the colored race . . . differed not one whit in manners, in taste or in appearance, save for the richer color of the skin, from any similar group of white people."[19] One black lawyer proudly offered a comparison:

> Suppose there gathered in one drawing room of a house representative members of Back Bay and Beacon Street culture. Let the lights be turned out, and you enter the room between the two drawing rooms. In one of the latter you will hear French, German, Spanish and Italian spoken; in the other drawing room you will catch precisely the same conversation. And you will not be able to distinguish in which room the Beacon Street people are.[20]

To the Brahmins the prestigious occupations were the professions and government service. The men in the top 20 families were merchant tailors, doctors, lawyers, and a judge.[21] Some members of the elite, like Dr. James T. Still, a physician born in New Jersey, urged educated young men to avoid the ministry in favor of careers in law, medicine, or business. Dr. Still was of distinguished lineage: His uncle was active in the underground railroad; his father was a physician. None but the caustic Dr. Still could have so deprecated the black ministry, whom he stereotyped as "the Rev. B.A. Doing-good, D.D., A.P.E., Professor of Infallible Hallelujah, true-colored-saving-religion, with his compeer, the Hon. Ego-Venerator-Self-Lauder, Seize-r-Opportunity for Self-Prominence . . . ."[22] To Dr. Still, the "lords of the golden slipper religion" constituted an unproductive

17. Francis L. Broderick, *W.E.B. DuBois: Negro Leader in a Time of Crisis* (Stanford, 1959), p. 18.

18. Ibid., p. 20.

19. Robert Woods, *Americans in Process: A Settlement Study by Residents and Associates of the South End House* (Boston and New York, 1902), p. 261.

20. "Boston as the Paradise of the Negro," *Colored American Magazine*, v. VII, No. 5 (May 1904), p. 313.

21. Unidentified Informant, Adelaide Hill, "The Negro Upper Class," pp. 101–102.

22. Dr. James T. Still, *Don't Tell White Folks, or Light Out of Darkness* (Boston, 1889), p. 30.

leadership, a "well-fed, richly-dressed hallelujah ministry, who never work, mentally or otherwise, for a dollar . . . ."[23] Dr. Still encouraged his race to enter the professions: "How is the negro family to rise to manhood and manliness through the barber's 'profession,' and the janitor's and messenger's 'callings,' any more than the white man has?"[24] Men like Dr. Still upheld the values of Peter Randolph—hard work, thrift, and personal honesty—but they added a preoccupation with status—a respectable occupation, rather than simply a decent income, and a conservative political ideology that was borrowed from Boston's other Brahmins. So, when the membership of the Garrison Lyceum debated whether "strikes benefit workers sufficiently to warrant their occurrence," they decided in the negative.[25]

At the churches of the black elite, the Charles Street African Methodist Episcopal or the Twelfth Baptist, black ministers preached the "social gospel," so favored in Boston's Protestant churches. One of the most successful of the new-style ministers was the Reverend J.T. Jenifer of the Charles Street A.M.E. church, an ex-slave who held his post for more than 30 years. He increased church membership from 260 in 1881 to 375 only 5 years later.[26] Jenifer invited protest organizations to meet at the church and preached on political subjects, favoring civil rights legislation, urging his congregants to vote for Blaine, and telling them that support for Irish independence was their "Christian duty." In a sermon opposing the Supreme Court's nullification of the Civil Rights Bill of 1875, Jenifer offered his own political solution: "Time, death, the schoolbook, Bible and Ballot will do for us everything."[27] (The catchy saying may also have been a Yankee influence: A New Haven black minister in this period was fond of preaching the fundamentals of "grace, grit and greenbacks."[28]) Reverend Jenifer even defended his political preaching against the opponents of secularism. He affirmed the importance of his sermons on "the great political questions agitating the people among whom we live" although he showed tolerance toward those who disliked "preaching on secular subjects . . . ."[29] Somewhat in

23. Ibid.
24. Ibid.
25. The *Hub* (July 26, 1885).
26. The New York *Freeman* (May 1, 1886).
27. New York *Age* (October 27, 1883); ibid. (March 20, 1886); ibid. (October 8, 1884); the *Hub* (November 10, 1883).
28. Robert Austin Warner, *New Haven Negroes: A Social History* (New Haven, 1940), p. 169.
29. The *Hub* (December 15, 1883).

compensation for his worldliness, he reserved Sunday evening "for the mixed congregation which attended his church" when he attacked "the evils of alcohol."[30] But northern ministers often found a way to combine secularism with tradition. At a special afternoon meeting at one of Chicago's A.M.E. churches, the subject was consumption and "care of the body," and at another Chicago church the minister began with tradition ("Get ready to leave this world") and ended with advice about homeowning.[31]

In cities throughout the North, the "blue veins" (those so light in color that the veins on the underside of the arm were visibly blue[32]) belonged to the same churches, clubs, and lodges. They lived on the edges of black neighborhoods or in white neighborhoods and made a living from respectable businesses, the professions or jobs with the government. They joined the Republican party, involved themselves in politics and sent their children to college. The few Southerners in the elite had usually lived in the North for decades. This pattern, repeated across the North, took on some interesting regional coloration: In New York City, the elite often had Dutch or English names; in Philadelphia they spoke, dressed, and even looked like Quakers; in Cincinnati they hosted lavish entertainments and spent thousands on elaborate wedding receptions; and in New Orleans the Creole Catholics snubbed the elite Protestants.[33]

The values of the black elite had even come to be held by the masses. The resentment ordinary Bostonians may have felt toward the "high-toned colored folks" who were "too lazy to wurk" and belonged to white Episcopal churches was often tinged with a strong feeling of envy.[34] The childhood of one black Bostonian vividly illustrates the penetration of white norms into black society.

Walter J. Stevens was a very light mulatto who was born in Boston in 1877. He published his autobiography, *Chip on My Shoulder*, in 1946 and described his Boston childhood in the first several chapters. His parents were Martin Stevens, a Massachusetts native (and a descendant of Crispus Attucks), and Mary, a French Canadian. Martin Stevens was a restaurant owner who made about $18 a week,

30. Ibid.

31. W.E. Burghardt DuBois, *The Negro Church* (Atlanta, 1903), p. 89.

32. David A. Gerber, *Black Ohio and the Color Line, 1860–1915* (Urbana, 1976), p. 129.

33. Ibid., pp. 123–128; Mary White Ovington, *Half a Man: The Status of the Negro in New York* (New York, 1911; New York, 1969), pp. 176–178; W.E.B. DuBois, *The Philadelphia Negro*, pp. 195–196.

34. Pauline Hopkins, *Contending Forces*, p. 186.

"at the time . . . a splendid income upon which to support a family of five."[35]

Along with pleasant memories of summer family vacations and wintertime sports, Walter also emphasized a vigilant, stern, and religious upbringing. His parents wanted him to keep away from "unruly elements" in the neighborhood, associate with people of his class, and follow a disciplined routine. On Saturday night he was immersed in the wash basin and scrubbed. The next morning the Stevens children were dressed in their clean, starched clothes (Walter in a blue serge suit and short pants) and marched down the hill to Sunday school at the Charles Street A.M.E. church. No churchgoer himself, Martin Stevens made his children attend Sunday school. After church he required them to sit quietly in the parlor while he and his wife conversed with visiting friends. Martin Stevens had other rules, which were enforced with occasional whippings: He insisted that the children return home at eight in the evening, and expected them to eat meals in silence.

Martin Stevens took an active interest in his son. By reading aloud from the Acts and Resolves of Massachusetts, he sought to instill a respect for the law and a love of the Commonwealth. He took Walter to the veterans' parades where they listened to the music of the black brass marching band. Walter regarded his father as a "strong, dominating, personable and vibrant man," but found his mother drab, a woman about whom "there is nothing much to say," he remarked, except that "she had absolutely no imagination." In her son's description, Mary Stevens emerges as a subdued, gentle-hearted woman who emphasized "the need for cleanliness" above all else. She never directly questioned or overruled her husband, but sometimes devised subterfuges to save her children "from the strict discipline and beatings of their father."[36]

The Stevens's respectable family life embodied the social ideals of black Brahmins: proper children, stern and upright fathers, gentle and religious mothers. Additional evidence, omitted by Walter Stevens from his autobiography, reveals another side of his family life. After Martin Stevens's death, Mary Stevens applied for a widow's pension. But her request was denied because the pension bureau claimed she had never been legally married to Martin Stevens. Bureau investigators located Martin Stevens's long-lost sister in New York City and a daughter in Troy, New York. Their affidavits challenged the sworn testimony of Mary Stevens and her son, Walter.

35. Walter J. Stevens, *Chip on My Shoulder* (Boston, 1947), p. 32.
36. Ibid., p. 25.

No native Bostonian, Martin Stevens was actually born in Troy, New York, in 1830, of seemingly undistinguished ancestry. At 16 he married a schoolmate, and had three children, all of whom died in infancy. Two years after his first wife's death, he remarried another native of Troy, and had two more children. He fought the Civil War as "Martin Williams," perhaps in order to receive a bounty for replacing another draftee. After his return from the war, his wife became pregnant for the third time and he took a job as a cook in a local hotel. There he met a 15-year-old white chambermaid, Mary Matilda Murray. They left Troy together for Boston around 1867. His daughter from his second marriage told the pension investigators that "he went off with a white French woman, and I have not seen him since."[37]

Martin Stevens never wrote to his kin or sent any money after he left Troy. His family, who thought he had died, learned otherwise when his sister, on a brief visit to Boston in 1894, accidentally encountered him and his new wife. They and their three children were living in Boston's West End. Stevens, who fixed stoves and took odd jobs, was active in the local veteran's post. At 72, his wife had him committed to the insane asylum in Boxboro, where he died.

Now penniless, Mary Stevens went to live with her son and applied for a pension as the widow of a Civil War veteran. But the affidavits of other Stevens relatives contradicted her sworn statements. She claimed to having known Martin Stevens for only 3 or 4 months before they married in 1875. Stevens's daughter from his second marriage testified that they had known each other since 1867. Mary Stevens denied ever having met any of her husband's relatives. But her sister-in-law swore that they met briefly once in Boston. There are also discrepancies between the information in these affidavits and in Walter Stevens's autobiography. He never mentioned his father's family in Troy or his father's death in an asylum. He omitted the story of his mother's failure to secure a widow's pension. He boasted of his paternal heritage—a father born in Boston and a descendant of Crispus Attucks, although his father's pension application indicated the birthplace as Troy, New York. The pension records did not substantiate his claim that his father was a restaurant owner.

Nonetheless, Walter Stevens skillfully wove some common assumptions about northern blacks into a convincing childhood reminiscence. From DuBois to Frazier, northern-born blacks have been

---

37. Affidavit of Mary M. Stevens, September 22, 1906, Civil War Pension of Martin J. Stevens, S.O. 826693.

consistently presented as the pillars of the community. The actual details of the family history would have made an exciting and fast-paced best seller in the hands of a Maya Angelou or Alex Haley. But Walter Stevens deliberately chose to emphasize his Boston heritage. In concealing part of his past from his largely white readership, he sought to avoid the prevalent racial stereotypes. His motives were as middle-class as his aspirations. Peter Randolph, too, had been ashamed of his congregants who "got happy" at a baptism in a white church. While both men were succumbing to the norms of Boston whites, the difference was one of degree. Boston had made a far deeper impression on Stevens than on Randolph. Walter Stevens's selective version of his past helps us gauge the enormous importance of middle-class morality for those who, in actual terms, were neither middle-class nor conventionally moral. His autobiography thus represents the natural outcome of the process of black acculturation in the North.

The relatively privileged background of northern-born blacks encouraged this process of cultural change. For one thing, they were more cosmopolitan in background than southern migrants. According to Boston marriage records, two out of five blacks from Canada's Maritime Provinces were born in the seaports of Halifax or St. Johns. One half of all blacks born in the Empire state came from New York City or Brooklyn and half of all Pennsylvania blacks were born in Philadelphia (Table IV-1). To be sure, some black Yankees came from rural New England, but, on the whole, about half of blacks from the North were urbanized, whereas only about a third of southern migrants were city-born.

Blacks from the North or Canada were also better educated than black Southerners.[38] As a group they had a higher rate of literacy than southern migrants—a small advantage for the men, a large one for the women (Table IV-1). A disproportionate number of them were also light in color. Only a third of Virginia-born migrants were

38. Northern-born blacks in Boston were a distinctly better-educated class than other black Northerners. The rate of illiteracy in 1870 among Boston blacks born in New Brunswick, Pennsylvania, and New York was compared with that among blacks in their home regions. Migrants to Boston were more likely to be literate than the blacks from each of their home locales. Similarly, the proportion of mulattoes in 1870 among black Bostonians was compared with the percentage of mulattoes in Pennsylvania and New York. Boston attracted a far higher than expected share of mulattoes from each of these states. It seems likely that the principle of migrant selectivity observed in Chapter III—the over-representation of the light-skinned, literate, and urban—was a general feature of black migration, whether from the South or the North.

TABLE IV-1
Urban Background, Color, and Literacy of Boston Blacks
by Selected Birthplaces, 1870

Birthplace	Urban back-ground[a]		Percentage of mulattoes				Percentage of illiterates			
			Males		Females		Males		Females	
Virginia	31	634	28	495	29	427	32	441	56	367
Pennsylvania	57	80	34	71	45	71	20	34	26	56
New York	73	79	50	61	42	73	24	46	34	42
Massachusetts	79	248	46	478	51	493	14	175	24	287
Canada	45	195	28	109	55	97	20	78	26	38

Sources: Boston Marriage Records, 1870–1879; U.S. Manuscript Census Schedules, Boston, 1870.

[a] Percentage of blacks from the Boston Marriage Records, 1870–1879, who were born in a town that had more than 10,000 inhabitants in 1850.

mulattoes, for example, whereas about half of all Massachusetts-born blacks were light-skinned.

Black natives of Massachusetts also had a certain bourgeois respectability. Among all the regional groups of blacks, those from Massachusetts were the least likely to enter city, county, or state almshouses, jails, or insane asylums.[39] There is no way of knowing whether they had a lower incidence of insanity, pauperism, and criminality or simply had a better strategy for remaining outside these institutions. But this pattern, whatever its sources, certainly distinguished them from the rest of black society.

This respectability was also a matter of occupational advantage. At the pinnacle of the black class structure were Massachusetts-born blacks (Table IV-2). Even among working women, where regional differences mattered less, the majority of bookkeepers, sales clerks, and other white-collar employees were born in Massachusetts. Among workingmen, the social distinctions by birth were much

39. In 1895 the rate of pauperism at the state almshouse was highest among migrants born in northern states other than Massachusetts (36 per 1000) compared with blacks born in Canada, the South, or Massachusetts, respectively 29, 20, and 25 per 1000. By 1900, southern migrants were more likely to enter city almshouses than blacks born elsewhere. In 1895 the proportion of Massachusetts-born black inmates at state asylums was also lower than among blacks born elsewhere (31 per 10,000 among the Massachusetts-born; 46 per 10,000 among foreign-born blacks). Massachusetts Bureau of Statistics of Labor, *Social and Industrial Condition of the Negro* (Boston, 1903), pp. 286–287.

TABLE IV-2

Occupational Distributions of Boston Black Male and Female Workers, by Regional Origins, 1870, 1880, and 1900[a]

Year and group	Professions and business	Sales and clerical	Skilled	Menial	N
MALES					
1870					
Southern migrants	1%	6%	9%	84%	744
Massachusetts born	3%	7%	13%	77%	176
Northern born	3%	6%	6%	85%	206
Canadian born	2%	6%	9%	87%	163
1880					
Southern migrants	2%	9%	5%	84%	1337
Massachusetts born	4%	7%	7%	82%	347
Northern born	3%	9%	4%	84%	273
Canadian born	3%	6%	8%	83%	192
1900					
Southern migrants	5%	4%	9%	82%	847
Massachusetts born	9%	8%	15%	77%	557
Northern born	4%	4%	9%	83%	2566
Canadian born	4%	4%	13%	79%	490
FEMALES					
1870					
Southern migrants	2%	3%	3%	92%	286
Massachusetts born	1%	8%	1%	90%	127
Northern born	9%	5%	0%	86%	91
Canadian born	1%	1%	0%	98%	70
1880					
Southern migrants	1%	1%	0%	97%	574
Massachusetts born	5%	2%	1%	92%	174
Northern born	3%	1%	0%	96%	148
Canadian born	2%	2%	1%	95%	127
1900					
Southern migrants	0%	0%	8%	92%	384
Massachusetts born	8%	4%	20%	69%	322
Northern born	2%	4%	8%	90%	1167
Canadian born	2%	0%	7%	91%	265

Sources: Manuscript Census Schedules, Boston, Suffolk County, 1870, 1880, and 1900; Massachusetts Bureau of Statistics of Labor, *Thirty-fourth Annual Report* (Boston, 1903), pp. 249–251. The statistics of the report seem suspect, at least in the proportion of southern-born blacks in the population. Presumably, many southern-born blacks were included along with the northern born. But the status of Massachusetts-born blacks was unaffected by any error of this kind and therefore the conclusion that Massachusetts-born blacks in 1900 were higher in status than other black workers still obtains.

[a] Information for 1900 includes West Indians along with Canadians.

greater. A disproportionate share of the blacks in the professions, clerical and sales jobs, and skilled trades were Massachusetts natives. This local domination of the trades, which had not been true in earlier decades, appeared distinctly by the turn of the century.

Still, Massachusetts-born blacks never became scions of wealth. In terms of the extent of property ownership in 1870, their advantage, as Table IV-3 demonstrates, was slight. In fact, if the comparison were restricted to the black propertied class, then southern black women were actually wealthier than Massachusetts natives, male or female. Furthermore, homeownership was as widespread among southern migrants as among blacks born elsewhere—8% of southern blacks and 6% of Massachusetts blacks secured a home mortgage or freely owned a home in 1900. Figures such as these suggest that the beliefs of Walter J. Stevens and his peers did not simply derive from material advantage. Like the characters in a novel by Henry James, northern-born blacks believed in ancestry and good breeding. They came from a long line of black Yankees.

In New England, African and Afro-American customs, on the wane as early as the American Revolution, declined precipitously thereafter. As early as 1741, blacks in Salem, Massachusetts, were celebrating Election Day with parades, elections of their own governors and kings, and dinners where " 'lection beer" and " 'lection cake" were served. Blacks in other parts of the Commonwealth and in Connecticut and Rhode Island at similar celebrations elected judges, sheriffs, and magistrates, who settled minor disputes between local blacks. Election Day festivities, which resembled the raucous

TABLE IV-3
Regional Origins and Per Capita Property Ownership among Adult Black Bostonians, 1870[a]

Group	Per capita wealth				Per capita wealth (for those with some property)			
	Males	N	Females	N	Males	N	Females	N
Southern born	$137.61	771	$115.82	627	$680.12	157	$2133.08	34
Northern born	$ 59.43	212	$ 64.28	252	$307.31	43	$ 857.89	20
Canadian born	$ 41.02	78	$ 5.84	38	$182.35	17	$ 112.50	8
Massachusetts born	$173.05	175	$109.54	287	$742.22	45	$1720.00	20

Source: U.S. Manuscript Census Schedules, Boston, 1870.
[a] Includes real as well as personal property.

carousing of lower-class whites, also bore a striking similarity to West African celebrations of the harvest, where kings were elected and crowned. In week-long revels blacks in New York City, Albany, and Brooklyn and on Long Island also celebrated Pinkster Day (on Whitsuntide). At one observation an African King ("Old Charley") beat on a sheepskin drum, "accompanied by singing some queer African Air." On July 4th blacks in many northern cities dressed in outrageous costumes, drank great quantities of rum and cider, and marched through the streets banging drums and blowing trumpets.[40]

Election Day, Pinkster Day, and raucous July 4th celebrations had all but disappeared by the 1830s. As early as 1811 the Albany Common Council prohibited "bacchanalian revels" by local blacks. Decades later New Haven black ministers and professionals were holding liquorless election day festivities and organizing temperance societies. Even the son of New Haven's African King, a graduate of a state normal school, taught his black pupils to be "intelligent, ambitious, well disciplined, and well behaved." Displeased white abolitionists and black leaders tried to tame the noisy black merrymakers on July 4th. In 1834 the abolitionist Lewis Tappan organized a church service for the holiday as an alternative to the African-style parade through New York's streets. Two choirs of blacks and whites sang hymns, including a special anthem written by John Greenleaf Whittier.[41]

Instead of celebrating July 4th, northern blacks commemorated August 1st, West Indian Emancipation Day. From New Bedford to Galesburg, Illinois, August 1st became an occasion for parades, picnics, speeches, daytime church services, and evening concerts of sacred music. Followed by brass bands, black uniformed militia companies paraded to the picnic grounds. White and black speakers read aloud from the Declaration of Independence or the West Indian Emancipation Act. The crowd was festive but sober in part because no beverage was served other than "pure and cold water."[42]

40. Joseph P. Reidy, " 'Negro Election Day' and Black Community Life in New England, 1750–1860," *Marxist Perspectives*, v. 1, No. 3 (Fall 1978), pp. 102–117; Herbert G. Gutman, *The Black Family in Slavery and Freedom, 1750–1925* (New York, 1976), pp. 333–334.

41. Bertram Wyatt-Brown, *Lewis Tappan and the Evangelical War against Slavery* (Cleveland, 1969), p. 117; Benjamin Quarles, *Black Abolitionists* (New York, 1969), pp. 118–123.

42. Benjamin Quarles, *Black Abolitionists*, pp. 118–129; Robert Austin Warner, *New Haven Negroes*, pp. 26, 74.

European hymn singing gradually replaced traditional black music. A Russian diplomat described the old-style practices in his visit to a Philadelphia black church in 1813: "The entire congregation, men and women alike, sang verses in a loud, shrill monotone. This lasted about half an hour. . . . Afterwards all rose and began chanting psalms in chorus, the men and women alternating, a procedure which lasted some twenty minutes."[43] After the completion of a new church building for Philadelphia's Bethel A.M.E. in the 1840s, some members wanted to introduce choral singing and hymns into regular services. Older members, who claimed that the devil had entered the church, fought unsuccessfully to continue the practice of singing improvised spirituals. But traditionalists in Chicago were able to fire the minister who introduced vocal and instrumental music into the church.[44] Ministers at the annual conference of the A.M.E. Church in 1841 passed a resolution "that our preachers shall strenuously oppose the singing of fuge [six] tunes and hymns of our composing in our public meetings and congregations."[45]

European elements appeared in black music as early as the 1740s. Slaves in colonial Boston played the flute and the violin, and some black enlistees in the militia took up the trumpet.[46] Cultural change began when the first African encountered the first Caucasian, but the pace of change was accelerated in the nineteenth century. In the antebellum black churches of the North the musical instruments, clarinets, trombones, violins, and oboes, were of European origin. Sometimes accompanied by an organ, a robed choir sang European hymns and the churches sponsored sacred music concerts in the evenings.

A black newspaper reprinted the program from one New York City concert in 1827. A white musician directed the chorus and played the organ, and a black composer led the orchestra. The congregation sang a familiar hymn, "Old Hundred," and the orchestra opened with an overture by an English composer. The chorus rendered a traditional English hymn, followed by a duet and two anthems. After the intermission, the organist played a voluntary, and

43. Dena J. Epstein, *Sinful Tunes and Spirituals: Black Music to the Civil War* (Urbana, 1977), p. 189.

44. Daniel Alexander Payne, *Recollections of Seventy Years* (Nashville, Tenn., 1888), p. 235.

45. Eileen Southern, "Musical Practices in Black Churches of Philadelphia and New York, ca. 1800–1844," *Journal of the American Musicological Society*, v. XXX, No. 2 (Summer 1977), p. 302.

46. Dena J. Epstein, *Sinful Tunes*, pp. 117, 119.

the choir sang two anthems, three arias by Handel, and a closing anthem ("Prayer for the Commonwealth").[47]

By the late nineteenth century, the black musical world had almost disappeared from New England. Some Boston blacks gladly greeted its departure, but others, like W.E.B. DuBois, yearned for the past. He recalled that when he first heard a spiritual, sung by a black choir from Hampton Institute visiting his hometown of Great Barrington, he "was thrilled and moved to tears."[48] Actually, the spiritual he heard had been denatured ("smoothed voices, altered grammar, proper tone") to make it more palatable to white audiences, but DuBois was apparently unaware of the difference. So vast was the cultural chasm that in 1899 an ex-slave who moved from Charleston to the North lamented, "De niggers heah ain't got no Holy Spirit and dey is singing no 'count songs—dese white songs from books."[49]

Before the 1840s the ring shout, a ritual dance which had been transferred from West Africa to the West Indies and the South, still found adherents in northern black churches. Worshippers formed a circle and, without ever crossing their feet or lifting them from the ground, shuffled along on their heels. The dancers kept time to the rhythm of a chant, sung in a minor key. A jerk of the body punctuated each stanza's conclusion. As the singing became faster and the clapping louder, the dancing grew quicker and wilder. A leader in the center of the circle, gesturing with his handkerchief, shuffled his feet in time to the music. Black ministers disapproved of the shout. Bishop Daniel Payne of the African Methodist Episcopal Church told his ministers to excommunicate any parishioner practicing it. Didn't they know that their singing and dancing were a "heathenish way to worship and disgraceful to themselves, the race, and the Christian name"?[50] Still, in 1896, DuBois wandered into a little mission in Philadelphia's Fifth Ward and found that the congregation had "entered the ring, and with clapping of hands and contortions led the devotions. Those forming the ring joined in the clapping of hands and wild and loud singing, frequently springing into the air, and shouting loudly."[51]

47. Eileen Southern, "Musical Practices," p. 306.

48. W. E. Burghardt DuBois, *Dusk of Dawn: Autobiography of a Race Concept* (New York, 1940; New York, 1968), p. 23.

49. Lawrence W. Levine, *Black Culture and Black Consciousness: Afro-American Folk Thought from Slavery to Freedom* (New York, 1977), p. 163.

50. Daniel Alexander Payne, *Recollections*, pp. 253–257.

51. W.E.B. DuBois, *The Philadelphia Negro*, p. 220.

Each individual instance of cultural change was part of a larger pattern. At a Philadelphia funeral procession a visiting Englishman was amazed to see blacks "behaving with the utmost decorum." Another visitor ridiculed Philadelphia's black women for dressing in the poke bonnets and plain smocks favored by Quaker women.[52] Episcopalian and Presbyterian ministers and their congregations led the way in introducing the new mores. They advocated the more sober celebrations of Election Day and the eradication of undisciplined black music and dancing from the churches. As they were helping to obliterate vestiges of African culture in the North, they were also seeking to introduce European practices: They formed debating and literary societies and organized libraries, and the women members of the churches began to sponsor female benevolent associations. By the 1830s black churches had established their own libraries, Sunday schools, and Bible classes. Church-related schools began to spread literacy among black adults and children. The debating societies gave blacks an opportunity to practice public speaking, a change which probably helped to eradicate black English from their speech. While many of the literary societies were short-lived—most lasted less than a decade—they had served as a training ground for blacks who went on to participate with whites in the temperance movement and then in abolitionism.[53]

Once the pattern of acculturation had been set in the 1840s, families passed along these values from one generation to the next. The three generations of the Paul family serve as an illustration. The grandfather, Thomas Paul, was born a freeman in New Hampshire. He joined a white Baptist church in Boston, but left to found the city's first black church in 1805. Under his leadership, the church established a Sunday school and taught reading and writing to adults as well as children. His daughter Susan, a well-known abolitionist and suffragist, founded a black women's temperance group and organized the Garrison Junior Choir.[54] Her son, Elijah W. Smith, worked as an apprentice in the office of the *Liberator*, became the headwaiter at Young's Hotel when it opened, married the daughter of a black abolitionist, and organized the Progressive Musical Union. Naturally

52. Edward Raymond Turner, *The Negro in Pennsylvania*, pp. 136, 141.

53. Dorothy B. Porter, "The Organized Educational Activities of the Negro Literary Societies, 1828–1846," *Journal of Negro Education*, v. 5, No. 4 (October 1936), pp. 555–576.

54. James Oliver Horton, "Generations of Protest: Black Families and Social Reform in Ante-Bellum Boston," *New England Quarterly*, v. XLIX, No. 2 (June 1976), pp. 245–248.

enough, Elijah Smith believed in racial integration. He even objected to the word "Negro," which suggested African origins. "What constitutes a native but birth on the soil?" he wondered. "We were born and toiled here. The proud title of Americans is ours, therefore, by birth, by blood, and by toil."[55]

Ironically, the long-term effect of the spread of these new views was to undermine the influence of the black church in the urban North. "A considerable part of the colored people," observed one white Boston social worker, "have no church affiliation whatever."[56] The further north one traveled, the lower the rate of black church membership. As has been previously noted, membership figures in Boston were only available for one black church. However, figures for membership in all Massachusetts black churches were compiled in 1890 and 1900. These were about the same as rates reported for Chicago and Philadelphia blacks. It seems reasonable to assume that these figures reliably estimate black church membership in Boston. When the rates of black church membership for different locales are contrasted in Table IV-4, the deleterious effect of the North becomes clear. Meanwhile in the South, southern blacks, urban or rural, joined black churches in near record proportions. In this respect, Xenia, Ohio blacks were more southern than northern. Otherwise across the North the black church was only a shadow of its former self.

It might seem that Northern black churches were having difficulties in recruiting members from among the southern migrants. To be sure, recent arrivals from the South may have found the mode of worship alien. But most of them still joined these churches. Indeed, it has already been noted that the majority of members in four Boston black churches were Southerners. This was probably true everywhere in the North. In antebellum Philadelphia, for example, the rate of membership was higher among migrants than among free-born blacks.[57]

Instead, it was black Northerners who were leaving the fold. Too often "the many paths of vice take hold . . . ," bemoaned one black minister, who noted greater attendance at the boxing match, music

55. The *Hub* (August 11, 1883); James M. Trotter, *Music and Some Highly Musical People* (Boston, 1881), p. 295.

56. Robert Woods, *Americans in Process*, p. 261.

57. Theodore Hershberg, "Free-Born and Slave-Born Blacks in Antebellum Philadelphia," in Stanley L. Engerman and Eugene D. Genovese, eds., *Race and Slavery in the Western Hemisphere: Quantitative Studies* (Princeton, 1975), pp. 395–426.

TABLE IV-4
Rates of Membership for Black Churches in Selected Cities and States, 1873–1902

Year	City	Percentage of blacks who belonged to churches
1902–1903	Cincinnati, Ohio	24[a]
1902–1903	Columbus, Ohio	24[a]
1902–1903	Springfield, Ohio	35[a]
1903	Chillicothe, Ohio	36[a]
1903	Portsmouth, Ohio	29[a]
1902	Xenia, Ohio	54[a]
1900	Chicago	26
1900	Philadelphia	21
1900	Richmond	48
1902–1903	Atlanta	45

Year	State	Percentage of blacks who belonged to churches
1890	Massachusetts	16
1906	Massachusetts	23
1890	Virginia	38
1906	Virginia	44
1890	North Carolina	52
1906	North Carolina	43

Sources: David A. Gerber, *Black Ohio and the Color Line, 1860–1915* (Urbana, Illinois, 1976), pp. 147–148; U.S. Bureau of the Census, *Report on Statistics of Churches in the United States at the Eleventh Census: 1890* (Washington, D.C., 1894), p. 49; U.S. Bureau of the Census, *Religious Bodies: 1906* (Washington, D.C., 1910), p. 550; W.E. Burghardt DuBois, *The Negro Church* (Atlanta, 1903), pp. 80, 86, 109.

[a] Among black adults only.

hall, or billiard contest than at his Sunday sermon.[58] Black ministers in Columbus, Ohio, saw their competition as "the saloons and houses of ill repute."[59] According to one black minister, black Bostonians were anxious to be cosmopolitan and undertook to "copy Boston, and to do this they must give religion a secondary place, if any at all."[60] He particularly chastised black women, who, instead of belonging to the church, went off "to the theaters and other fashionable resorts."[61] Ministers throughout the North were concerned about the decline in

58. *New York Age* (March 15, 1890).
59. David Gerber, *Black Ohio and the Color Line*, p. 157.
60. Rev. R. F. Hurley, "The African in New England," p. 437.
61. Ibid.

membership. A Cleveland black minister urged "heroic efforts . . . to be put forth with a view of winning this vast multitude to Christ."[62]

Black Northerners were not wholly devoid of religion; some of them found white churches more to their liking. Black ministers believed that many young people and some of their elders "seem more happy in the occupancy of a back seat in a white church than in official positions in a church of their own race."[63] Black Bostonians belonged to the elite Episcopal church in Back Bay, Trinity Church in Copley Square: There were even black Catholics, Unitarians, Swedenborgians, Spiritualists, and Christian Scientists.[64] A few of them may have joined white churches in order to dispel racial stereotypes.[65] One white social worker claimed that the motive was status: "The woman who can claim membership in Trinity parish is apt to feel socially superior to her female neighbor attending the Zion Methodist or Twelfth Baptist. . . ."[66] But a black minister also suspected that blacks were joining white churches in order to "escape that immediate religious oversight and observation they would be under were they to unite with a church of their own race. . . ."[67]

The tradition of interracial association, beginning with abolitionism, often had a strong overtone of paternalism. White abolitionists helped deserving blacks secure jobs with Yankee employers. The young Harvard graduate William Monroe Trotter found a position in the Boston real estate firm of Holbrook and Company through the aid of a white man who had been an officer in his father's regiment, the Massachusetts 54th.[68] Robert Morris, the son of an abolitionist, studied law in the office of one of his father's friends. Edgar Benjamin's law practice depended on the patronage of white firms. He explained, "I am sole counsel for many large firms and corporations, and business associations, many of which are white and perhaps do work for the larger portion of piano concerns of the city."[69] An unusual example of white abolitionist patronage could be found in the life of Archibald Grimké, the child of a South Carolina plantation owner and his slave concubine. When the abolitionists

62. Kenneth L. Kusmer, *A Ghetto Takes Shape: Black Cleveland* (Urbana, 1976), p. 93.

63. Rev. R. F. Hurley, "The African in New England," p. 437.

64. John Daniels, *In Freedom's Birthplace*, p. 277.

65. Boston *Guardian* (October 25, 1902).

66. Robert Woods, *Americans in Process*, p. 261.

67. Rev. R. F. Hurley, "The African in New England," p. 435.

68. Stephen R. Fox, *The Guardian of Boston: William Monroe Trotter* (New York, 1971), p. 25.

69. John Daniels, *In Freedom's Birthplace*, p. 62.

Angelina and Sarah Grimké learned that the boy was their nephew, they welcomed him into their Hyde Park home and helped pay his expenses at Harvard Law School. But his aunts wanted him to practice in the South, and he wanted to remain in Boston. He stayed in Boston and apparently his aunts became reconciled to his decision.[70]

Only a few members of the elite passed judgment on the degree of association with whites. One young Bostonian, Christine Lee, whose father ran a catering business, recognized that her friends were "strong when it comes to the purely social."[71] In her account of women's wardrobes ("Mrs. U.A.R. was regal in the new black flowered silk") and the dancing of the quadrille at the Bachelor's "At Home" dance, the young black society woman confided in her letters to a friend that "everyone of color so merge themselves in the affairs and functions of the whites that it seems to sap all independence and strength from the colored people, especially the better class."[72]

Throughout the North the old coalition between white abolitionists and blacks also contributed to philanthropy. The alliance could be traced back as far as the early nineteenth century. While black parents had provided the meeting room for the African School, the teacher's salary was paid by whites, including the president of Harvard College and the Unitarian minister, William Ellery Channing. Prior to the hiring of a permanent black schoolteacher, Harvard undergraduates provided the instruction. Even after an all-black primary school had opened, white sponsors were making weekly donations of clothing, shoes, and books to the school. Boston's Home for Aged Colored Women, established in 1862, was also the product of this interracial alliance. Its board of directors throughout the century included famous abolitionist families; among the trustees and major benefactors were Lewis Tappan, Jr., Thomas Wentworth Higginson, Lydia Maria Child, and numerous Cabots, Lowells, Howes, and Homans. Only an occasional black served on its board of directors. Black donations to the home were small, but community service clubs regularly visited the residents, and church choirs and musical clubs performed there.[73] The philanthropic interracial alliance could be found throughout the North. A white benefactor

70. Angelina W. Grimké, "A Biographical Sketch of Archibald H. Grimké," *Opportunity*, v. III, No. 26 (Fall 1925), pp. 44–47.
71. Letter from Christine Lee to Mary Church Terrell, February 25, 1896, Mary Church Terrell Papers, Box 1, Library of Congress.
72. Ibid.
73. *Report of the Home for Aged Colored Women* (Boston, 1877); Arthur O. White, "The Black Leadership Class," pp. 509, 510.

donated his estate as a home for aged colored men in Cincinnati, and the Colored Orphan Asylum there subsisted on white philanthropy (although under the direction of a black board of trustees). The Ann Arbor Women's Club helped secure new quarters for Detroit's Phyllis Wheatley Home. Philadelphia's Home for the Aged, founded by a black lumber merchant, was run by blacks and whites.[74]

The attraction of mixing freely with whites extended even to the most intimate form of association. In 1877, 38% of all Boston black marriages were to whites, a figure worthy of note as the highest recorded rate of interracial marriage in American history, 18 percentage points above the next highest, for Hawaii's blacks in 1964.[75] (Nationwide the rate of interracial marriage in 1970 was 1%). Boston's rate, which fluctuated from decade to decade, as Table IV-5 shows, did not decline sharply until 1909. In these decades interracial marriage was illegal in most southern states: even in New Orleans, noted for its Creole quarter, only 2% of black marriages were interracial. While most northern states permitted intermarriage, the rate was only a few points higher in Cleveland, Cincinnati, Pittsburgh, Philadelphia, or Cambridge, Massachusetts than in New Orleans. For some reason, a few northern cities in the late nineteenth century stood out as virtual melting pots, a group which included (along with Boston) New York, Milwaukee, Buffalo, and Detroit.[76]

74. David A. Gerber, *Black Ohio and the Color Line*, p. 327; David M. Katzman, *Before the Ghetto: Black Detroit in the Nineteenth Century* (Urbana, 1973), pp. 154–155; W.E.B. DuBois, *The Philadelphia Negro*, p. 230.

75. The rate for Hawaii, incorrectly reported as the highest recorded rate of interracial marriage, can be found in David M. Heer, "The Prevalence of Black–White Marriage in the United States, 1960 and 1970," *Journal of Marriage and the Family*, v. 36, No. 2 (May 1974), pp. 246–259.

76. Elizabeth H. Pleck, "Interracial Marriage in American Cities, 1850–1970," unpublished paper delivered at The Conference on the History of Blacks in Pennsylvania, April 1978. These rates were computed by dividing the total number of black marriages by the number of interracial marriages. The rates for Boston were based on the examination of Boston marriage records. Figures for other cities were reported in the following seven studies: Herbert G. Gutman and Laurence A. Glasco, "The Buffalo, New York, Negro, 1855–1875: A Study of the Family Structure of Free Negroes and Some of Its Implications," unpublished paper, 1968; William T. Vollmar, "The Negro in a Midwest Frontier City," unpublished M.A. thesis, Marquette University, 1968, p. 8; Paul J. Lammermeier, "The Urban Black Family of the Nineteenth Century: A Study of Black Family Structure in the Ohio Valley, 1850–1880," *Journal of Marriage and the Family*, v. 35, No. 3 (August 1973), p. 446; John Blassingame, *Black New Orleans, 1860–1880* (Chicago, 1973), pp. 240–241; Thomas P. Monahan, "Are Interracial Marriages Really Less Stable?" *Social Forces*, v. 48, No. 4 (June 1977), pp. 997–1010; Thirty-fourth Annual Report of the Massachusetts Bureau of Statistics of Labor, *Social and Industrial Condition of the Negro in Massachusetts* (Boston, 1904), pp. 262–264;

TABLE IV-5
Rate of Interracial Marriage: Overall and According to the Regional Birthplace of Black Husbands, 1870–1900[a]

	1860	N	1870	N	1880	N	1890	N	1900	N
(1) Overall (as in the Marriage Records)	24	86	12	95	16	120	14	126	16	183
(2) By husband's region of origin[b]										
Southern migrants			6[c]	333	10	677	8[c]	88	8[c]	146
Massachusetts born			18	77	15	97	29	38	35	37
Other northern born			10	87	12	138	n.a.		n.a.	
Canadian born			11	38	8	50	n.a.		n.a.	

Sources: U.S. Census, 1870 and 1880, Manuscript Census Schedules, Boston, Suffolk County; Boston Marriage Records, 1890 and 1900.

[a] Omits the less than 10 marriages in this period between black women and white men.

[b] Data for 1870 and 1880 from the manuscript census schedules; all other figures from the marriage records.

[c] Significantly different from Massachusetts born.

Cities at one end of the spectrum differed from those at the other in two significant ways, an excess supply of black men, and an excess demand for husbands, especially from immigrant (or second-generation) women. A city's racial atmosphere also contributed, although the liberalism of Hyde Park, for example, must be distinguished from the racial climate in the rest of Chicago. In Boston, too, most of the interracial couples, who met at work in service or in neighborhood taverns and dance halls, lived in black enclaves in the West End.

The results of acculturation, which all along were most pronounced among the northern-born, were reflected in the patterns of interracial marriage. Throughout these years, most of these marriages involved black men and white women. Among the men, the rate of interracial marriage was highest among blacks born in Massachusetts, intermediate for those from other northern states or Canada and lowest among the Southerners.[77] Between 1870 and 1900, rates of

Albert J. Mayer and Sue M. Smock, "Negro–White Intermarriage for Detroit, 1899–1957," *Population Index*, v. 26 (July 1960), pp. 210–211.

77. Black men in menial jobs were more likely to intermarry than black men in higher status jobs. According to tabulations based on Boston marriage records from 1870 to 1879, 23% of menial grooms had white brides, compared with 11% of nonmenial grooms. Furthermore, within each regional grouping, interracial marriage was

interracial marriage among southern blacks ranged from 6 to 10%, whereas those for Massachusetts-born blacks varied from 18% in 1870 to 35% in 1900.[78] In a sense, since southern-born women were in short supply, men born in the South had more of an excuse for outmarrying, but they seemed to prefer marriage partners from the South. While some Boston blacks were displeased with the prevalence of interracial marriage, others saw it as the inevitable future of the race. William Wells Brown, the abolitionist and temperance advocate, believed that the British had triumphed because of their mixed race and thought that racial amalgamation was "the great civilizer of the races of man."[79]

Thus the origins of black acculturation in the North began in earnest during the antebellum decades. This viewpoint was passed down through several generations of northern black families. By the late nineteenth century it had already become a tradition, but even traditions, even in a city that believed in them, needed to be nourished. Without the all-encompassing embrace of the black church, it was easier to adopt a new way of life, which was also continually encouraged by the unusual degree of interracial association.

Overassimilation of this kind sometimes led some to pass as white. No one can ever know how often this happened, although most blacks could recount stories of friends who had "gone over to white."[80] A light-skinned Cincinnati woman had even learned Italian in order to claim immigrant ancestry.[81] But most had pragmatic reasons for passing. Anita Hemmings posed as white during her undergraduate years at Vassar College. Upon returning to Boston, she reclaimed her racial identity. DuBois recounted the story of a light-skinned Philadelphia painter who could not gain admission to the union. When he omitted any mention of his race, he easily secured a union card. In order to avoid any one discovering the race of his wife and children, he secretly left his home in the morning and returned after nightfall. The painter admitted, "The thing finally became un-

more common among menial than among nonmenial workers. Boston Marriage Records, 1870–1879.

78. Boston may have been exceptional. Among Philadelphia blacks in 1897, the rate of interracial marriage was higher among southern migrants than among Pennsylvania natives. W.E.B. DuBois, *The Philadelphia Negro*, p. 364.

79. William Wells Brown, *My Southern Home* (Boston, 1882), pp. 248–250.

80. Ray Stannard Baker, *Following the Color Line: American Negro Citizenship in the Progressive Era* (New York, 1908; New York, 1964), p. 162.

81. David Gerber, *Black Ohio and the Color Line*, p. 166.

bearable; no decent man could stand it. I preferred to be a Negro and hold up my head rather than to be a sneak."[82] He forfeited his painting job and became a janitor. Because of the alienation and deception involved, many blacks, like this painter, probably found passing unacceptable.

As a matter of fact, acculturation led less often to a denial of race than an assertion of it.[83] Blacks born in the North, rather than the South, were most conscious of racial discrimination. The "smart Negro," the city-bred black, responded quickly to racial slights. An example from early twentieth-century Boston was furnished by a white settlement house worker. She had asked her student to pick up the handkerchief she dropped. He refused and she sternly rebuked him. The youth shot back, "The days of slavery are over."[84] In *Contending Forces*, an elderly character (Mrs. Davis) recounted the rude behavior of young women on the streetcar who were, she remarked indignantly, "a trampin' onto the feet of every white man an' woman in the car to show the white folks how free they was."[85] It seems more than a coincidence that, in the racial rebellions of the 1960s, a far higher proportion of Newark or Detroit rioters were born in the North rather than the South.[86]

It may seem paradoxical to think that the adoption of white values and beliefs could have stimulated black consciousness. But blacks had to first regard themselves as the social equals of whites before they could recognize the need for group solidarity. Their personal encounters with racial discrimination came as a rude awakening. William Monroe Trotter wrote in his Harvard class report, "I had been out of college and in real estate mortgages, when I realized that democracy which I had enjoyed at dear old Harvard was not secure for Americans of color just because of their pigmentation. So I

82. W.E.B. DuBois, *The Philadelphia Negro*, p. 361.

83. August Meier has argued that dependence on white customers and patrons and the lingering abolitionist tradition kept protest alive in two northern cities, Boston and Cleveland. These factors, while certainly valid, fitted into the larger pattern of black acculturation. Meier sees the protest tradition as an upper-class tradition, but such sentiments were far more widely shared. August Meier, *Negro Thought in America, 1880–1915* (Ann Arbor, 1966), pp. 154–155.

84. Ray Stannard Baker, *Following the Color Line*, p. 126.

85. Pauline Hopkins, *Contending Forces*, p. 111.

86. Robert L. Crain and Carol Sachs Weisman, *Discrimination, Personality and Achievement: A Survey of Northern Blacks* (New York, 1972), pp. 14, 43; David O. Sears and John B. McConahay, "Participation in the Los Angeles Riot," *Social Problems*, v. 17, No. 1 (Summer 1969), pp. 3–20; Nathan S. Caplan and Jeffrey M. Paige, "A Study of Ghetto Rioters," *Scientific American*, v. 219, No. 2 (August 1968), pp. 15–21.

plunged in to contend for full equality in all things, governmental, political, civil, and judicial, as far as race, creed, or color are concerned." Even the style of protest copied Boston: The black leadership held meetings, circulated petitions, and sponsored resolutions. Because of their special advantages, they felt compelled to provide the leadership for the race. At an anti-lynching meeting held on the ninety-ninth anniversary of John Brown's birthday, black leaders drafted an open letter to President McKinley protesting racial massacres and lynchings in the South. They told him, "The silence of death reigns over our people and their leaders in the South, we of Massachusetts are free, and must and shall raise our voice to you and through you to the country."[87]

Blacks born in the North believed themselves to be different, even superior to, the southern migrants. But as tempting as it is to emphasize their differences, these groups were not polar opposites— the one traditional, the other modern—so much as they were each more or less modern, responding to change, but at a different pace. But southern migrants had preserved more of their traditional life: They belonged to black churches, married other blacks, and lived in migrant neighborhoods. Black Northerners were less often church members (or belonged to white churches), they lived among other blacks (but not in distinctive regional neighborhoods), and they married blacks from other regions or they married whites. Above all else, these children of the North were Americans who were also people of color, and that consciousness of "twoness" often moved them into the front ranks of race leadership.

Sociologist Milton Gordon makes the distinction between the first stage of acculturation, where the subordinate group accepts the norms and outward behavior of the dominant society, and the second, where the subordinate group joins white clubs, resides in integrated neighborhoods, and intermarries.[88] Southern migrants belonged somewhere in the first stage, while northern blacks were well along the way in the second. Their total disappearance as a group might have been expected, had racial animosity not intervened, but because whites so often drew the color line, they were forced to withdraw behind their own.

Northern-born blacks, who had erased from their memories most

87. Harvard Class of 1895, *Secretary's Report No. 4* (Cambridge, 1895), p. 199; Herbert Aptheker, ed., *A Documentary History of the Negro People in the United States* (New York, 1964), pp. 787–791.
88. Milton Gordon, *Assimilation in American Life: The Role of Race, Religion, and National Origins* (New York, 1964), pp. 69–71.

of slave culture, were absorbing the values and beliefs of native whites. In the second generation, every American immigrant group undergoes a somewhat similar process. The unique feature of the black experience was that acculturation had occurred without significant economic advance. It is often claimed that some kind of cultural deficit—rural background, illiteracy, the slave heritage—contributed to racial poverty, but if lack of acculturation was the reason for black disadvantage, then almost complete acculturation should have been a major economic asset. Yet, even among blacks born in Massachusetts, 8 out of 10 were employed in menial jobs. Middle-class cultural values should have propelled them forward, but, as it will soon be seen, persistent racial prejudice held them back.

CHAPTER V

EMPLOYMENT

The first-class ditcher can seldom become foreman of a gang; the hod carrier can seldom become a mason; the porter cannot have much hope of being a clerk, or the elevator boy of becoming a salesman. Consequently we find the ranks of the laborers among Negroes filled to an unusual extent with disappointed men, with men who have lost the incentive to excel, and have become chronic grumblers and complainers, spreading this spirit further than it would naturally go. At the same time this shutting of the natural outlet for ability means an increase of competition for ordinary work.

W. E. B. DuBois
The Philadelphia Negro

No other group of Bostonians was as concentrated in menial jobs as blacks. Eight out of ten black workers in late nineteenth century Boston were in menial jobs at the bottom of the pay scale: Servants made $5 or $6 a week, janitors and laborers about $9. One Boston black porter said it all: Blacks "are given . . . the work that white folks don't want."[1] It is easy to see that blacks were poor because so many of them were in low-wage jobs.[2] But how did it happen that most of them became confined to these jobs, and why was upward mobility so limited?

In *The Other Bostonians*, Stephan Thernstrom analyzed the lack of economic progress among black Bostonians up to 1940, and he relied especially on a comparison of Boston blacks and Irish between 1880 and 1900. Thernstrom's work bears mentioning here, since he helped to eliminate four possible reasons for the higher concentration of blacks than Irish in menial jobs. First, he argued that rural background was not a fundamental source of black inequality. Former Irish peasants were no more trained for urban occupations than southern blacks; nonetheless, Boston's Irish immigrants in 1880 were less often to be found in menial jobs than southern black migrants. Furthermore, the blacks who were presumably the most urbanized, those born in the North and Canada, were still behind Irish immigrants in occupational status. At the time these comparisons were made, Thernstrom was unaware of the urban background of so many southern blacks. Since many Southern migrants were already urbanized, it is even less likely that rural background was a fundamental reason for the concentration of blacks in menial jobs.

Thernstrom next dismissed the suggestion that educational deficiencies contributed to the poor economic showing of Boston's blacks at the turn of the century. Black children in 1900, he pointed out, were attending Boston's public schools in about the same pro-

1. "The Race Problem in Boston, Mass.," *Zion's Herald*, reprinted in *Liberia Bulletin*, No. 9 (November 1896), p. 13.
2. A calculation of racial differences in wage distributions for blacks and immigrants around 1900 is reproduced in Table A-2.

Chapter opening photo
Black stewards in casual dress, in between trips on a Maine coastal steamer.

portion as the native-born children of immigrant parents. He suggested that an inferior education burdened Irish peasants or southern Italians as much as blacks. He ruled out a third alternative, that confinement to ghettos was a serious economic handicap for black workers. Residential segregation, he found, bore little or no relationship to occupational standing for several groups of Boston workers: Highly clustered groups like the Jews were rising rapidly in occupational status, while the Irish, spread throughout the city, made only sluggish economic progress, and the greatest economic advance for black Bostonians came in the 1940s and 1950s, despite their high level of residential segregation.

Finally, Thernstrom doubted the idea that fatherless families were a significant deterrent to black occupational advance. He noted that female-headed households (in a 1960 study) were more often to be found among the white and black poor and that, if economic differences were held constant, the male-absent household was only slightly more common among blacks than whites. Moreover, contemporary survey data available subsequently to the publication of *The Other Bostonians* cast doubt on any link between mother-headed families and subsequent poverty; when family income was taken into account, the presence or absence of a father in the childhood home did not significantly affect a man's job history as an adult.[3] The elimination of these four alternative explanations compelled Thernstrom to conclude that the major barrier to black economic achievement was racial prejudice, "overt racial discrimination in many industries," which "left most blacks with little choice but to accept traditional jobs."[4] But he doubted that discrimination played a significant role in the failure of blacks in businesses. Brahmin bankers were as likely to refuse credit to Irish immigrants as to blacks. Thernstrom, who argued that black culture never embraced the virtues of the Protestant ethic, concluded that cultural deficiencies rather than racial discrimination explained the under-representation of blacks in business.

3. Rearing in a broken family had actually less impact on black men's occupational status than the number of siblings in the family of origin. And, no family variable came anywhere near race as an important variable predicting adult occupational status. Otis Dudley Duncan, David L. Featherman, and Beverly Duncan, *Socioeconomic Background and Achievement* (New York, 1972), p. 67. A convenient summary of current research on this topic is contained in Heather L. Ross and Isabel V. Sawhill, *Time of Transition: The Growth of Families Headed by Women* (Washington, D.C., 1975), pp. 145–149.

4. Stephan Thernstrom, *The Other Bostonians: Poverty and Progress in an American Metropolis, 1880–1970* (Cambridge, 1973), p. 218.

Thernstrom's account is incomplete in several respects. While he eliminated four possible explanations for greater Irish than black economic progress, he failed to consider the importance of differences in the proportion of recent arrivals or in absolute size. Each of these factors has often been considered to be significant in determining the level of a group's achievement. But a complete explanation, in addition to considering these two additional factors, must also resolve the paradox of the inherent tension between economic competition and racism. In an ideal scenario, black workers, by virtue of being crowded into menial jobs, became available as a supply of cheap labor. The firm that replaced expensive white labor with cheap black labor reaped higher profits and undersold its competitors, who would eventually be compelled to hire black labor. In reality, black workers suffered when they failed to compete and when they began to compete, as the analysis to follow explains.

Those black workers able to compete with whites had lived in Boston for many years. Classing all Boston blacks together would tend to slight the achievements of this group. Therefore, all subsequent comparisons make the distinction between two different groups of black workers: newcomers to the city and long-time residents. Each of these groups is also contrasted with a similar group of white immigrants. In this way, groups more nearly alike in their privileges (or handicaps) are compared.

BLACK NEWCOMERS

The belief is firmly held, and generally confirmed by studies of America's immigrants, that fresh arrivals to the city must make their way by accepting jobs at the bottom rung of the occupational ladder. After a few years of residence in the metropolis, it is said that they secure a promotion or rely on their new-found contacts to help them find more promising jobs. But if most southern blacks had moved to Boston between 1865 and 1870, and most Irish immigrants had arrived a decade earlier (during the famine years), then a comparison of the two groups in the 1870s or 1880s would overemphasize black disabilities, simply from the over-inclusion of large numbers of recent southern migrants. Remove these newcomers from the tabulations of occupations, it is suggested, and the groups would more nearly resemble each other.

A black newcomer, as identified in Table V-1, was an employed man or woman listed in the 1880 manuscript census schedules for

TABLE V-1

Occupational Status of Employed Black Newcomers, Immigrants, and Irish in Late Nineteenth-Century Boston[a]

Group	Years of residence in Boston	Professionals	Clerical, sales, and business	Skilled	Semiskilled	Menial	N
MALES							
Southern-born blacks	1–10	5	5	6	3	81	1,269
Immigrants	1–6	2	17	25	24	32	13,502
Irish immigrants	n.a.	2	7	28	7	56	25,556
Northern-born blacks	1–10	4	12	23	0	61	542
American-born Irish	n.a.	3	18	30	19	30	315
FEMALES							
Southern-born blacks	1–10	1	1	2	1	95	613
Immigrants	1–6	0	4	7	1	88	16,825
Irish immigrants	n.a.	1	5	0	6	88	28,673
Northern-born blacks	1–10	3	1	27	1	68	317
American-born Irish	n.a.	7	12	29	9	43	135

Sources: U.S. Manuscript Census Schedules, 1870 and 1880; Boston Death Records, 1870–1880; published Massachusetts census, 1895; Carroll D. Wright, *The Census of Massachusetts: 1880* (Boston, 1883), pp. 366–367.

[a] Occupational distributions for Irish-American workers based on a sample taken from the manuscript census schedules; all other tabulations represent the occupational status of the entire group.

Boston whose name had not appeared in Boston's census a decade
earlier. Thousands of names, addresses, and other personal characteristics of blacks as listed in the 1870 census were matched with
the same identifying information in the 1880 census, but, instead
of attempting the same kind of tedious record linkage for white
workers, a reasonable substitute was found. The Massachusetts
state census in 1895 listed occupations for immigrants who had
arrived in Boston 1 to 6 years previously. Because the overall distribution of jobs in Boston had remained much the same between
1880 and 1895, a comparison of data separated by a 15-year interval
still seemed reasonable. But a second difficulty with the 1895 state
census was its failure to distinguish nationalities: The unskilled Sicilian laborer cannot be separated from the Jewish leather dealer or the
Swiss glass blower. It is likely that the inclusion of so many Northern
European immigrants tended to raise the overall occupational status
of immigrant workers. To offset this bias, data about the occupational status of the Irish, Boston's lowliest white workers in 1880 was
added, even though it was lacking information about their length of
residence in Boston. It should be kept in mind that the inclusion of
long-term residents in these figures tends to inflate the occupational
status of Irish workers.

Table V-1 shows that the burden of adjustment, the trials of
finding a job in a foreign country, and the difficulty in learning new
customs and a new language were no more than temporary difficulties for most European immigrants in late nineteenth-century Boston. The immigrant who had lived in Boston from just 1 to 6 years
had already started a small business, practiced a craft, or worked in a
factory; in only one out of three instances was he a menial laborer.
Irish immigrants were not as well off as other foreigners, but they
were still doing much better than southern black newcomers: 81% of
southern black immigrants were in menial jobs, compared with 56%
of all Irish immigrants. By considering only recent arrivals from
Ireland, a few points might have been shaved off this difference of 25
percentage points. But it still seems likely that Irish immigrants
would have enjoyed a considerable lead. Among working women, the
choices were fewer and the degree of inequality smaller. Although
most young women, from Richmond or County Donegal, entered
service, proportionately more black than Irish women were channeled in this direction.

A second group of black newcomers, those who came to Boston
from elsewhere in the North or Canada, also confronted the problems
of strangers in a new city, but, as we have seen, they were urbanized,

mostly literate, and free born. If the critical factor placing them in an inferior economic position was not so much race as recency of arrival, then the occupational status of this group of blacks should have been on a par with American-born Irish who had just settled in Boston.

But, from these matched comparisons, it was a disappointment to learn that northern-born black workingmen were twice as likely to be employed in menial jobs as the sons of Irish immigrants. Furthermore, none of them were factory operatives or held other than semi-skilled positions, but 19% of Irish-American men held such posts. Again, the status of black and Irish-American working women was more equal. Nevertheless, black working women were still one and a half times more likely to enter jobs in domestic service (classified in Table V-1 as menial jobs) than American-born Irish women. Unfair as it was, the typical European immigrant who had just arrived in Boston had a far better chance of securing a higher-paying job than a black whose ancestors had been in the North for generations.

It involves a certain sleight of hand to view Boston as an empty stage awaiting a succession of newcomers, when in fact the stage was already filled with players. Surely numbers made a difference, and, because of sheer size alone, Boston's Irish could have established footholds in certain jobs, thus raising their status and making it more difficult for other, smaller groups of newcomers, white or black. But if the small size of the black population in Boston reduced black opportunity, then a large black population should have enhanced it. This kind of premise can easily be checked, by ranking cities according to the percentage of black men employed in menial labor alongside the percentage of black and foreign born in the work force. As Table V-2 shows, the proportion of black workingmen in menial jobs in 1900 did not correlate with the size of the black (or immigrant) population. Blacks formed a proportionately larger share of the population of New York City, Philadelphia, Kansas City, and Baltimore than in Boston. Yet in each of these cities the percentage of black workingmen in menial jobs was actually higher than in Boston. Even two cities equally matched in terms of the proportions of black and immigrant inhabitants still differed in the opportunities available for blacks. A comparison of black workers in Cleveland and Boston is a case in point. Blacks were 2% of the population of Cleveland as well as of Boston in 1900; immigrants made up 45% of the labor force in Boston, 47% in Cleveland. Despite these similarities, Cleveland blacks had the advantage of a smaller proportion of workmen in menial jobs and a substantially larger proportion of artisans, including even a large number of black plumbers.

TABLE V-2
Percentage of Black Men Employed in Menial Labor, in Relation to
the Proportions of Blacks and Immigrants in the Male Work Force, 1900

City	Percentage of black men in menial labor	Blacks as a percentage of the male work force	Foreign born as a percentage of the male work force
Boston	77	2	45
New York City	79	.1	51
Philadelphia	79	5	30
Pittsburg	69	7	39
Cleveland	66	2	47
Cincinnati	74	5	24
Indianapolis	75	10	14
Chicago	75	2	49
Kansas City, Mo.	77	11	16
St. Louis	74	7	28
Baltimore	81	15	19
Richmond	60	36	5
Charleston	57	55	7
Savannah	67	51	10
Atlanta	62	35	5
Louisville	70	21	14
Memphis	68	45	7
Nashville	66	35	6
New Orleans	72	26	15

Source: U.S. Bureau of the Census, *Special Reports: Occupations at the Twelfth Census* (Washington, D.C., 1904), Table 43, pp. 486–711.

Some of the common explanations for the occupational disadvantage of black workers have been found wanting. Thernstrom concluded that four characteristics often found among lower-class blacks, rural background, inferior education, ghetto residence, or male-absent households, were relatively insignificant barriers to economic opportunity. Two additional explanations, the excess of black newcomers and the small size of the black population, appeared to have little impact on the level of black achievement. Having failed to locate any substantial non-racial barrier, it seems clear that the one overriding disadvantage blacks faced was the deeply rooted racial prejudice of their fellow Bostonians.

In one blatant form of racial discrimination, blacks receive less than whites for equivalent work. The classic case was the black train engineer who was paid $2.60 for the run from Atlanta to Greenville, South Carolina, for which a white engineer earned $3.25. Data about racial differences in wages came from a survey of Cambridge blacks

in 1896 and were compared with wage rates for Boston white workers
in 1903 and 1905. Given that the survey of Cambridge blacks was
undertaken during one of the worst years of a depression, one might
expect that black wages would be lower than usual. Nonetheless, the
wages of blacks in 1896 were equal to those of whites in 1903 and
1905. The average black laborer made only 5 cents less than the white
laborer. The black clerk, bricklayer, or mason received slightly more
than a comparable white, although the black painter, paper hanger,
or carpenter earned somewhat less.[5]

The kind of racial discrimination to be found in Boston was more
subtle; it involved crowding black workers, especially newcomers,
into low-wage labor. For the most part, this process of "exclusion"
consisted of racial bias in the policies of city government, department
stores, trade unions, and manufacturers.[6]

5. Robert Higgs, *Competition and Coercion: Blacks in the Economy, 1865–1914*
(Cambridge, England, 1977), p. 89 describes the case of the two train engineers, but
argues that even in the South, blacks usually earned the same wages as whites. Wage
data from the Cambridge and Boston surveys are given below:

Occupation (sex)	Weekly wages for blacks ($)	N	Weekly wages for whites ($)	N
Unskilled				
Waiter (M)	8.00	4	9.10	83
Porter (M)	10.00	2	10.18	274
Janitor (M)	10.00	1	9.05	5
Cook (M)	8.00	2	6.71	8
Laundress (F)	6.00	4	5.33	3
Laborer (M)	10.27	44	10.32	65
Teamster (M)	9.00	1	11.46	49
Skilled and clerical				
Mason (M)	17.33	3	17.12	9
Bricklayer (M)	17.58	2	15.87	253
Painter (M)	12.58	6	13.69	62
Paperhanger (M)	10.00	1	17.11	9
Carpenter (M)	13.40	5	15.37	384
Clerk (M)	12.00	1	9.76	106

"Condition of the Negro in Various Cities," *Bulletin of the Department of Labor*, v. II, No.
10 (May 1897), pp. 318–320; *Thirty-third Annual Report of the Bureau of Statistics of
Labor* (Boston, 1903), pp. 120–122; *Thirty-fifth Annual Report of the Bureau of Labor*
(Boston, 1905), p. 15.

6. I have used the term exclusion because of its simplicity. Some economists refer
to this process as "the crowding model" of job segregation. It is explained by Barbara
R. Bergmann in "The Effect of White Incomes on Discrimination in Employment,"
Journal of Political Economy, v. 79, No. 2 (March–April 1971), pp. 294–313.

The city of Boston hired very few blacks. Despite the reluctant adoption of some Civil Service reforms, most jobs in city employ were patronage plums, controlled by aldermen or city department heads. City laborers constituted "the aristocracy of the skilled" because they were paid about 25 cents more than laborers in private employ and were less likely to be fired. Even menial jobs with the Boston Elevated Railway or the gas company were rewards for loyal Democratic voters.[7] Boston social worker Robert Woods estimated that one third of Irish families in Boston's West End included a breadwinner employed through patronage.[8] The Irish completely dominated the city's police and fire departments. In 1888, the city published a list of its employees, the poorly paid lamplighters and janitors along with the relatively prosperous sheriffs, librarians, and city councilmen. Page after page listed Ahearns, O'Connors, and Faheys, and, almost as an afterthought, 10 blacks, one a policeman and most of the rest messengers.[9]

Boston department stores also refused to employ blacks. One black Bostonian said that "of the thousands of clerks in Boston I do not know a single Negro behind the counter."[10] Even in the lowliest jobs in these stores, such as the cash boys or girls who carried money from the customer to the cashier, blacks encountered almost castelike restrictions, as if an invisible barrier kept them from handling merchandise or money. The cash boys and girls were often promoted to sales jobs, and thus this exclusion locked blacks out of better jobs. Department stores claimed that customers refused to have blacks wait on them. The Wendell Phillips Club, a group of prominent black Republicans, investigated the complaints of black women and men who were denied jobs as clerks. But they never succeeded in changing hiring practices. In addition to the handicap of base racial prejudices, potential black employees also lacked an organized group of black consumers to demand their employment. A shrewd black lawyer recognized the problem: "The seventy-five thousand clerks, parceltiers, salesmen and other employees who come into Boston every morning have their friends who shop where they are employed. The shrewd Yankee recognizes the value of this."[11] The same difficulties

7. Robert A. Woods, *The City Wilderness: A Settlement Study by Residents and Associates of the South End House* (Boston and New York, 1899), p. 88.

8. *Ibid.*

9. Robert A. Woods, ed., *Americans in Process: A Settlement Study by Residents and Associates of the South End House* (Boston and New York, 1902), p. 121.

10. "The Race Problem in Boston, Mass.," p. 13.

11. New York *Freeman* (November 19, 1887).

probably confronted Italian or Jewish immigrants; it was a difference of degree. Department stores hired 4169 employees in 1900, and the city gave jobs to another 6500. These two avenues of employment, which generally excluded blacks, formed about 5% of all Boston jobs.[12]

The policies of trade unions added even more restrictions. Racial covenants in national union constitutions excluded blacks as cigarmakers, railway conductors, cutting makers and die makers, railroad carmen, locomotive firemen or engineers, iron shipbuilders or helpers, and wire weavers. Although the Boston carpenters and joiners local had two black members, even the president of the union acknowledged that there were many shops "where a black man is not allowed to work, no matter how good a workman he is."[13] Some of Boston's locals adopted policies different from those of their national unions. Boston locals of cigarmakers and iron and steel workers did not follow their national union's policy of racial exclusion. At the same time, those of streetcarmen, boilermakers, and machinists refused to admit blacks, despite the nondiscriminatory policies of their national unions.[14] If a list is made of the jobs where Boston blacks were barred from membership in trade unions, it adds up to 6000 jobs or another 2% of the entire Boston workforce.

Blacks were also kept out of the skilled trades by other practices. Most trades required an apprenticeship lasting from 3 to 7 years. At a time of declining demand, craftsmen restricted the number of apprentices to help raise their wages. The printer's union, for example,

12. John Daniels, "Industrial Conditions among Negro Men in Boston," *Charities*, v. XVI, No. 1 (October 7, 1905), pp. 35–39; *Thirtieth Annual Report of the Bureau of Statistics of Labor: March, 1900* (Boston, 1900), p. 36.

13. Bernard Mandel, "Samuel Gompers and the Negro Workers, 1886–1914," *Journal of Negro History*, v. XL (January 1955), p. 250.

14. All three of the major national unions after the Civil War—the National Labor Union, the Knights of Labor, and the American Federation of Labor—officially maintained a nondiscriminatory labor policy, but in practice most locals banned blacks. Sterling D. Spero and Abram L. Harris, *The Black Worker: The Negro and the Labor Movement* (New York, 1931), pts. 1–4; Frank E. Wolfe, *Admission to American Trade Unions* (Baltimore, 1912), ch. 6; Julius Jacobson, ed., *The Negro and the Labor Movement* (Garden City, N.Y., 1968), chs. 1–4; Gerald N. Grob, "Organized Labor and the Negro Worker, 1865–1900," *Labor History*, v. I (Spring 1960), pp. 164–176; Herman D. Bloch, "Labor and the Negro, 1866–1910," *Journal of Negro History*, v. L (July 1965), pp. 163–184; Sumner Eliot Matison, "The Labor Movement and the Negro during Reconstruction," *Journal of Negro History*, v. XXXIII (October 1948), pp. 426–468; Sidney Kessler, "The Organization of Negroes in the Knights of Labor," *Journal of Negro History*, v. XXXVII (July 1952), pp. 248–276; Bernard Mandel, "Samuel Gompers and the Negro Workers," pp. 234–260.

only allowed the training of 2 apprentices for every 10 employees.[15] Apprentices were offered meager wages and sometimes boarded with the employer and received meals; apprentices to bakers, leather curriers, and tanners lived in the employer's home. Immigrant parents were especially anxious (and successful) in placing their sons in these positions. As a result, most apprentices were the American-born children of immigrants. Masters, who often took white apprentices into their homes, treated them like their own sons. Few wanted this kind of intimacy with blacks. As a result of these practices, the exclusion of black apprentices was almost complete: By 1890 there were only 6 blacks out of 1356 apprentices in Boston.

Black artisans were unable to train many black apprentices because they could only afford to offer apprentices subsistence wages. The son of a poor family was more inclined to become a waiter or a servant than an apprentice. One black politician urged parents "to make sacrifices and allow their children to learn trades at $1.50 to $2.00 until they have finished their time, when they will get better wages, as the white boys and girls do,"[16] but black families, close to subsistence, could not afford to invest in training future craftsmen.

Many factories also closed their doors to black employees. In 1900 no blacks could be found at the gas works or at factories making carpets, furniture, rope and cordage, rubber, textiles, hosiery, or silk. A few manufacturers employed an occasional black man or woman, often as a janitor or night cleaner. Foremen generally hired their own helpers; some workers even bribed them to find jobs for their relatives. The ethnic composition of the workshop often resembled the nationality of the foremen. About half the Boston foremen in 1900 were Yankees and another quarter were immigrants; only three were blacks. In a Cambridge publishing office, a printer noted, "I find that quite a large proportion of the [female] labor of the composition room . . . consists of the relatives—the daughter, sister or cousins, or aunts of the men working at the trade."[17] The power of the foremen over hiring had to be undermined to secure the employment of blacks at Philadelphia's Midvale steel plant in the 1890s. Integration was achieved there by destroying single-nationality work groups.[18]

In a small way, family and friends also helped to perpetuate

15. U.S. Senate, *Report of the Committee of the Senate upon the Relations between Labor and Capital*, v. 1 (Washington, D.C., 1885), pp. 590–591.

16. New York *Freeman* (May 15, 1887).

17. U.S. Senate, *Report of the Committee of the Senate*, p. 42.

18. W.E.B. DuBois, *The Philadelphia Negro: A Social Study* (Philadelphia, 1899; New York, 1967), pp. 130–131.

black employment in menial work.[19] They directed newcomers to the
jobs they knew were available. When southern black men and women
first arrived in Boston, they entered service or worked as waiters in
hotels. The importation of southern blacks first began with the
Freedman's Bureau in 1864 and continued with labor contractors
after that. Several black-owned employment agencies placed domestics (mostly southern women) with clientele in the Boston area and at
New England resorts. Black headwaiters, employed by the hotels,
recruited southern migrants. At the sixth annual ball of the black
headwaiters in 1883, 14 men were honored, 13 of whom were born in
the South.[20] No doubt, these special recruitment efforts contributed
to the large percentage of southern black newcomers employed as
servants and waiters. These kinds of connections may not have been
as important among blacks born in the North, who more often found
jobs outside of service, but they, too, headed for jobs in unskilled
labor. With unfailing regularity, then, black newcomers from every
region were excluded from many avenues of employment and recruited into menial work. Shunted aside in the competition for
better-paying jobs, they constituted instead an isolated and marginal
segment of the labor force.[21]

19. Since some black workers were incapable of heavy labor and grew ill from
work in inclement weather, they may have preferred low wages in service to outdoor
work injurious to their health. Moreover, a job in service was easy to secure; servants
were relatively protected from slack seasons and unemployment. Among Massachusetts workers in 1885, servants had the lowest rates of unemployment: Three quarters
of the boot- and shoemakers and half the teachers and woolen mill operatives were
unemployed, but only 1 out of 10 domestics was unemployed. Lucy Maynard Salmon,
Domestic Service, p. 105.
20. New York *Age* (June 13, 1883).
21. The conclusion that exclusion operated, irregardless of the state of the
economy, runs contrary to the more familiar belief that blacks make progress in good
times and fall back in bad times, in other words, that black workers function as a
"surplus labor force". At least in late nineteenth-century Boston, they were not used
this way. Census tabulation of black occupations in late nineteenth-century Boston
were generally carried out in a year of business expansion, with the exception of the
census of 1900. Industrial and commercial production was substantially lower in 1900
than a decade earlier, and the number of Massachusetts relief recipients in 1900 was
20,000 greater than in 1890. Only a selected tabulation of occupations was published in
the 1890 census, and, for a strict comparison, the same 79 occupations were studied a
decade later. During business expansion, black men were slightly more likely to enter
skilled trades or to open small businesses; black women were somewhat more likely to
take skilled jobs. From boom to bust, the number of black men in menial jobs increased
by only 4% and that for black women by just 3%. U.S. Bureau of the Census, *Report on
the Population of the United States at the Eleventh Census: 1890, Part II* (Washington,
D.C., 1897), Table 118, p. 638; U.S. Bureau of the Census, *Special Report, Occupations at
the Twelfth Census* (Washington, D.C., 1904), Table 43, pp. 494–499.

JOB TURNOVER AND OUT-MIGRATION

The effect of this concentration in menial jobs was dissatisfaction. Men and women, who often changed jobs, rarely moved up the occupational ladder. Servants and cooks had low rates of unemployment—households did not have slack seasons comparable to those in industry—but employees never remained very long.[22] Black domestics often quit or were fired. An employer could dismiss a servant for stealing food, entertaining a friend, violating a curfew, drinking at work, or other infractions of the rules. From the servants' point of view, there were a hundred distasteful aspects to the job, ranging from sexual abuse by an employer to accusations of theft. A Philadelphia domestic explained, "Yes, they say long service is good service but sometimes you can't *stay* at places; some of the ladies and gentlemen's not very *pleasant*."[23] And so they quit. The lower the standing of the job and the more meager the wages, the higher the rate of turnover. Among black coachmen, the best paid of domestic servants, stability was common; the majority of coachmen traced in the manuscript census schedules from 1870 to 1880 were still in this line of work, and a certain *esprit de corps* could be found among the members of the Benevolent Fraternity of Coachmen, which met regularly.[24] Among the worst-paid black servants, turnover was common. Over the decade 1870 to 1880 just one out of every four black servants located in the manuscript census schedules at both dates remained in service, and most of the rest moved into jobs in unskilled labor.

Turnover was common among all servants, black as well as white, who relied on service as temporary work during the slack

22. Unemployment rates derived from the manuscript census schedules for 1880 indicate that blacks were less likely than the Irish to be unemployed. The rate of unemployment for Irish workingmen was twice that for blacks, and the same disparity applied to working women. In 1900 the black unemployment rate (18% for men; 11% for women) simply equaled that for Boston whites. Higher unemployment rates appeared among blacks in southern cities. In 1880 among blacks in New Orleans, Atlanta, Charleston, Mobile, Norfolk, Richmond, and Savannah, the rate of unemployment was slightly higher for blacks than for whites. But the whole concept of "unemployment" must be questioned: It is a phenomenon more appropriate to the manufacturing sector of the economy than to the labor market for service and unskilled, hired-by-the-day labor. Was the floating hand at the docks, who worked a few hours one day and none the next, employed, unemployed, or, as modern economists would say, underemployed?

Rates of black unemployment for southern cities can be found in Claudia Goldin, "Female Labor Force Participation: The Origin of Black and White Differences, 1870 and 1880," *Journal of Economic History*, v. XXXVII, No. 1 (March 1977), pp. 87–112.

23. W.E.B. DuBois, *The Philadelphia Negro*, p. 48.

24. New York *Age* (May 10, 1890).

season. Even the average white Boston domestic in the 1880s remained at the same job for only a year and a half.[25] Blacks associated service with slavery. How much this discontent affected their tenure with any employer cannot be known. But the level of dissatisfaction, whatever its source, was higher among blacks than whites. Among New York City black servants in 1909, the average duration of service with any one employer was just 6 to 11 months.[26]

High job turnover meant a constant shift from service to other jobs. One measure of this turnover was the number of servants taking other work. A 1-year turnover rate was determined by tracing black employed men from the manuscript census schedules for 1870 or 1880 to Boston city directories for the following year. Because women's occupations went unnoted in the city directories, this trace was only done for men. It indicated that three quarters of male servants left their jobs within the space of a year to become laborers, waiters, cooks, or sailors. When asked about his work experience, John Harris, for example, mentioned "peddling, farming and light work at anything I was able to do."[27] John Glover explained, "My poverty, ill health, and domestic trouble made me drift from place to place frequently, and at irregular periods—I am and have been for 25 years a poor broken down colored man with no regular occupation, working at building fires, cleaning windows, and such work for hundreds of people, many of them unknown to me by name."[28] Julia Frazier, an ex-slave from Virginia, took one job after another. "I've travelled quite a lot. Of course, that was aftuh the war. I worked in service everywhere. Sometimes I'd quit an' go on my own an' sell books. . . . Made good money too. I been to St. Louis, Ohio, Massachusetts, an' a thousan' other places I reckon."[29]

The concentration of blacks in service jobs contributed to a vicious cycle. Low wages in these jobs led to unstable work habits, which made potential employers wary. It might have been different if blacks were offered higher wages and greater job security. But without tangible economic incentives, many lacked a reason for preferring one job to another. And so they quit and moved out of Boston, and the cycle continued.

25. Lucy Maynard Salmon, *Domestic Service* (New York, 1897), p. 11.

26. George Edmund Haynes, *The Negro at Work in New York City: A Study in Economic Progress* (New York, 1912), p. 85.

27. Record Group No. 15, Civil War Pension Application Files, Civil War Pension of John H. Glover, S.C. 548761.

28. Ibid., Civil War Pension of John H. Harris, S.C. 220161.

29. Charles L. Perdue, Jr., Thomas E. Barden, and Robert K. Phillips, *Weevils in the Wheat: Interviews with Virginia Ex-Slaves* (Charlottesville, Virginia, 1976), p. 97.

As a matter of fact, most blacks left Boston after a few years of residence. They were part of a vast army of vagabonds tramping across the country, but, at least in northern cities, transiency was far more common among blacks than among whites. In late nineteenth-century Boston, blacks were far less rooted in the city than whites. Between 1870 and 1880, only 29% of black men and 24% of black women stayed in Boston in the decade, 1870 to 1880. But in the next two decades, the rate of out-migration was cut in half: 20% of adult black men and 19% of adult black women remained in Boston from 1880 to 1900. In contrast, 64% of employed white workingmen in a single decade (1880 to 1890) persisted in the city.[30] The rate for white men was derived from a sample that excluded men with common names. Without this exclusion other studies of urban white work-ingmen in Waltham, Omaha, Los Angeles, and elsewhere have re-ported rates of persistence in the range of 40 to 50%. Even by these standards, the rate of persistence among black Bostonians was still extremely low. Blacks in other northern cities were also exceptionally transient: No more than a third of Poughkeepsie's blacks remained in that city from one decade to the next.[31]

Were ex-Bostonians moving to comfortable neighborhoods in Medford or Newton or to the back alleys of New York or Philadel-phia? Different conclusions can be drawn depending on the desti-nations of these out-migrants. An alphabetical index of Massachu-setts residents for the 1900 census made it possible to trace black Bostonians as listed in the manuscript census schedules to their destinations within Massachusetts two decades later. (Those blacks who were registered in Boston's death records in the intervening decades were eliminated from the trace.) About one quarter of the ex-Bostonians could be located in other parts of Massachusetts, most of them in the greater Boston area, especially in Cambridge and Chelsea.[32] Three quarters of the out-migrants could not be found. It is

30. Stephan Thernstrom, *The Other Bostonians*, Table 9.1, p. 222. It might be suggested that the underenumeration of blacks in the census would invalidate these results, but Appendix C indicates that the age reporting for black men was actually more accurate than for whites, thereby suggesting that these differences could not have been simply the artifact of underenumeration. To be sure, a more accurate survey of white men might have reduced but would certainly not have eliminated this differ-ence.

31. Clyde Griffen, "Social Mobility in Nineteenth Century Poughkeepsie," *New York History*, v. II, No. 5 (October 1970), Table XI, p. 498.

32. A few of the out-migrants ended up in the asylums, almshouses, and state farms in Danvers, Westboro, Tewksbury, Bridgewater and Salem; another small group of out-migrants were live-in domestics in Newton, Wellesley, Hingham, Weston, and

possible to suggest the destinations of this missing group from examining the published federal census between 1870 and 1900, which listed the lifetime relocations among those blacks born in Massachusetts who had permanently settled in another state. Most of them were living in four states: New York, Connecticut, Pennsylvania, and Rhode Island. The published federal census for one year, 1870, also listed city destinations of Massachusetts-born lifetime migrants, and it can be seen from comparing the city and state destinations that about half of the out-migrants to Rhode Island had moved to Providence; half of the out-migrants to Pennsylvania went to Philadelphia, and so forth.[33]

Was it a wise decision to leave Boston? We know the occupational status of blacks born in northern states who had moved to Philadelphia, a group that includes some ex-Bostonians. Eight out of ten were employed in menial jobs, a pattern which virtually repeated that of Boston.[34] Low wages, seasonal employment, and unsteady habits of work propelled black workers out of Boston. In their new homes in other northern cities, they were excluded from jobs of higher pay and pushed back into menial labor. It was regrettably apparent that blacks across the North were moving about without much moving up or down.

LONG-TIME RESIDENTS OF BOSTON

For the majority of black Bostonians the city was a mere resting place from their travels. Only a small group of permanent residents ever came under the influence of Boston. Their occupational history offers a glimpse of the fate that awaited those who were willing to settle in a single black community.

These permanent residents were identified from information in

Swampscott. However, the most sizable cluster of out-migrants had settled in Cambridge, Melrose, Medford, Everett, Chelsea, Newton, and Somerville. U.S. Manuscript Census Schedules, Boston, 1880, and selected Massachusetts towns and cities, 1900.

33. U.S. Bureau of the Census, *The Ninth Census*, v. I (Washington, D.C., 1872), Table VIII, pp. 384–391; U.S. Bureau of the Census, *Population*, Part I (Washington, D.C., 1883), p. 489; U.S. Bureau of the Census, *Population*, Part I (Washington, D.C., 1895), Table 28, p. 576; U.S. Bureau of the Census, *Population*, Part I (Washington, D.C., 1900), Table 29, p. 702.

34. Theodore Hershberg, "Mulattoes and Blacks: Intra-Group Color Differences and Social Stratification in Nineteenth-Century Philadelphia," unpublished paper delivered at the annual meeting of the Organization of American Historians, 1974, no page.

several different censuses. Black workers in the 1880 census were traced to the 1870 census. Those linked at both censuses constituted a definable group of 10-year residents. Although a similar trace of employed black women was carried out, the results are not reported here. Most of them were no longer employed, and even those who continued to work had not been promoted. Movement up or down the occupational ladder was, for the most part, a phenomenon limited to the work of men.[35]

Employed black men who had settled in Boston were advancing, if ever so slowly. It was previously noted that among the newcomers, 8 out of 10 were employed in menial jobs: among these permanent residents 7 out of 10 Southerners and 6 out of 10 Northerners were in menial jobs[36] (see Table V-3).

The small cause for celebration to be found in the higher standing of these permanent residents in Table V-3 must certainly be diminished when their achievement is measured against their white counterparts.[37] The occupational status of black 10-year residents was compared with first- and second-generation Irish workers who had lived in Boston at least a decade. Irish immigrants held jobs of higher occupational status than southern black migrants. This racial disparity increased among the natives of New England. Blacks born in the North were twice as likely to be employed in menial jobs as the American-born sons of Irish immigrants. As has so often been ob-

---

35. Elizabeth H. Pleck, "A Mother's Wages: Income Earning among Married Italian and Black Women, 1896–1911," in Michael Gordon, ed., *The American Family in Socio-Historical Perspective*, second edition (New York, 1978), pp. 490–510.

36. If it could be demonstrated that putting down roots in Boston was the reason for improvement, then it might follow that restlessness was a major source of black poverty in the urban North. The assumption behind a conclusion of this kind would be that stable residents had slowly climbed into better-paying jobs after they had become familiar with Boston employment opportunities. While southern-born blacks had edged up slightly in occupational status, northern-born blacks had actually fallen back quite a bit, and if both groups are combined occupational status at mid-career appears only slightly above what it had been when these men had secured their first jobs. What, then, of the undeniable fact that stable black residents do appear so much better off than the floating group of black workers? What seems to have happened is that holding a higher-status job was the *reason* for remaining in Boston, and not the product of having done so.

37. A less complete method was employed in tracing Irish workers. A sample of employed Irish men from the 1880 manuscript census schedules was followed to the alphabetical listings of the Boston city directory. Doubtless if the cumbersome census-to-census trace had been performed, a somewhat larger group could have been found. But it seems unlikely that the occupational status of the men in a much larger sample would have been that much below the status of the men traced to the city directory.

TABLE V-3
Occupational Status among 10-Year Black and Irish Male Residents in Late Nineteenth-Century Boston

Group	Job after 10 years of residence[a]					
	Professionals and semiprofessionals	Business, clerical, and sales	Skilled	Semiskilled	Menial	N
Southern-born blacks	5	11	8	7	69	176
Irish immigrants	4	14	19	5	59	111
Northern-born blacks	3	8	11	17	61	109
Second-generation Irish	14	17	33	10	26	42

Sources: U.S. Census Manuscript Census Schedules, Boston and Cambridge, 1880; Boston, 1870; Boston City Directory, 1890; Vital Statistics of Massachusetts, Death Records, 1870–1880.

[a] Definition of stable residence was measured by tracing black Bostonians in the 1870 and 1880 censuses. A stable black 10-year resident was a workingman enumerated in the Boston or Cambridge manuscript census schedules in 1880 who had also been present in the manuscript census schedules for Boston in 1870. A stable Irish worker was a man enumerated in the Boston manuscript census schedules for 1880 who could be located 10 years later in the Boston city directory. The occupational status reflected here is a tabulation of the worker's jobs at the second time of observation—in essence, mid-career job standing.

served here, the small gap in economic status between black and Irish in the first generation had widened enormously by the second.

Why did these black workingmen fare so much worse than the Irish? No longer raw recruits to the city, they now possessed adequate information to search out those employers who could offer them better-paying jobs. If there was demand for cheap labor in manufacturing, at the gas company, or in the shipyard and a ready supply of black labor, why were so few hired?

It is true that competition is only effective if the rival groups are more or less equally matched. That requirement appears to have been met in the case of Boston's blacks and Irish, whose levels of literacy were almost identical. According to the manuscript census schedules for 1880, adult illiteracy was 12% for black men, and it was 11% in a sample of Irishmen. The educational handicaps of black women were also those of Irish women: 18% of adult black women and 19% of Irish women were unable to read and write.[38] After these adults came the next generation of workers being educated in the Boston public schools. Although Irish children were more likely to attend school (below age 15) than blacks in antebellum Boston, this was no longer true by 1870. Black Boston, which had again fallen behind by 1900, was still an educational leader: the rate of blacks attending high school in Boston was higher than in New York, Philadelphia, or Cleveland.[39]

Of course, black workers in Boston, who had received very little training in the jobs they held, were unprepared to become supervisors or managers. But Boston employers rarely set rigid require-

38. Sample of Boston Irish from the Manuscript Census Schedules, Boston, 1870 and 1880. All black adults (21 and over) in the manuscript census schedules, Boston, 1880.

Nonetheless, Boston's rate of adult black literacy resembled that in other cities. To some extent, the similarity arose from the fact that no black community was self-contained: The presence of southern migrants in city after city tended to lower the overall rate. In 1880, the rate of black literacy was about the same in Boston as in Philadelphia. Two decades later black adult literacy in Chicago, Milwaukee, or Cleveland had reached the Boston standard, although black Bostonians were still more literate than their counterparts in New York or Philadelphia. U.S. Bureau of the Census, *The Negro Population in the United States, 1790–1915* (Washington, D.C., 1918), Table 32, p. 435.

39. In 1850 58% of black children between the ages of 4 and 16 and 62% of Irish-born children were attending the Boston public schools. Janet Riblett Wilkie, "School Status, Acculturation and School Attendance in 1850 Boston," *Journal of Social History*, v. 11, No. 2 (Winter 1977), p. 182. Figures for 1900 computed from data in U.S. Bureau of the Census, *Population, 1900*, Part II (Washington, D.C., 1902), Table 54, p. 396.

TABLE V-4
Rate of Upward Mobility into Nonmenial Jobs among
Boston Blacks in Service and Unskilled Labor, Compared
with Upward Mobility among Irish Unskilled Laborers, 1870–1890

Group and decade	First job	Rate of upward mobility into nonmenial jobs	N
Southern-born blacks, 1870–1880	Service	21%	48
Northern-born blacks,[a] 1870–1880	Service	13%	15
Southern-born blacks, 1870–1880	Unskilled labor	14%[b]	56
Irish immigrants, 1870–1880	Unskilled labor	3%[c]	63
Irish immigrants, 1880–1890	Unskilled labor	6%[c]	54
Northern-born blacks, 1870–1880	Unskilled labor	16%[b]	19
American-born Irish, 1880–1890	Unskilled labor	29%	7
Boston whites, 1880–1890	Unskilled labor	32%	75

Sources: U.S. Manuscript Census Schedules, Boston, 1870 and 1880; Boston City Directory, 1880 and 1890; Stephan Thernstrom, *The Other Bostonians: Poverty and Progress in the American Metropolis, 1880–1970* (Cambridge, 1973), Table 4.3, p. 57.

[a] Blacks born in Massachusetts, other northern states, or Canada.
[b] Significantly lower than for Boston whites.
[c] Significantly lower than for southern-born blacks.

ments for the jobs they were filling. The man who began in Boston as a menial laborer had a reasonable chance of being hired in a higher-status job—in fact, as Table V-4 shows, one chance in three for the typical white (of any nationality) or the typical American-born Irishman. Boston companies were more than willing to promote men without special job training—if they were white.[40] The chances to rise were much fewer for the black menial laborer.[41] Table V-4 displays

40. By the late nineteenth-century Boston was growing more slowly than cities in the Midwest or South. As a result, the chances for rising from a blue-collar to white-collar job were lower there than in South Bend, Atlanta, Omaha, or even Holland, Michigan! But a relatively more stagnant rate of growth probably depressed opportunity for the entire working class, not just one segment of it. Gordon W. Kirk and Carolyn T. Kirk, "The Immigrant, Economic Opportunity, and Type of Settlement in Nineteenth-Century America," *Journal of Economic History*, v. XXXVIII, No. 1 (March 1978), pp. 226–234.

41. Others might recognize these restrictions on upward mobility as a "dual labor market," but I have avoided using what I consider a confusing term. If by a dual labor

the rates of upward mobility among southern- and northern-born blacks in two kinds of menial jobs, unskilled labor and service. The black man in service had the same chance of rising as his Irish counterpart in unskilled labor. (These chances were far less than those of other white men). When blacks and Irish immigrants in menial labor are compared, blacks actually do better. Nonetheless, black advance was still limited by prejudice.[42] If race had been irrelevant, then in all likelihood northern-born black menials would have moved up as often as Irish-Americans. Instead, they lagged behind, and so it is fair to conclude that blacks were the only group where prejudice significantly limited opportunities well into the second generation.

But the whole notion of a race makes it seem as if blacks were poised at a starting line, ready to enter the iron works, piano factories, or shops of the garment manufacturers downtown. Actually, black upward mobility, as Table V-5 makes clear, was confined to the edges of the economy. Among the better-paying jobs held by ex-

market we mean extreme job segregation, then that was precisely what existed for black Bostonians. But many dual labor market theorists insist on another definition, which depends on the fact that (a) mobility between a secondary and a primary labor market is extremely limited and (b) immobility results from some unfavorable consequence of secondary employment (e.g., it offers low wages, provides no on-the-job training, or teaches unsteady work habits). My disagreement is with the first premise, that intersectoral mobility was restricted, and because that was too extreme a position the second premise (about the unfavorable characteristics of secondary jobs) also falls. It should be added that more recent empirical tests of dual labor market theory using contemporary data have also found that upward mobility into primary jobs was not as restricted as was first imagined. In this regard, I was struck by the many similarities between my findings and those reported by Samuel Rosenberg, "The Dual Labor Market: Its Existence and Consequences," unpublished Ph.D. dissertation, University of California at Berkeley, 1975.

Among the many explications of dual labor market theory, I have found the most interesting to be Peter B. Doeringer and Michael J. Piore, "Equal Employment Opportunity in Boston," *Industrial Relations*, v. 9 (May 1970), pp. 324–329; Peter B. Doeringer, *Internal Labor Markets and Manpower Research* (Washington, D.C., 1970); David M. Gordon, *Theories of Poverty and Underemployment* (Lexington, Mass., 1972); Barry Bluestone, "The Tripartite Economy: Labor Markets and the Working Poor," *Poverty and Human Resources*, v. 5 (July–August 1970), pp. 15–35; Harold M. Baron and Bennett Hymer, "Racial Dualism in an Urban Labor Market," in David M. Gordon, ed., *Problems in Political Economy: An Urban Perspective* (Lexington, Mass., 1977), pp. 188–194.

42. A separate analysis of the career mobility of semiskilled black workers has not been reported here, simply to avoid a repetition of what has been said about the constricted opportunities for menial laborers. It is enough to say that semiskilled black workers had about the same rate of upward mobility into jobs above that level as menial laborers and that they often fell back into menial jobs.

TABLE V-5
Mobility Routes for Ex-menial Laborers among
Black Bostonians, 1870–1900[a]

Self-employed (tailor, caterer, carpet layer, newspaper and tobacco seller,
   minister, real estate sales, undertaker, printer, club manager, grocer, clothes
   cleaner, carpet cleaner, huckster, jobber, clothing
   store owner, musician)   34

Large companies (railroads, gas companies, newspapers, bookbinderies)   9

Small shops, offices, and taverns   14

Government   8

Craft shops   7
                                                                                                                    ——
                                                                                                                    72

Sources: U.S. Manuscript Census Schedules, Boston, 1870, 1880, 1900.
[a] The 1880 jobs of upwardly mobile menial workers in the 1870 census and the jobs in 1900 of
upwardly mobile menial workers traced from the 1880 census.

menials, half were in small business, and the other half were spread
out across shops, offices, utility companies, and the government.
Even at these large firms, only a few blacks were hired.

What has happened to the shrewd Boston Yankee whose desire
for higher profits has led him to employ cheap labor? He was largely
a fiction of the imagination for several reasons. For one thing, the
employer was willing to offer a customary wage, an agreed-upon
price for labor because he had more to gain from ensuring a steady
and reliable work force than from securing the cheapest supply of
labor.[43] For another, he perceived blacks as inferior workers who
would be costly to hire: His prejudice blinded him to the opportunity
for profit. Social worker John Daniels published his study of Boston
blacks, *In Freedom's Birthplace*, in 1914. He interviewed some em-

43. The daily wage for industrial workers in Boston could not be budged. From
1870 to 1898, the highest daily wage for a boilermaker in Boston was $2.60 and the
lowest was $2.15. Similarly, in other industrial occupations listed below, the extent of
wage fluctuations was minimal:

Railroad firemen	$0.40
Machinists	$0.43
Compositors	$0.58
Railroad conductors and engineers	$0.77
Iron moulders	$0.90
Pattern makers	$1.49

"Wages in the United States and Europe, 1870 to 1898," *Bulletin of the U.S. Department of
Labor*, No. 14 (January 1898), pp. 670–683.

ployers of blacks who claimed that "many individuals of this race
. . . have exceptional qualifications, but as a class they were 'unreli-
able and incompetent.' "[44] Daniels apparently agreed. Few black
workers, he felt, "displayed initiative, resourcefulness, and persistence."[45] Attitudes like these helped to exclude black workers from
Boston's factories. Even unprejudiced manufacturers, who assumed
that white workers would object to hiring blacks, sought to avoid the
risk of disruption. Every employer could cite examples of white
workers who had walked off the job when blacks were hired. But
most Boston employers never had to face the choice of whether to
discriminate. For every black worker who tried to find a job in their
factories and was turned away, there were hundreds who assumed
employers were hostile and never applied. For these reasons, only a
few black workers ever entered a Boston factory.

Two barriers kept blacks from occupational advance, the first
from entry into nonmenial work and the second from permanent
security in nonmenial jobs. About one in five of the stable black
residents of Boston had advanced past the first barrier only to encounter the second. These were the barbers, other craftsmen, clerical
or sales employees, and professionals. Each of them had managed to
evade the forces of prejudice in reaching a position of reasonable
reward and prestige. Yet so often they were expendable.

The first group of blacks to fare unsuccessfully in competition
with whites were the barbers. Immigrants were driving them out. In
1870 17% of Boston's barbers were black; in 1900, only 5%. The
decline of Boston blacks in this skilled trade actually appears far
more gradual compared with black losses in Cleveland, Philadelphia,
or Detroit, but the trend was occurring everywhere, even in southern
cities, although it was especially strong in the North (Table V-6).

The displacement of black barbers suggests that black workers
suffered from competition even *within* black-dominated jobs. It is
true that after American men began using the safety razor at home
the trade of barbering declined, but black barbers should still have
been able to hold onto their share of a declining market.[46] One black
Boston barber offered his explanation: "The white man doesn't want
to be handled by the Negro."[47] However, the decline of blacks was far

---

44. John Daniels, *In Freedom's Birthplace: A Study of the Boston Negroes* (Boston,
1914), p. 320.

45. Ibid., p. 319.

46. David Manners Katzman, *Before the Ghetto: Black Detroit in the Nineteenth
Century* (Urbana, 1973), pp. 115–117.

47. "The Race Problem in Boston," p. 12.

TABLE V-6
Displacement of Black Male Barbers in Nine Cities, 1870–1900[a]

Year	Cleveland	Boston	Poughkeepsie	Detroit	Philadelphia	Richmond	Savannah	Birmingham	New Orleans
1870	43	17	19	55	31	n.a.	43	n.a.	37
1880	n.a.	14	3	n.a.	10	93	82	100	30
1890	15	11	n.a.	24	14	89	n.a.	80	30
1900	16	5	n.a.	22	11	83	n.a.	68[b]	26

Sources: Kenneth Kusmer, A Ghetto Takes Shape: Black Cleveland, 1870–1930 (Urbana, 1976), pp. 75–76; U.S. Manuscript Census Schedules, Boston, 1870 and 1880; U.S. Bureau of the Census, Population, v. 1 (Washington, D.C., 1872), p. 778, 784, 785, 792, 794; U.S. Department of the Interior, Census Office, Population, v. 1 (Washington, D.C., 1883), pp. 864, 894; U.S. Department of the Interior, Census Office, Population, Part II (Washington, D.C., 1897), pp. 638, 654, 702, 718; U.S. Bureau of the Census, Special Report, Occupations at the Twelfth Census (Washington, D.C., 1904), pp. 494–499; Clyde and Sally Griffen, Natives and Newcomers: The Ordering of Opportunity in Mid-Nineteenth-Century Poughkeepsie (Cambridge, 1978), p. 213; David M. Katzman, Before the Ghetto: Black Detroit in the Nineteenth Century (Urbana, 1973), p. 116; Theodore Hershberg, Mulattoes and Blacks: Intra-Group Color Differences and Social Stratification in Nineteenth-Century Philadelphia," unpublished paper delivered at the annual meeting of the Organization of American Historians, April 1974, no page; Herbert G. Gutman, The Black Family in Slavery and Freedom, 1750–1925 (New York, 1976), p. 480; John Blassingame, "Before the Ghetto: The Making of the Black Community in Savannah, Georgia, 1865–1880," Journal of Social History, v. 4 (Summer 1973). p. 467; Paul B. Worthman, "Working Class Mobility in Birmingham, Alabama, 1880–1914," in Tamara K. Hareven, ed., Anonymous Americans: Explorations in Nineteenth-Century Social History (Englewood Cliffs, New Jersey, 1971), pp. 176–179; John Blassingame, Black New Orleans, 1860–1880 (Chicago, 1973), pp. 230–233.

[a] The values are for blacks as a percentage of all barbers.

[b] For 1898.

greater in northern than in southern cities, where customers were presumably less prejudiced. The extent of decline appears to have been dictated less by racism than by the strength of immigrant competition and the oversupply of black barbershops (one on every corner, it used to be said). In Poughkeepsie, Germans edged out blacks; in Philadelphia and Boston, it was Germans and then Italians.[48] Immigrant barbers charged less than black barbers, and when blacks responded in kind the price war that resulted often inadvertently helped to undermine less competitive black barbers. In a shrinking market, many black barbers could not even depend on the black trade because for years they had succumbed to white prejudice and had refused to serve black customers. A Boston black barber explained, "I'd lose my [white] trade if it was known I did any work for a Negro."[49] This displacement of black barbers was in a small way helping to perpetuate black poverty in Boston. If blacks had maintained their share of the trade, then, by the turn of the century, there would have been 350 black barbers in Boston instead of 106. This single change would have decreased the concentration of blacks in menial jobs from 77% to 72%.

Black craftsmen comprised a second group of workers who were pushed out. The artisanal class as a whole was declining in this period, but black artisans were far more vulnerable than whites.[50] The rates of downward mobility of craftsmen (including barbers) were calculated for blacks and several groups of Boston's whites (first- and second-generation Irish and a sample of "whites" of undesignated nationality). The rate of downward mobility among black craftsmen was twice as high as among the Irish (first or second

48. W.E.B. DuBois, *The Philadelphia Negro*, pp. 115–116; Clyde and Sally Griffen, *Natives and Newcomers: The Ordering of Opportunity in Mid-Nineteenth-Century Poughkeepsie* (Cambridge, 1978), p. 213.

49. "The Race Problem in Boston," p. 12.

50. Robert Higgs refers to "the myth that black employment in skilled occupations declined during the postbellum period." Between 1870 and 1900 black craftsmen were losing out in five cities, but not in eight others. The obvious sorts of explanations for this variation do not offer much insight. The degree of decline was unrelated to (a) region, (b) the liberal reputation of the city, (c) the size of the immigrant work force, or (d) the size of the black population. The view that black craftsmen were being undermined was put forward by Herbert G. Gutman, *The Black Family in Slavery and Freedom, 1750–1925* (New York, 1976), pp. 627–628, and Kenneth L. Kusmer, *A Ghetto Takes Shape: Black Cleveland, 1870–1930* (Urbana, 1976), p. 75. See also Robert Higgs, *Competition and Coercion: Blacks in the American Economy, 1865–1914* (Cambridge, England, 1977), p. 81. The percentages of urban black men employed in crafts in 13

generation) and nine times greater than among the sample of white workers (Table V-7). Those most immune to failure tended to be concentrated in highly specialized crafts: the carriage-maker, the wigmaker, the silverplater, and the silversmith. Others were not as protected. Of the nine carpenters who could be traced from 1870 to 1880, six were still in the trade, two were porters, and one was a hackdriver. Two brickmasons in the same decade kept at their work, but a third had become a laborer. During the winter, black tradesmen fell back into service jobs. DuBois recorded the same fate for skilled artisans in Philadelphia: "The Negroes of the city who have trades either give them up and hire out as waiters or laborers, or they become job workmen and floating hands, catching a bit of carpentering here or a little brickwork or plastering there at reduced wages."[51]

The same problems appeared in the careers of blacks employed in shops and offices. Throughout the late nineteenth century, Boston blacks enjoyed one of the highest concentrations in clerical jobs, as

cities between 1870 and 1900 are presented below:

Year	Boston	Buffalo	Philadelphia	Pittsburgh	Cleveland
1870	22		5		32
1875		15			
1880	14		9	9	
1900	7	6	7	14	14

	Cincinnati	Louisville	Richmond	New Orleans	Atlanta
1870				24	19
1880	7	5	15	22	
1890	6	8	13	3	18

	Savannah	Baltimore	Detroit
1870	39	9	10
1880	15		12
1890	1	7	9

Sources: U.S. Manuscript Census Schedules, Boston, 1870 and 1880; Theodore Hershberg, "Mulattoes and Blacks," Table 22.2 and 22.3, no pages; Paul J. Lammermeier, "The Urban Black Family of the Nineteenth Century: A Study of Black Family Structure in the Ohio Valley, 1850–1880," *Journal of Marriage and the Family* (August 1973), p. 445; Thomas J. Goliber, "Cuyahoga Blacks: A Social and Demographic Study, 1850–1880," unpublished master's thesis, Kent State University, 1972, pp. 64–96; Herbert G. Gutman, *The Black Family*, p. 480; John W. Blassingame, *Black New Orleans, 1860–1880* (Chicago, 1973), pp. 224–228; David M. Katzman, *Before the Ghetto*, pp. 217–219.

51. W.E.B. DuBois, *The Philadelphia Negro*, p. 130.

TABLE V-7
Selected Rates of Downward Mobility into Menial
Labor: Boston, Atlanta, and Birmingham, 1870–1900

Group	City	Decade	Percentage	N
I. Former craftsmen employed as menials				
First-generation Irish	Boston	1880–1890	19	21
Second-generation Irish	Boston	1880–1890	14	14
All whites	Boston	1880–1890	4	164
Blacks	Boston	1870–1880	36	36
Blacks	Boston	1880–1890	21	19
Blacks	Atlanta	1870–1880	23	65
Blacks	Atlanta	1880–1890	9	68
Blacks[a]	Birmingham	1880–1890	43	7
Blacks[a]	Birmingham	1890–1900	29	28
II. Former clerical and sales workers employed as menials				
First-generation Irish	Boston	1880–1890	0	0
Second-generation Irish	Boston	1880–1890	0	4
All whites	Boston	1880–1890	1	157
Blacks	Boston	1870–1880	17	6
Blacks	Boston	1880–1890	53	17
Blacks[b]	Atlanta	1870–1880	0	3
Blacks[b]	Atlanta	1880–1890	33	3
III. Former professionals employed as menials				
First-generation Irish	Boston	1880–1890	0	1
Second-generation Irish	Boston	1880–1890	0	3
All whites	Boston	1880–1890	2	52
Blacks	Boston	1870–1880	17	6
Blacks	Boston	1880–1890	53	17
Blacks	Atlanta	1870–1880	0	3
Blacks	Atlanta	1880–1890	33	3

Sources: U.S. Manuscript Census Schedules, Boston, 1870, 1880, and 1900; Boston City Directory, 1890; Stephan Thernstrom, *The Other Bostonians: Poverty and Progress in the American Metropolis, 1880–1970* (Cambridge, 1973), Table 4.3, p. 57; Richard Joseph Hopkins, "Patterns of Persistence and Occupational Mobility in a Southern City, 1870–1920," unpublished Ph.D. dissertation, Emory University, 1972, Table 4-6, p. 119; Paul Worthman, "Working Class Mobility in Birmingham, Alabama, 1880–1914," in Tamara K. Hareven, ed., *Anonymous Americans: Explorations in Nineteenth-Century Social History* (Englewood Cliffs, N.J., 1971), Table II, p. 198.

[a] Men in semiskilled jobs were considered as menials.

[b] Includes businessmen.

bookkeepers, agents, stenographers, and sales clerks. In 1870, Boston, with about 3% of blacks employed in these jobs, was far ahead of other northern cities (like Cleveland) as well as southern ones (Atlanta, Savannah, New Orleans, and Denver). By 1900 5% of all black men were in clerical jobs, a proportion equaled only by New York City blacks. Some other northern cities (for example, Chicago and

Detroit) stood close, while clerical workers were a smaller proportion of the labor force in most southern cities.[52] Despite this strong show-ing in national terms, individual black workers in Boston could not hold onto their jobs.

There were too few Irish workers in clerical and sales jobs to offer much of a basis for comparison. But it can be easily seen that blacks enjoyed less security in jobs than Boston whites (of all nationalities). Only 1% of Boston white workingmen dropped down to menial labor in the decade between 1880 and 1890. In the previous decade, 17% of black workingmen fell that far. It is true that the rate of failure increased greatly toward the end of the century, but it is simply speculation to think that the color barrier in shops and offices was tightening, when the number of blacks who could be traced was so small. Nonetheless, whatever the interval being considered, a black clerk or sales employee was always less likely to keep his job than a white.

Countless examples of this process can be cited. In tracing all black clerks from 1880 to 1900, a category that included those in postal service as well as those in private employ, three were still clerks, one had no occupation, two were waiters, two held odd jobs, and one was a cook. Blacks failed to retain other white-collar jobs. The single black employed as a cashier in 1880 was too sick to work at all two decades later; of the three former office workers who were traced, one was a caterer and two were porters. Even a former gov-ernment official had taken a job as a cook. Several motives might be suggested for the firings of these men: Mulattoes, passing as whites, may have been discovered and promptly dismissed; others may have been edged aside by whites who coveted these jobs, and government workers may have been given their notices after a change in adminis-trations.

Even in the professions, where the representation of blacks was equal to that of the Irish, there was a retreat.[53] Again, the information

52. Thomas J. Goliber, "Cuyahoga Blacks," pp. 64–96; John W. Blassingame, *Black New Orleans*, pp. 224–228; John W. Blassingame, "Before the Ghetto: The Making of the Black Community in Savannah, Georgia, 1865–1880," *Journal of Social History*, v. 6, No. 4 (Summer 1973), pp. 463–488; Richard J. Hopkins, "Patterns of Persistence and Occupational Mobility in a Southern City: Atlanta, 1870–1920," unpublished Ph.D. dissertation, Emory University, 1972, Table 4.8, p. 176; Robert M. Tank, "Occupational and Geographic Mobility in Denver, 1870–1890," unpublished paper, 1975; U.S. Bureau of the Census, Special Reports, *Occupations at the Twelfth Census* (Washington, D.C., 1904), Table 43, pp. 480–763.

53. Boston had a reputation as the best city for black professionals, but that distinction probably belonged to Buffalo, with the largest black professional class for

available regarding the careers of Irish professionals is too minimal to form a conclusion, but, compared with whites of all nationalities, black professionals were eight times more likely to go under, as indicated in Table V-7. Some of the actors, musicians, and even clergy were so marginal to begin with that they could earn more as a coachman or pullman porter than in their original callings. A patron could die or retire and that left even the professional man vulnerable. But whatever the individual reasons behind the dismissal of these men of talent, the universal principle was that "the Negro suffers in competition more severely than white men."[54]

Losing out in competition with whites, as Table V-7 shows, was a consistent pattern for educated and skilled urban blacks. The rate of downward mobility has been studied for black workers in late nineteenth-century Atlanta and Birmingham, and, again, only the most severe kind of occupational skidding, downward mobility into the lowest status of jobs, menial labor, was considered. Because the black population in all of these cities was so transient, the number of workers whose careers could be traced was very small. Despite this problem the pattern of failure was being repeated in city after city.

Being forced into menial labor was a common predicament for black craftsmen in Birmingham and Atlanta as well as in Boston. (In a single decade, Atlanta craftsmen managed to hold their own.) It is doubtless true that prejudice against blacks was greater in Birmingham than in Boston, but the kind of racial animosity that pushed marginal black craftsmen out of their trades was as strong in one as in the other. Only tentative intercity comparisons can be made about the fate of blacks in clerical and sales work and in the professions. No information was available about the extremely small group of white-collar workers or professionals in Birmingham. Still, in At-

---

its day (8.5% of black Buffalo workers in 1875 and 6% in 1900). The early favorable showing of Boston blacks was lost by 1900. In 1870 the Boston black professional class comprised 3% of the black labor force and thus ranked above Cleveland, Denver, Atlanta, New Orleans, and Savannah. By 1900 Boston blacks could take less pride: The black professional class was on a par with that in Atlanta, Cincinnati, Indianapolis, or Nashville, but was behind those of Cleveland, Detroit, New York, Chicago, or Buffalo. Herbert G. Gutman and Laurence A. Glasco, "The Buffalo, New York Negro, 1855–1875: A Study of the Family Structure of Free Negroes and Some if Its Implications," unpublished paper, 1968, p. 12; Robert M. Tank, "Occupational and Geographic Mobility"; Thomas J. Goliber, "Cuyahoga Blacks," Table 38, p. 82; Richard J. Hopkins, "Patterns of Persistence," Table 4.8, p. 146; John W. Blassingame, "Before the Ghetto," pp. 463–488; John W. Blassingame, *Black New Orleans*, pp. 224–228; U.S. Bureau of the Census, Special Reports, *Occupations at the Twelfth Census*, Table 43, pp. 480–763.

54. W.E.B. DuBois, *The Philadelphia Negro*, p. 323.

lanta dismissal of black clerks and salesmen was as common as in
Boston. The doctors, lawyers, and other professionals in black Atlanta, who were just as prone to failure as the black professionals of
Boston, had not gained any major advantage from the South's segregation of the races.

Unsuccessful competition of this kind was a racial barrier just as
powerful as a union's policy of admitting only whites, and it was, in a
sense, far more destructive because it dashed the future of the
middle-class. Black workers were at a disadvantage in securing
better-paying jobs and in holding on to them. Access to higher-status
jobs was something of a revolving door: Some blacks were allowed to
enter, but many of them were sent back. Doubtless, a year-by-year
trace of black workers would show ever more rapid rates of movement. But even the crude measures used here make clear that stable
black residents advanced somewhat but often fell back, in this two-
stage process of unsuccessful competition.

BLACKS IN BUSINESS

Prejudice operated against almost every black worker, the ill-
educated ex-slave and the college-educated black Brahmin, the newcomer and the long-time resident of Boston. But the existence of twin
racial barriers, the exclusion of black newcomers and the unsuccessful competition of stable residents, is still not a complete explanation
for the persistence of black poverty in Boston. The Chinese and the
Japanese established their own businesses and hired members of
their race, despite the prejudice they faced. Even if employers and
unions consistently discriminated against blacks, did not the failure
of black businesses betray some inner weakness?

Much has been written about the inability of blacks to develop a
business class. E. Franklin Frazier argued that slavery robbed blacks
of an opportunity to develop entrepreneurial skills and that the subsequent oppression of the race reinforced an emphasis on immediate
consumption rather than on saving and self-denial. He found that
blacks were unable to generate even the small amount of capital
needed to open businesses. Others have argued that young blacks
lacked successful role models, the black equivalents of Rockefeller
and Carnegie. Even the black man who preached the business ethic
was a southern college president, not a financier or industrialist.
Daniel Moynihan and Nathan Glazer have added that black culture is
missing a certain "clannishness," a willingness to buy black, com-

parable to that found in other ethnic groups.[55] All of these factors are brought forward to explain why blacks opened businesses less often than European immigrants, or even than Chinese or Japanese.

It is true that black Bostonians were less likely to open retail stores than European immigrants, but they did develop service businesses.[56] Of the 197 Boston black businesses in 1900, 70 were in wholesale or retail trade, 107 were in personal service, and 20 were in other lines of work (printers, landlords, newspaper publishers, cigar manufacturers, and a banker). The personal service category included tailors, undertakers, caterers, livery stable keepers, boarding and lodging house keepers, owners of restaurants, barbershops, laundries, and bootblack stands.

It might be thought that black business failed because of the small size of the black community. Or that black business in the South succeeded because of a vast market of black consumers. Actually, the fate of the black business class did not rest on the size of a city's black population. On a per capita basis, more black entrepreneurs could be found in Boston than in Cleveland, Denver, Savannah, Atlanta, or New Orleans in 1870. Black Boston had lost its lead by 1900. But the cities with a large business class were northern (Chicago, Cincinnati, and Philadelphia) as well as southern (Baltimore, Charleston, and Richmond).[57]

55. E. Franklin Frazier, *The Negro in the United States* (New York, 1949), p. 411; E. Franklin Frazier, *Black Bourgeoisie: The Rise of a New Middle Class* (New York, 1957); Eugene P. Foley, "The Negro Businessman: In Search of a Tradition," *Daedalus*, v. 95 (Winter 1966), pp. 107–144; Nathan Glazer and Daniel Patrick Moynihan, *Beyond the Melting Pot: The Negroes, Puerto Ricans, Jews, Italians and Irish of New York City* (Cambridge, Mass., 1963), p. 33. Apparently influenced by E. Franklin Frazier, Thernstrom also argued that black deficiencies in business stemmed from a unique "cultural pattern—an emphasis on consumption rather than savings." Unfortunately, his conclusions were based on the tabulations from the published federal census of "merchant, retail," "merchant, wholesale," and "huckster and peddler," and thus he failed to recognize the stronger showing of blacks in personal service businesses. A similar assumption lies behind the analysis to be found in Robert Higgs, *Competition and Coercion: Blacks in the American Economy*, pp. 91–93. Stephan Thernstrom, *The Other Bostonians*, p. 217.

56. Black businessmen were less likely to open retail stores than European immigrants. Black retailers had to compete with white merchants who could offer more credit and a greater variety of merchandise than black retailers, and, as a consequence, many black consumers patronized white merchants. This "consumer demands" explanation can be overstated: No group is self-sufficient in meeting its own consumer needs. But still, it seems likely that blacks *were* less likely to enter retailing than other groups.

57. Thomas J. Goliber, "Cuyahoga Blacks," Table 38, p. 82; Robert M. Tank, "Occupational and Geographic Mobility"; John W. Blassingame, "Before the Ghetto,"

Even in comparison with Boston's Irish, black Bostonians were quite business-minded. From the manuscript census schedules, the number of men and women indicating a business as their occupation was tabulated. Southern-born blacks were more than three times as likely to establish businesses as Irish immigrants in 1870 or in 1880 (13% for blacks and 4% for Irish immigrants in both decades). Although the second generation among both groups tended to enter other lines of work, business enterprise was still stronger among blacks than Irish (about 9% for second-generation blacks versus 3% for second-generation Irish in 1870 and again in 1880). Even a small-scale study in 1909, conducted by the U.S. Immigration Commission in the older neighborhoods of the city, found that 45% of Jews, but only 5% of first-generation Irish and 3% of the second generation were in "business for profit."[58]

The unique problem of blacks was not a failure to cast down their bucket in race enterprise but the fact that the bucket so often came up empty. Many studies of business mortality have relied on the detailed yearly credit ratings by Dun and Bradstreet. The Boston branch of this firm rated only three black businesses (the largest three) in this period. Actually, the manuscript schedules of the census are the best source of the history of black enterprise.[59] The rate of failure in business was calculated by tracing blacks with entrepreneurial occupations (e.g., merchant, coal and wood dealer, caterer) from one census to the next. Because the federal manuscript census schedules for 1890 had been destroyed by fire, black entrepreneurs in the decade from 1880 to 1890 were traced from the census to the Boston city directory. This decade-by-decade measure does not detect small periodic fluctuations (the merchant who declares bankruptcy and then reopens a year or two later) but does measure permanent failure in business (the merchant who a decade later becomes a laborer). In the late nineteenth century, the chances of a black business surviving were at best two in three and at worst, one in three. The rate of survival for Boston's Irish was at least twice as high (Table V-8).

In fact, blacks failed in business more often than any other group of American entrepreneurs. Comparative figures in Table V-8, derived

---

pp. 463–488; Richard J. Hopkins, "Patterns of Persistence," Table 4.8, p. 176; John W. Blassingame, *Black New Orleans*, pp. 224–228; U.S. Bureau of the Census, Special Reports, *Occupations at the Twelfth Census*, Table 43, pp. 480–763.

58. U.S. Senate Reports, 62nd Congress, first session, *Reports*, v. 26 (Washington, D.C., 1911), pp. 475–476.

59. Dun and Bradstreet Collection, Manuscript Division, Baker Library, Harvard Business School.

TABLE V-8
Rate of Business Failure, 1870–1900

Locale	Years	Group	Rate of failure[a]	N
Boston	1870–1880	Blacks	36	11
	1880–1890	Blacks	63	27
	1890–1900	Blacks	53	17
	1880–1890	Irish	27	11
Poughkeepsie	1870–1880	Irish	27	44
	1870–1880	British	15	33
	1870–1880	Native whites of native parents	13	333
Russell County, Alabama; Gwinnett, Twiggs, and Worth counties, Georgia; Rankin and Tunica counties, Mississippi	1870–1880	White country store owners	20	133

Sources: U.S. Census, 1870, 1880, and 1900, Manuscript Census Schedules, Boston; Massachusetts Vital Statistics, Boston, 1870–1900; Boston City Directory, 1890; Clyde and Sally Griffen, *Natives and Newcomers: The Ordering of Opportunity in Mid-Nineteenth-Century Poughkeepsie* (Cambridge, 1978), Table 6.1, p. 120; Roger L. Ransom and Richard Sutch, *One Kind of Freedom: The Economic Consequences of Emancipation* (Cambridge, England, 1977), pp. 142–145.

[a] Entrepreneurs who died or moved were eliminated from this category; those whose second job was other than business were considered business failures.

from census-based studies of country store owners in southern crossroads and small-scale entrepreneurs in Poughkeepsie confirm the popular impression of Yankee ingenuity. Poughkeepsie's Irish and the southern merchants were less successful. But if the generous Irish saloon keeper who passed out too many free drinks was a stereotype with a bit of truth, then by comparison with the average black in business, he was a veritable J.P. Morgan.

Unsuccessful entrepreneurs of any race can usually find in their competitor's ruthlessness, their own inexperience, or the blind prejudice directed at them some reason for failure. But if some deficiency of this kind can be pointed to, it must be shown to be unique among blacks, not some general malady common to all small entrepreneurs. And therein lies the problem for most of the explanations usually advanced. To blame competition from whites for black business failure seems to partake of exactly this kind of thinking. Surely Irish grocers were losing out to the A & P and Jewish peddlers were being undermined by the department store. It would seem difficult, off-hand, to make a case that the competitors of black enterprises were somehow a unique breed of ruthless operator.

It seems equally unfair to cite inexperience as the source of difficulty for black businesses. To be sure, Poughkeepsie's Yankee merchants had acquired first-hand knowledge from previous jobs as store clerks or accountants. But most Irish grocers or saloonkeepers in Poughkeepsie were formerly common laborers.[60] Quite frankly, most immigrants had no previous experience in business, and so the deficiencies of blacks were general, not unique.

It is also claimed that an increase in white prejudice beginning in the 1890s helped to undermine black businesses dependent on white customers—the caterers, barbershop owners, tailors, and so forth. The hatred and fear of the Chinese led to the Exclusion Act of 1882, the prejudice against the Japanese resulted in California's Alien Land Law. The first of these passed in 1913 forbade Japanese from acquiring land in their own names, and yet Chinese and Japanese businesses survived. By 1919, half of the hotels and one quarter of the grocery stores in Seattle were owned by Japanese. Very few Chinese or Japanese grew rich from these enterprises but most remained in business until other opportunities opened after the end of World War II.

The best possible clue to the distinct problems of blacks in business is an understanding of the reasons for success among the Chinese (less evidence is available about *urban* Japanese). They kept their laundries and restaurants going, despite competition from larger, white-controlled firms, despite the absence of managerial experience, and despite color prejudice. The extent of their success may be exaggerated simply because no empirical studies have been conducted showing the rate of business failure among the Chinese. But the fact that, by 1920, one half of all the Chinese in the United States were employed in Chinese-owned restaurants and laundries suggests considerable business acumen. After World War I washhouses faced stiff competition from mechanized steam laundries. Many white laundries went bankrupt but the Chinese remained in business. They began their own steam laundries, which still apportioned some of the laundry to the washhouses. Chinese success depended on rigorous community organization. Trade guilds of Chinese merchants not only fixed prices and wages, but oversaw working conditions and prohib-

60. Clyde and Sally Griffen, *Natives and Newcomers*, p. 107.

ited excess competition between Chinese enterprises. They even specified that at least ten doorways must separate Chinese laundries. Under the requirements of the laundrymen's guild, only men who had undergone an apprenticeship and paid dues to the guild were permitted to open laundries. Violators were driven out of business by hired thugs or by disastrous price wars with guild-owned laundries. Funds from a rotating credit association probably supplied the capital for the purchase of steam equipment. In this form of capital-by-lottery operation, participants contributed small weekly sums for the chance of winning the entire pot. In the United States Chinese, Japanese, and West Indians, all groups that have been noted for their business skill, have operated pools of this kind.[61]

Other small businesses, without resorting to Chinese-style community regulation, devised somewhat similar techniques. With somewhat more gentility than the Chinese, southern country store owners still sought to minimize competition. New owners chose locations distant from other stores and established merchants exerted considerable pressure to maintain their dominance of the market. But it is doubtful that Irish saloonkeepers or grocers were ever able to freeze out their competition. The best that can be said is that a monopoly of trade was a sufficient but not absolutely necessary ingredient for business success.

What was necessary was a sufficient supply of capital. As a general rule, the greater the amount of capital investment, the lower the rate of business failure.[62] Although few Irish in business ever received bank loans, they tapped sources of capital which were largely unavailable to blacks. First, they were able to acquire first or second mortgages on real estate, whereas blacks often encountered discrimination in the purchase of homes. Second, wholesalers were probably more willing to extend an initial line of credit to an Irish retailer. Finally, successful small businesses could invest their profits in other enterprises. One Boston Irish saloonkeeper in East Boston used his profits to open a retail and wholesale trade in whiskey. That success story of an American president's grandfather was surely that of Irish businessmen other than Patrick Kennedy. It is a maxim of

---

61. Ivan Light, *Ethnic Enterprise in America: Business and Welfare among Chinese, Japanese, and Blacks* (Berkeley, 1972), pp. 89–92.

62. The risk of failure among southern country store owners was greatest among the small firms, those with less than $10,000 in assets. Similarly, Poughkeepsie firms with more than $10,000 in capital were more likely to survive than enterprises with smaller assets. Roger L. Ransom and Richard Sutch, *One Kind of Freedom: The Economic Consequences of Emancipation* (Cambridge, England, 1977), pp. 144–145; Clyde and Sally Griffen, *Natives and Newcomers*, pp. 110–111.

American enterprise that the more you have, the more you get. Because the Irish were more prosperous than blacks, they could begin businesses with a greater supply of capital, which gave them a better chance for survival. Once the business began to flourish, its profits could be invested in other enterprises. But black enterpreneurs did not have as many resources as the Irish. They could still have succeeded, but they needed to resort to the Chinese formula for success: regulate competition and rely on a system of rotating credit.

CONCLUSION

The roots of black poverty have been located in the racial discrimination practiced by Boston employers and workers. Racial discrimination exists whenever race is a factor in predicting an individual's opportunities.[63] Racial discrimination in employment can take several forms: The kind described in this chapter was not a case of blacks receiving lower wages for the same kind of work as whites, but of blacks of presumably equal productivity with whites being channeled into a set of jobs that paid lower wages, carried considerable social stigma, and involved high turnover. The twin processes of racial discrimination that produced this job segregation were exclusion of black newcomers from all but menial labor and the unsuccessful competition of stable residents for better-paying jobs.

Exclusion was the process of discrimination that affected the largest part of the black work force, those blacks who had just arrived in the city. Entry barriers to employment in factories, craft shops, department stores, offices, and city departments kept black newcomers locked out of many parts of the economy. In addition, black migrants were recruited into jobs—mostly in service—by their own friends and relatives and by employment agents. The effect of exclusion was that large numbers of black workers shifted between jobs and, as a consequence, developed unstable work histories and work habits.

Unsuccessful competition, a second form of racial discrimination against black workers, affected those blacks who had permanently settled in Boston. Blacks lost in competition in two respects. First, because of racial discrimination in the prospects for promotion, black upward mobility into many sectors of the economy was blocked, and aspiring blacks were forced to pull themselves up largely by their own bootstraps. But the second phase of the competitive cycle was the dismissal of many of those blacks who managed to make their

63. Lester C. Thurow, *Poverty and Discrimination* (Washington, D.C., 1969), p. 2.

way into better-paying jobs: displacement of barbers, and the wholesale firing of other black artisans, clerks, and even professionals. The sorriest cases of unsuccessful competition were the businessmen and businesswomen who went under, in large part because they were not well enough organized to regulate competition within the black community or to pool their meager capital resources.

Thus it was that the overwhelming majority of blacks found themselves in the market for unsteady, low-paying jobs. Many immigrants also accepted the same kinds of jobs, and many immigrants were stuck in these jobs. But soon after the Civil War most Irish immigrants and their American-born children had come to be employed in jobs in manufacturing, with the city, or in the skilled trades that offered slightly higher wages and slightly greater chances for promotion, although somewhat greater risks of unemployment.

Why were blacks kept out of semiskilled and manufacturing jobs, especially when they were employable at such low wages? It turned out that Boston employers were less interested in hiring low-wage labor than has been commonly thought. They were more than able to fill their positions with the available supply of labor, and they chose to keep their wages at almost a fixed rate and shore up their profits by dismissing their work force during slack periods. They maintained smooth functioning of production by selecting new workers from the family and friends of the current employees and by promoting acculturated children of immigrants from the ranks of menial labor. They feared the disruption involved in hiring large numbers of blacks. Boston employers did not want to tarnish their good reputations on Beacon Hill or in Brookline by the forced importation of black labor. Even if black workers had actively sought factory jobs (which they rarely did), it is unlikely that many employers, weighing the potential benefits against the real costs, wanted to hire them.

Some blacks were able to move out of menial jobs. It is therefore incorrect to think of them as the Sons of Ham, perpetually condemned to be only the haulers of wood or the drawers of water. Theirs was a much more dynamic situation: They were more like Sisyphus, forever pushing a rock slowly up the hill, then falling back, only to begin again. Stable black residents in Boston did move up, not as much as Irish-Americans to be sure, but certainly enough to challenge the notion that they were totally entrapped in menial jobs. Ambitious menial workers were hired one or two at a time by diverse employers, and, for the most part, they pursued the immigrant strategy of self-employment. However, among those who tried, only a few succeeded: The rate of failure was alarmingly high in all types of better-paying jobs.

In a story of this kind, where racial barriers appear not just in securing a well-paying job but in keeping it and in being promoted, it is reasonable to try to search out those groups who stood to profit from the occupational segregation of blacks. White shipbuilders gained because they were able to break the strikes of caulkers and freight handlers and force them to work longer hours at the same level of wages.[64] White hotel owners benefited from being able to replace white waiters with blacks.[65] Given the restricted nature of black opportunity, the employers of porters, waiters, janitors, laundresses, and domestic servants saved money because they could pay low wages but still have a ready supply of labor at their command. Some white builders profited from using black artisans on their projects when white labor was in short supply and in being able to readily dismiss these black employees. And many employers derived some kind of advantage from the threat to white unionism that the importation of southern blacks, beginning with the efforts of the Freedman's Bureau, posed. How much this threat acted to thwart white union demands in general is difficult to tell, but certainly in the aftermath of the Civil War white workers did perceive the expected influx of ex-slaves as a major threat to their status. But if we are trying to uncover a grand and purposeful divide-and-conquer strategy on the part of Boston employers, it has not appeared; we have only a diverse group of employers, uncoordinated in purpose, who had something to gain from racial discrimination in Boston.

Many white workers also derived economic advantages from racial discrimination in Boston. Those whites who were protected from the fact that black newcomers could not freely compete with them for jobs gained: the men and women in the protected part of unskilled labor, in manufacturing jobs, crafts, city employ, and in the department stores. Another group benefited because they were the victors in competition with blacks: white businesses, clerks, craftsmen (again), immigrant barbers, even professionals, and those menial laborers who had an easier time in moving up because black competition had been hamstrung. It seems unnecessary to try to compute exactly how much each of these groups was enriched. But because Boston's black population was so small, occupational integration in Boston could have been accomplished without cataclysmic changes for any group of white workers. Any attempt to calculate

64. Frederick L. Hoffman, *Race Traits and Tendencies in the American Negro* (Washington, D.C., 1903).
65. Blacks replaced striking white waiters at a downtown dining room and white bellmen at the Tremont House. New York *Age* (May 25, 1889); New York *Freeman* (July 31, 1886); ibid. (February 19, 1887).

how much white workers gained from discrimination must also sub-
tract what they lost from racial divisions in their ranks, which
weakened attempts to unionize and to secure better working conditions and wages.[66] If one could devise some kind of elaborate accounting scheme to take all of these factors into account, it would probably
turn out that a substantial group of white employers *and* white
workers in Boston were still gaining from racial discrimination, but
not by all that much. Clearly, there were whites who, as beneficiaries
of racial discrimination in Boston, had an interest in perpetuating it,
but American racism has always been entangled with questions of
power, status, and sexual threat, which go far beyond simple economic loss.

While exactly how many whites actually benefited from racial
discrimination is imprecise, it is abundantly clear that one group
consistently lost—Boston's blacks. (Since there were only a few black
businesses that depended on a segregated clientele, the number of
blacks who stood to profit from discrimination was negligible.) It is
impossible to weigh the impact of one kind of loss, being consistently
shut out, as against the other, being allowed to move up and then
being pushed back. Because of these racial barriers, more blacks than
immigrants were living in poverty. The family, which stood between
the individual and the economy, was forced to find new ways to cope
amidst these conditions of poverty.

66. The view that capitalists exploit racial antagonism to divide and conquer the
working class is the orthodox Marxist position. The opposing opinion, that white
workers actively act to exclude blacks and that capitalists are neutral, goes by the
name of the "split labor market" theory. In the capitalist exploitation model,
capitalists gain, and white workers lose; in the split labor market theory, white
workers gain (when they are able to exclude blacks) and white capitalists lose. There
have been attempts to demonstrate each position empirically. Some researchers have
tried to figure out how much whites would lose if blacks were integrated in the
economy (assuming current levels of education and skill). But it seems impossible to
measure how much all workers, white along with black, stood to gain from solidarity
between them. Furthermore, it seems unwarranted to make the *a priori* assumption
that for workers to gain, capitalists must lose, or *vice versa*.

The orthodox Marxist position is best explained by Michael Reich in "The Eco-
nomics of Racism," in David M. Gordon, ed., *Problems in Political Economy*, pp.
183–188. Edna Bonacich originated the idea of a split labor market in "A Theory of
Ethnic Antagonism: The Split Labor Market," *American Sociological Review*, v. 37
(October 1973), pp. 547–559, and applied it to the abolitionist era in her article
"Abolition: The Extension of Slavery and the Position of Free Blacks: A Study of Split
Labor Markets in the United States," *American Journal of Sociology*, v. 37 (November
1975), pp. 601–628. Two different, but equally intelligent, efforts to compute white gains
from racial discimination are Barbara R. Bergmann, "The Effect of White Incomes on
Discrimination in Employment," pp. 294–313, and Lester C. Thurow, *Poverty and Discrimination*.

CHAPTER VI

FAMILIES

The economic difficulties arise continually among young waiters and servant girls; away from home and oppressed by the peculiar lonesomeness of a great city, they form chance acquaintances here and there, thoughtlessly marry and soon find that the husband's income cannot alone support a family; then comes a struggle which generally results in the wife's turning laundress, but often results in desertion or voluntary separation.

W. E. B. DuBois
The Philadelphia Negro

During the winter of 1883, Joseph Dickason worked in Baltimore for 8 months and then returned to his wife in Boston. Within the same decade Mrs. T. and her daughter were given a place to stay by a West End black woman who found them wandering the streets. When Susan Jackson, 6 months pregnant, was abandoned by her husband, she went to live with her father and stepmother. All the years that Lizzie Johnson worked as a domestic, she left her young daughter in the care of an aunt.[1] All of these individuals found a means to ensure personal and family survival, ranging from temporary marital separation to reliance on kin. The circumstances of each individual were unique, but the problems they confronted were more general.

Ever since the publication of the Moynihan Report in 1965—and perhaps much before that—the adaptation of the black family to poverty and urbanization has been a subject of controversy. But the reason for considering it here is not simply to contribute some fresh evidence to a long-standing debate but to explore the effect of black urban poverty on the most fundamental unit of black life, the family.

The impact of poverty was probably most strongly felt by one type of family grouping, the female-headed household. Among Cambridge black households in 1896, the only year for which exact income figures were available, the median income for female-headed households was $432.75, compared with $696.10 in a two-parent household. Because of the higher incidence of poverty, women heading these households were often forced to become wage earners. In 1880 over half of all Boston black women heading households were employed, compared with just 17% of wives with husbands present.[2]

1. Record Group No. 15, Records of the Veterans' Administration of the National Archives, Civil War Application Files, Civil War Pension of Joseph Dickason, C.W. 652869; *Third Annual Report of the Associated Charities of Boston: November, 1882* (Boston, 1882), p. 42; Civil War Pension of Elias Hall, C.W. 634126; Civil War Pension of Charles H. Johnson, W.C. 50151.

2. "Condition of the Negro in Various Cities," *Bulletin of the Department of Labor,* v. II, No. 10 (May 1897), pp. 318–320; U.S. Census, 1880, Manuscript Census Schedules, Boston.

Chapter opening photo
Picnic in a Boston park, c. 1890.

Children from such households were being raised in the most abject circumstances, often without adequate food, clothing, and medical care. Some contemporary studies have suggested that "father absence" also has many long-term negative consequences (poor school performance, juvenile delinquency and in adulthood diminished occupational status), but most subsequent examinations of such claims have failed to show significant differences between father-present and father-absent children, when other relevant factors are considered.[3] Children raised in such households, it can be said, have gained as well as lost, benefiting from an emphasis on sharing, training in independence, and involvement with kin. One can admit that creativity often grew out of adversity, but still investigate the conditions that sometimes gave rise to creativity.

The Moynihan Report suggested that illegitimacy and female-headed households were common among poor blacks in the 1960s. (The rate of female headed households subsequently increased; in 1975 41% of Boston black households were headed by females.) Moynihan traced the rising incidence of female-headed households to the legacy of slavery, racial discrimination, and high levels of unemployment among black husbands. He wrote: "At the heart of the deterioration of the fabric of Negro society is the deterioration of the Negro family. It is the fundamental source of the weakness of the Negro community at the present time."[4] The critics objected to his view of the lower-class black family as a "tangle of pathology," especially to the charge that the male-absent family, rather than poverty and unemployment, was the fundamental source of community weakness. More recently, scholars have argued that the extended family, a grouping of kin and fictive kin spread across several households who cooperated together in economic undertakings and child care, is a more meaningful family unit in black life. Anthropologists, including Joyce Aschenbrenner, Carol Stack, Elmer and Joanne Martin, and Demtri Shimkin and his collaborators Gloria Louie and Dennis Frate, have shown that extensive daily sharing, adoption of

3. Heather L. Ross and Isabel V. Sawhill, *Time of Transition: The Growth of Families Headed by Women* (Washington, D.C., 1975), pp. 129–157; Elizabeth Herzog and Celia Sudia, "Children in Fatherless Families," in Bettye M. Caldwell and Henry N. Ricciuti, eds., *Review of Child Development Research*, v. 3 (Chicago, 1973), pp. 141–233.

4. Office of Policy Planning and Research, U.S. Department of Labor, *The Negro Family: The Case for National Action* (Washington, D.C., 1965), p. 5. Many of the criticisms of the Moynihan Report are summarized in Lee Rainwater and William L. Yancey, eds., *The Moynihan Report and the Politics of Controversy* (Cambridge, 1967).

orphans and strangers, and obligations of mutual aid form the basis of a black extended family system.[5] In *The Black Family in Slavery and Freedom*, Herbert Gutman located its origins in the system of plantation-based obligations that cemented ties of kinship among slaves. While this new research gives a much needed counterpoint to the old theme of marital instability, the one does not negate the other. The black extended family often functioned as a substitute for the stable nuclear family. It is worthwhile to consider first the stability of the marital unit and then the duration of kin ties, before examining each in relation to the other.

In the article entitled "The Two-Parent Household: Black Family Structure in Late Nineteenth-Century Boston," I explored the first theme.[6] Evidence about the household composition of Boston black families, based on the federal manuscript census schedules in 1880, showed that 8 out of 10 Boston black couples lived in a two-parent household. I concluded that the black family (actually, the census household) withstood the pressures of poverty with few signs of what had been termed a tangle of pathology. This conclusion was based on census information about black household composition in a single year. Subsequent examination of evidence from birth records, charity applications, and longitudinal data derived from the manuscript census schedules led me to conclude that the household was a transitory living arrangement, that many blacks marriages were short-lived, and that children were sometimes raised by foster parents; the succession of evidence that led to this new conclusion can be briefly summarized here.

To be sure, illegitimacy was just slightly higher among Boston black than Irish women. Birth records without the designation of the father's name were considered illegitimate. By this definition, 7% of black births and 4% of Irish births between 1875 and 1880 were out of wedlock.[7] But charity applications of deserted wives were far more

5. Carol Stack, *All Our Kin: Strategies for Survival in a Black Community* (New York, 1974); Demitri B. Shimkin, Edith Shimkin, and Dennis A. Frate, eds., *The Extended Family in Black Societies* (Chicago, 1978); Carol B. Stack, "The Kindred of Viola Jackson: Residence and Family Organization of an Urban Black American Family," in Norman E. Whitten and John F. Szwed, eds., *Afro-American Anthropology: Contemporary Perspectives* (New York, 1970), pp. 303–312; Joyce Aschenbrenner, *Lifelines: Black Families in Chicago* (New York, 1975); Elmer P. Martin and Joanne Mitchell Martin, *The Black Extended Family* (Chicago, 1978).

6. Elizabeth H. Pleck, "The Two-Parent Household: Black Family Structure in Late Nineteenth-Century Boston," *Journal of Social History*, v. VI, No. 2 (Fall 1972), pp. 3–36.

7. This rate was computed from data in the *City Registrar's Report: 1875* (Boston,

common among blacks than immigrants. In 1896, the Associated Charities, Boston's largest relief agency, tabulated the nationality and race among applicants who identified themselves as "deserted wives." In a city where blacks were only 2% of the population, black deserted wives were 8% of the charity applicants. The rate of application was higher than among white immigrant women: for blacks, 27 per 10,000; for Irish immigrants, 7 per 10,000, and for second generation European immigrants of various nationalities, .8 per 10,000.[8] This is suggestive but not conclusive proof of a higher incidence of desertion; black women may simply have been more willing to apply for charity. Far greater weight, then, must be given to the more representative family patterns to be found in analysis of the census.

These indicated that father-absent households were more common among black than Irish children. Under the age of 6, 14% of black youngsters in 1870 but only 8% of Irish children (in my sample of 3000) were missing a parent. In 1880 about 12% of black youngsters but 9% of Irish children (in a second sample of 3000) were living apart from at least one parent.[9] This was probably the general pattern for blacks across the North. In Philadelphia the incidence of fatherless black children in 1880 was 8 points higher than in Boston.[10] It is unlikely that a higher mortality rate among black than Irish fathers accounted for these differences because the mortality rate for Boston black males in the 1880s was only slightly above that for Irish males. Furthermore, the names of absent parents (fathers or mothers) were checked against Boston's death records between 1870 and 1880. Only about one out of seven names of missing parents could be found. In all likelihood, these missing parents were alive, but living apart from their families.

1875), p. 8; *City Registrar's Report: 1876* (Boston, 1876), p. 8; *City Registrar's Report: 1879* (Boston, 1879), pp. 6–7; *City Registrar's Report: 1880* (Boston, 1880), pp. 5–6. The rate of illegitimacy among Boston blacks in 1914 was three and a half times greater than among whites. James E. Teele and William M. Schmidt, "Illegitimacy and Race: National and Local Trends," *The Millbank Memorial Fund Quarterly*, v. XLVIII, No. 2 (April 1970), pp. 132–135.

8. Zilpha D. Smith, *Deserted Wives and Deserting Husbands* (Boston, 1901), pp. 1–7. Only in work relief were the Irish overrepresented as charity applicants. At the Industrial Aid Society for the Prevention of Pauperism, which dispensed jobs in day labor, the rate of applications was slightly higher for Irish than blacks between 1883 and 1897. *Annual Report of the Industrial Aid Society for the Prevention of Pauperism* (Cambridge, 1883–1897).

9. U.S. Census, 1870 and 1880, Manuscript Census Schedules, Boston.

10. Claudia Goldin, " 'The Philadelphia Negro' in 1880: Some New Findings and Comparisons," unpublished paper, 1978.

TABLE VI-1
Proportion of Female-Headed Households among Boston
Blacks and Irish, by Migrant Generation, 1870 and 1880

Group and year	Percentage of female heads[a]	N
1870		
Blacks, southern migrants	18	393
Irish, immigrants	22	377
1880		
Blacks, southern migrants	21	520
Irish, immigrants	22	468
Blacks, second generation[b]	31	243
Irish, second generation[b]	16[c]	115

Sources: U.S. Census, 1870 and 1880, Manuscript Census Schedules, Boston.
[a] Only households with children were included.
[b] Born in Massachusetts, other northern states, or Canada.
[c] Significantly different from second-generation blacks.

Census figures further indicated that the female-headed household was more common among blacks than among the Irish. If the comparison is restricted to the first generation (southern blacks versus Irish immigrants), Table VI-1 shows that the rates were about the same. Divergent trends appeared only in the second generation, where the rate of female-headed households was 16% for the Irish and 31% for blacks. The effect of city residence, then, was to widen the initially small differences between Irish and blacks. The reasons for this difference will be considered more fully later on.

Measures such as these provide an understanding of family circumstances at one moment in time. But they do not provide evidence about the permanence of any particular living arrangement. That requires evidence derived from a linkage of records; in the case of black Bostonians, it involved locating the names of Boston black married couples listed in the census for 1870 in the 1880 census for Boston and Cambridge. Similarly, the names of Boston black married couples, enumerated in the 1880 census, were checked against an alphabetical index of the names of all Massachusetts residents enumerated in the 1900 census. The deaths of husbands and wives, as recorded in Boston death records from 1870 to 1900, were noted, thereby eliminating widows and widowers from the trace. The results of this linkage indicated that fully one third of black marriages dissolved between 1870 and 1880 and that two out of five ended between 1880 and 1900. Among black children under 6 in 1870, one third were living apart from at least one parent by the next decade.

SOURCES OF MARITAL DISSOLUTION

What accounts for the dissolution of black marriages and the absence of many black fathers? The evidence for black Boston and other nineteenth-century black communities permits evaluation of three explanations considered to be significant in previous studies.

1. *The Legacy of Slavery.* In *The Negro Family in the United States,* E. Franklin Frazier claimed that in the immediate aftermath of slavery two traditions arose: Those with "stable marital arrangements as slaves persisted without much disturbance to the routine of living," whereas slave marriages of convenience "broke easily during the crisis of emancipation."[11] In *Beyond the Melting Pot,* Daniel Moynihan and Nathan Glazer insisted, "The experience of slavery left as its most serious heritage a steady weakness in the Negro family. There was no marriage in the slave family—husbands could be sold away from wives, children from parents. There was no possibility of taking responsibility for one's children for one had in the end no power over them. One could not educate them, not even, in many cases, discipline them."[12] Recent research has tended to overturn each of these judgments. Using household information drawn from the manuscript census schedules in many southern and northern communities just before and after the Civil War, Herbert Gutman argued that emancipation revealed "no steady weakness" in the black family because a two-parent household could be found throughout the South.[13]

Ex-slaves in late nineteenth-century Boston, although more privileged than other ex-slaves, still confronted the general problem of being newcomers to the northern city whose ties to the South had been severed. It is natural to think that their marriages would show the strains of this new life, especially when compared with blacks who had been free for generations. But their family life stubbornly defied these expectations. A significantly lower proportion of Boston female-headed households in 1850, 1870, and 1880 could be found among southern migrants than among blacks born in other regions (Table VI-2).

2. *The Surplus of Women.* The female-headed household, some

11. E. Franklin Frazier, *The Negro Family in the United States* (Chicago, 1939; Chicago, 1966), p. 88.

12. Nathan Glazer and Daniel Patrick Moynihan, *Beyond the Melting Pot: The Negroes, Puerto Ricans, Jews, Italians and Irish of New York City* (Cambridge, 1963), p. 52.

13. Herbert G. Gutman, "Persistent Myths about the Afro-American Family," *Journal of Interdisciplinary History,* v. 6, No. 2 (1975), pp. 181–210.

TABLE VI-2
Proportion of Boston Black Female-Headed Households,
By Migrant Generation, 1850, 1870, and 1880[a]

Group and year	Percentage of female-headed households	N
1850[b]		
Southern migrants	17	140
Massachusetts, northern, and		
Canadian born	30[c]	228
1870		
Southern migrants	18	393
Second generation	36[c]	277
Massachusetts born	40[c]	112
Other northern born	30[c]	110
Canadian born	40[c]	55
1880		
Southern migrants	21	520
Second generation	31[c]	243
Massachusetts born	36[c]	92
Other northern born	23	98
Canadian born	40[c]	53

Sources: U.S. Census, 1870 and 1880, Manuscript Census Schedules, Boston; Janet Riblett Wilkie, "Social Status, Acculturation and School Attendance in 1850 in Boston," *Journal of Social History*, v. II, No. 2 (Winter 1977), Table 5, p. 186.

[a] Only households with at least one child were included. In two-parent households, generational status was determined by the husband's place of birth.

[b] Households with children under 4 and over 16 were excluded. Since very few black households included children over 16, that restriction should not bias these figures. However, the rate of female-headedness was probably higher for mothers with children under 4. Therefore, the true rate of female-headed households in 1850 was probably slightly above these figures.

[c] Significantly different from the southern born.

have claimed, results from an imbalanced sex ratio—an excess of women to men—which often contributed to illegitimacy, prostitution, and a host of social problems. Because of the demand for domestic servants and the higher rate of male than female mortality, many black urban populations in the late nineteenth and early twentieth centuries were virtual female metropolises. Herbert Gutman has argued that the female-headed household was uncommon in the southern countryside, but more common in southern cities because of the surplus of women.[14] Upon closer inspection, however, this connection

14. Ibid.; Jacqueline J. Jackson, "But Where Are the Men?" *Black Scholar*, v. 3 (December 1971), pp. 30–41. Some obvious explanations for the growth of female-headed households can also be easily dismissed. For one thing, few female-headed

appears spurious. Rates of female-headed households were compared with the sex ratio in each of eight northern and southern cities between 1850 and 1925. It is quite correct, as Gutman pointed out, that in several postbellum southern cities, low sex ratios went hand in hand with high proportions of black female-headed households Nonetheless, in Evansville, Indiana, a high sex ratio was accompanied by a high proportion of black female-headed households. Table VI-3 gives two more contrary instances: a moderate rate of female-headed households in Philadelphia, despite the surplus of women, and a high rate of such households in New York City, despite the numerical balance of the sexes.

    3. *Deaths of Black Husbands.* In their study of Philadelphia black households between 1850 and 1880, Frank Furstenberg, Jr., Theodore Hershberg, and John Modell argued that the female-headed household was more common among blacks than immigrants because "black women lost their spouses and did not remarry."[15] At first glance, the same argument could be made for Boston's blacks. The proportion of female-headed households was highest among the elderly and lowest among those under 30. It was also true that about 7 in 10 Boston black women heading such households identified themselves as widows. Moreover, widows had fewer opportunities to remarry, in fact, half as many, according to rates of remarriage computed from the Boston marriage records between 1870 and 1880.

    But this evidence is misleading. In studying Philadelphia blacks, DuBois insisted that "a large number of these widows are simply

---

households were the result of teenage marriages. Actually, blacks in late nineteenth-century Boston married late: on the average, black brides married at 25 and grooms at 30. Few of these female-headed households had been divorced. Among Boston blacks, there were only 2 divorced men and 11 divorced women in 1890; by 1900, the total number of divorced men and women was only 30.

    It is true, as Appendix C indicates, that underenumeration of blacks in the census was substantial. The argument had been made that the underenumeration of black men explained the prevalence of female-headed households. This seems doubtful for two reasons. First, the black husbands being classified as separated or deserting in the census-to-census trace had already been enumerated once by the census. Their chances of appearance in the census a second time were probably greater than those of men who had been missed altogether. Second, if black men had been undercounted, then one would expect an overabundance of husbandless women. The reverse was actually the case: More husbands were missing wives than wives were missing their husbands.

    15. Frank F. Furstenberg, Jr., Theodore Hershberg, and John Modell, "The Origins of the Female-Headed Black Family: The Impact of the Urban Experience," *Journal of Interdisciplinary History*, v. VI, No. 2 (1975), p. 221.

TABLE VI-3
Relationship Between the Sex Ratio and the Percentage of
Black Female-Headed Households in Eight Cities, 1850–1925

City	Date	Percentage of female-headed households	N	Sex ratio
Philadelphia	1850	23[a]	1,739	68
	1880	26	2,886	66
Mobile	1880	34	2,791	73
Boston	1870	26	670	108
	1880	24	763	108
St. Johns, New Brunswick	1871	35	73	59
Evansville, Indiana	1880	31	403	106
Richmond	1880	70	4612	80
New York City	1905	33	3014	98
	1925	30	10,732	98
Buffalo	1905	39	105	76
	1925	14	73	48

Sources: See the citation for Appendix Table D-1.
[a] For the population aged 15–44.

unmarried mothers and thus represent the unchastity of a large number of women."[16] Shorn of its Victorian prudishness, DuBois's statement appears reasonable. At least some black couples, husbands as well as wives, misrepresented their marital status to the census taker. Harriet Young, for instance, called herself a widow in 1900 while her partner from 1880, still a resident in Boston, had remarried. Richard and India Wilder, husband and wife in the 1880 census, were by 1900 each claiming to be widowed. Elizabeth Williams, a Bostonian who had moved to Worcester, told the census taker in 1900 that her husband was dead; meanwhile, her partner, according to the 1880 census, was living in Boston with a "wife." Kate and Darby Hill, a married couple in the 1880 census, were designated as widowed in the 1900 census, although they were living only a few blocks apart. The motives for these deceptions were probably the same as those of Mary Williamson, who explained in her application for a widow's pension, "I went by the name of 'Black' all the time; never changed

16. W.E.B. DuBois, *The Philadelphia Negro* (Philadelphia, 1899; New York, 1967), p. 68. See also E. Franklin Frazier, *The Negro Family in the United States*, p. 247.

the name till I married Phillips. I had done wrong once but I did not again and I did not want to publish what I had done, so I continued to use Black's name after we separated."[17]

These examples fit with more solid evidence of a different sort. The probabilities of widowhood were calculated based on four demographic facts about Boston's blacks: the number of deaths among husbands, among wives, and among both parents and remarriages of widows. Table VI-4 reports the "expected" number of widows based on these calculations for different age cohorts of black married women. The expected number was just a tenth of the actual proportion for women between 20 and 40, slightly more than that for middle-aged women, and close to the actual proportion among women over 50. Although the rate of adult male mortality among blacks was high, it was not high enough to account for the large number of "widows" under the age of 50.[18] On the other hand, the rate of adult mortality among blacks in Philadelphia was high enough to account for the expected proportions of widows there. It appears that the match between the expected and actual proportions of widows in Philadelphia was less a question of cause and effect than of sheer coincidence.

Additional evidence makes it unlikely that most of the heads of male-absent households were widows. In the nineteenth century, the system of death registration in Massachusetts was the finest in the country. Clerks canvassed every Boston neighborhood and compiled figures about yearly deaths from the hospitals and the morgue.[19] Because of the quality of their work, it makes sense to assume that most deaths of blacks in Boston had been recorded. Yet only a third of the black husbands and wives missing in 1880 could be located in Boston's death records. Some of the absent may have died elsewhere in Massachusetts, but it is doubtful that this group was large enough to account for such a large disparity.

If none of the common explanations for the prevalence of black female-headed households—the legacy of slavery, the imbalance of

17. Affidavit of Mary A. Williamson, April 11, 1921, Civil War Pension of Williamson, C. W. 902002.

18. These calculations assume a stable population of widows, balanced between in-migrants and out-migrants. In fact, the rate of in-migration was probably slightly higher than the rate of out-migration. Nonetheless, it would take an extreme imbalance in the size of the two population streams to call these findings into question.

19. Robert Gutman, "Birth and Death Registration in Massachusetts," *Milbank Memorial Fund Quarterly*, v. 36 (January and October 1958), pp. 58–74, 373–402; ibid., v. 37 (July and October 1959), pp. 297–326, 384–417.

TABLE VI-4
Probability of Widowhood among Boston Black Women, 1880[a]

Age	(a) Number of black married women	(b) Husband's death	(c) Married woman's death	(d) Widow's death[b]	(e) Joint death of husband and wife[b]	(f) Re-marriage[c]	Expected number of widows	Actual number of widows	"Expected" proportion of widows as a percentage of actual reported widows
21–30	469[a]	7	9	0	0	1	6	61	10
31–40	454	7	6	0	0	1	12	117	10
41–50	442	14	16	1	0	5	30	86	35
51–60	416	22	21	3	8	1	50	69	72
61+	363	37	38	9	5	0	78	89	88

[a] The number of widows $= a - b + f$; the number of married women $=$ the previous cohort of married women $- b,c,d,e + f$.
[b] Calculated from the death rates for Boston blacks published in the U.S. Department of the Interior, *Vital Statistics of Boston and Philadelphia* (Washington, D.C., 1895), Table 6, p. 5.
[c] Calculated from Massachusetts Vital Statistics, Boston, 1870–1880.
[d] The number of married women and married women with spouse absent in the manuscript census schedules, Boston, 1880.

the sexes, or the high death rate among black husbands—are satisfactory, then what explains it? Several types of evidence can be used, but an especially valuable kind of evidence derives from following a group of couples over time. The evidence to be reported on here consisted of longitudinal data about married couples, traced from the 1870 to the 1880 manuscript census schedules and again from the 1880 to the 1900 manuscript census schedules. Stable married couples were compared with those in which one spouse was missing to determine differences in economic status, demographic condition, and regional origins.[20] One extraordinary and unexpected finding emerged; wives actually left their husbands more often than husbands left their wives. It made sense then to examine the correlates of separation and desertion separately for each sex.

The Moynihan Report argued that the high rate of unemployment among black males placed an unusually large burden on their marriages. That suggestion was borne out by the Boston evidence: Husbands who were unemployed in 1880, as Table VI-5 shows, were significantly more likely to leave their wives than fully employed men, a 9 percentage point difference that was statistically significant. Because this finding appears significant even in admittedly crude data, one might expect that it would emerge with even greater clarity if a more accurate measure of black unemployment was available.

Black husbands employed in menial jobs were twice as likely to leave their wives as men in better-paying jobs (Table VI-5), a rate of separation and desertion of 10% for blacks in nonmenial jobs and 19% for husbands in menial work. Unsteadiness in work also contributed to disruption, as Alvan Sanborn, a Boston social reformer, realized in describing the condition of the *Irish* poor: "For the man with steady low wages at least knows what *not* to depend on, and given a fair amount of intelligent will power, will cut his garment according to his cloth, while the man fitfully employed is always on the brink of a precipice."[21] Often the husband employed in an un-

20. The largest group consisted of husband–wife couples, where both partners were no longer living in Boston. If it could be shown that these couples remained together more often than the couples under study, then a substantially different conclusion would be reached. But it is doubtful that this group had more stable marriages than the others. In fact, men employed in menial jobs were more likely to leave Boston than higher status black workers, and such men were also more likely to separate or desert. It is sensible to think that marital instability was at least as common—and probably more common—among this non-persisting population as among the couples represented in Table VI-5.

21. Alvan F. Sanborn, "The Anatomy of a Tenement Street," *The Forum* (January 1895), pp. 554–572.

TABLE VI-5

Proportion of Separations and Desertions among Black Married Couples, 1870–1900[a]

	Percentage of separating and deserting husbands													
	Nativity	*N*	*Childless*	*N*	*With children*	*N*	*Menial occupation*	*N*	*Nonmenial occupation*	*N*	*Unemployed*[b]	*N*	*Employed*[b]	*N*
Overall[c]	11	338	14	85	9	249	19	274	10	109	21	19	12	144
Southern migrants	11	228	19	55	8	168	15	178	13	60	19	16	12	101
Second generation														
Massachusetts born	17[d]	30	13	6	10	23	57	30	14	12	0	1	25	8
Northern born	6	52	0	12	8	43	10	31	5	21	0	1	8	24
Canadian born	28[d]	18	15	9	14	10	17	12	17	6	100	1	14	7

	Percentage of separating and deserting wives													
	Nativity	*N*	*Childless*	*N*	*With children*	*N*	*Employed*	*N*	*Not employed*	*N*	*Husband menial worker*	*N*	*Husband nonmenial worker*	*N*
Overall[c]	20	232	23	86	11	226	21	38	10	313	10	235	11	101
Southern migrants	9	192	17	41	8	123	10	20	9	160	7	162	14	55
Second generation														
Massachusetts born	20[d]	49	36	11	13	40	29	7	14	42	24	17	20	15
Northern born	17	54	18	17	15	39	25	4	16	51	13	32	17	24
Canadian born	18	34	27	15	10	20	33	6	12	26	29	14	17	6

Sources: U.S. Census, 1870, 1880, 1900; Manuscript Census Schedules, Boston, Suffolk County and Massachusetts Vital Statistics, Boston Death Records, 1870–1900.

[a] A combination of blacks persisting from the 1870 to the 1880 census and those persisting from the 1880 to 1900 census. Deserters are a residual category, including all missing or separated spouses. Black couples where one partner died (as indicated in Boston's death records) or where both had moved out of Boston were eliminated from the trace. The spouse in the couple who was missing from the census has been considered as the partner who decided to separate or desert.

[b] Applies only to blacks first appearing in the 1880 census.

[c] Includes blacks born in the West Indies and other foreign countries.

[d] Significantly different from southern-born blacks.

steady job picked one of several alternatives: moving his family elsewhere, staying in the city and living off his wife's earnings, stealing, or deserting. He had probably tried several of these at one time or another. A more refined accounting of husband's occupations (unreported in Table VI-5) indicated that desertion or separation was especially common among black waiters. The rate was about 40% among waiters and about 20% for men in other menial jobs. Some waiters were briefly separated from their families, during the summer when they took jobs at summer resorts, while others were permanently absent.

Childless husbands were also more inclined to desert. The rate of separation or desertion was 9% for fathers and 14% for childless husbands, as indicated in Table VI-5. (Among black women, childlessness was far more strongly linked with separation or desertion). According to a profile drawn from the records of the Boston Associated Charities in 1903, the usual male deserter was an unemployed immigrant menial laborer and the father of two or three young children.[22] While the typical black deserter did not have the family burdens of the white deserter, neither did he have the joys of fatherhood or the security of assistance from grown children in old age.

City life in some way also seemed to foster separation and desertion. At least it can readily be seen from Table VI-5 that it was far more common among blacks born in Massachusetts or in Canada than among those born in other regions. This conclusion has already been anticipated by the evidence about black household composition from 1850 to 1880, where it was shown that the female-headed household was proportionately more frequent among black Northerners than Southerners. An explanation for this difference defies simple economic causation, since a straight line from economic immiseration to marital breakup would lead precisely to the expectation of a higher frequency of separation and desertion among blacks born in the South rather than in the North. It also defies a simple demographic explanation, such as a higher incidence of teenage marriage among northern-born blacks. Marriage records for late nineteenth-century Boston indicate that the median age of marriage for men and women was about the same among blacks born in various regions. A medical explanation, for example, a higher rate of disease and death among northern than southern-born blacks, also runs counter to a more reasonable inference of higher mortality among those most abject in occupational status, the southern born.

22. Zilpha D. Smith, *Deserted Wives and Deserting Husbands*, pp. 1–7.

The northern city, it must finally be recognized, had added new temptations and eroded old beliefs and ways of living. Familiar customs had persisted in the rural South for generations. As late as the 1930s blacks on St. Helena's Island, South Carolina, preferred to take minor disputes before church rather than legal courts. The island's black churches worked in concert with neighbors to enforce strong "social pressure toward sex morality." Neighbors rebuked parents who failed to discipline children properly by spreading rumors "to the effect that children of the particular parents concerned are only half brought up."[23] Even in southern cities, neighbors and churches had scrutinized every aspect of personal life. Slave churches, such as the First African Baptist in Richmond, punished adulterers and tried to keep marriages together. During the Civil War a Camden, South Carolina, black church, described by a plantation mistress as a "keen police court," expelled thieves, drunks, and adulterers. Most of these social controls in the South were reimposed by southern migrants in the North, who libed within the tightly knit world of church-going, kin, and neighborhood gossip. But for others in the urban North, neighborhood life was more anonymous, less personalized and probing: Couples like Mary and Martin Stevens could pass as man and wife without excessive questioning. Blacks born in the North had left behind the kind of life that helped keep marriages together.

Wives actually separated from their husbands more often than husbands left their wives. The rate of separation or desertion was 20% for wives, but 11% for husbands. Table VI-5 makes clear that the missing wife was, more often than not, born in Massachusetts (but not in Canada) and childless. Since this was also the profile of the missing husband, no special emphasis need be added here, and we can turn our attention to the one distinctive motive for wives' absence from the family.

Desertion was more often the remedy for the working woman. Employed wives were twice as likely to separate from their husbands as non-employed wives, according to Table VI-5. Women like these, earning on the average $154 a year in 1896 (or about one third of what their husband's made) were still dependent on their husbands. A wife's wages, it must be admitted, were less a steady sum for a start in a new life than a source of tension in the old one. Edwin Harwood and Claire Hodge have suggested that the black domestic, exposed to

23. Clyde V. Kiser, *Sea Island to City: A Study of St. Helena Islanders in Harlem and Other Urban Centers* (New York, 1932), pp. 62–63, 201–202; T. J. Woofter, Jr., *Black Yeomanry* (New York, 1930), pp. 205–207; Herbert Gutman, *The Black Family*, p. 70.

the higher standard of living in her employer's home, tended to devalue her own meager circumstances and belittle her husband's worth as a provider.[24] That exposure to wealthy whites was the major source of discontent seems oversimplified, especially since the laundress who stood over a tub at home was just as likely to separate or desert as was the woman who went out in service. Moreover, it has already been noted that the black domestic, far from demonstrating loyalty to her white mistress, often quit her job after only a few months of employment.

The roots of discontent had more to do with dissatisfaction at home. Taking a job often followed rather than preceded marital problems. After Sarah Barnett had her husband arrested for beating her, she became a domestic in Boston. When she learned that he got a young Irish girl pregnant, she left him. Lucretia Manuel, the wife of an itinerant preacher, took a job during one of her husband's absences, and when he returned from a trip to Nova Scotia— accompanied by two women—she refused to take him back. She explained, "I saw him about two or three times after he left me, once in Lynn and once in Boston. He wanted to return to live with me but I wouldn't have him." Frances Douglass's reasons for separation can only be inferred from the pages of the manuscript census schedules. She supported herself and her children while her husband was an inmate at the Suffolk County House of Correction. After his release, she divorced him and continued to provide for her children by taking in laundry.[25]

Dissatisfaction was probably compounded by conflict about a wife's employment. It is true that contemporary studies, such as a 1970 national survey, found more favorable attitudes toward working wives among black than white men and that another national survey 4 years earlier reported that even black husbands born prior to 1911 were less opposed to the employment of mothers with school-age children than were comparable white men. Nonetheless, during Reconstruction black husbands demanded a wage sufficient to support their families and wanted their wives to remain in the home. Many ex-slave wives also sought to leave field labor to the men and believed that their husbands should provide from them.[26] The sentiments of

24. Edwin Harwood and Claire C. Hodge, "Jobs and the Negro Family: A Reappraisal," *The Public Interest*, No. 23 (Spring 1971), pp. 125–131.

25. Civil War Pension of America Barnett, C.W. 724156; Civil War Pension of William Manuel, M.C. 157824; Civil War Pension of Charles M. Moore, C. W. 564774; U.S. Census, 1870, 1880, and 1890, Manuscript Census Schedules, Boston.

26. Karen Oppenheim Mason and Larry L. Bumpass, "U.S. Women's Sex Role

black husbands in the North are unknown, and, although some may have accepted economic necessity, others may have resisted, with the now-familiar sequence of events: an undermining of the husband's self-esteem, frustration for the wife, mutual grievances, and eventual separation or desertion.

Sickness may also have forced couples to separate. This motive, unapparent from examination of statistical evidence, appeared in case histories of black applicants for Civil War pensions. Mary Burns was compelled to live alone after her husband entered the insane asylum in Worcester. Isabella Moore had to become a live-in servant during her husband's illness. She recalled: He "began to have hemorrhages during the Fall of 1886 and got so bad in health that he couldn't do any work for about three weeks before he died. Then I had to break housekeeping and I went to work in South Boston, and [he] lived with Spencer Williams and from there he went to the Consumptive's Home and died there about a week after entering there. I visited him while he was there but he died while I was at work and so note was sent to me."[27] When Alexander Phillips, a coachman, developed pneumonia, he left his wife in Boston and went to his parents' farm in Otsego, New York. His wife, working as a domestic, sent him money, but her letters were returned unopened, and she soon learned that he had died before reaching the farm.[28]

Desertion and separation were the products of poverty, childlessness, sickness, and city life. It is obvious that these conditions were bound up together, interconnected so as to form a system more than a set of isolated instances. Consider, for example, the employment of black married women. It not only contributed to marital dissolution but also derived from conditions of poverty, ranging from a woman's childlessness to her husband's illness, unemployment or low wages.[29]

Ideology, 1970," *American Journal of Sociology*, v. 80, No. 5 (March 1975), pp. 1212–1219; James Morgan, J. Sirageldin, and Nancy Baerwaldt, *Productive Americans: A Study of How Individuals Contribute to Economic Progress* (Ann Arbor, 1966), Figure 19-4, p. 330; Herbert Gutman, *The Black Family in Slavery and Freedom*, p. 168; Gerda Lerner, ed., *Black Women in White America: A Documentary History* (New York, 1973), p. 292; Theodore Rosengarten, *All God's Dangers: The Life of Nate Shaw* (New York, 1974), p. 128; Vernon Burton, "Black Household Structure in Edgefield County, South Carolina," unpublished paper, 1976; Robert Abzug, "The Black Family during Reconstruction," in Nathan J. Huggins, Martin Kilson, and Daniel M. Fox, eds., *Key Issues in the Afro-American Experience* (New York, 1971), pp. 26–41.

27. U.S. Census, 1900, Manuscript Census Schedules Boston; Civil War Pension of Charles M. Moore, C.W. 564774.

28. Civil War Pension of William Williamson, C.W. 1153203.

29. U.S. Census, 1870 and 1880, Manuscript Census Schedules, Boston. A slightly

Childlessness can also be seen as part of this family system. The published federal census in 1910 tabulated the number of black women past childbearing age (over 45) who had never given birth. Childlessness was a city (especially a northern city) condition; only 4% of southern rural women but 10% of southern urban black women and 16% of northeast urban black women were barren.[30] Even figures as high as these underestimate the extent of childlessness in black Boston. The federal manuscript census schedules in 1900 inquired about the number of children a women had ever borne. In order to isolate the effect of long-term city residence, only those women who had lived in Boston for 20 years were considered. Life in the city drastically reduced black fertility, since in this group the rate of childlessness was 28%.[31]

It seems hard to believe that so many black women wanted to remain childless. Even women who resorted to abortions (or to infanticide) probably eventually had children. Most women using spermicides or douches were trying to space the size of their families, and few of them intended to remain childless throughout their lives. There are a number of medical explanations for sterility, such as genetic defects, mumps in childhood, psychosomatic illness, or a woman's advanced age. It is highly unlikely that any of these factors were more common among blacks in the North than among those in the South. Moreover, frequent separation or desertion, far from leading to barrenness, often had the opposite effect, of increasing the

different point of view can be found in Elizabeth H. Pleck, "A Mother's Wages: Income Earning among Married Italian and Black Women, 1896–1911," in Michael Gordon, eds., *The American Family in Socio-Historical Perspective* (New York, 1978), p. 501. Virginia Yans-McLaughlin has offered an argument very similar to the one presented here. Among first-generation Italians in Buffalo between 1905 and 1925, illegitimacy, female-headed households, and acceptance of charity were uncommon. McLaughlin claimed the importance of the Catholic church and of strong ethnic neighborhoods, and the absence of wives' employment contributed to family stability. Virginia Yans-McLaughlin, *Family and Community: Italian Immigrants in Buffalo, 1880–1930* (Ithaca, 1977).

30. Within the North and West, childlessness was as common among southern migrants as among women born elsewhere, according to the federal census of 1910. For black women past childbearing age (over 45) who were living in northern cities, 13% of southern migrants and 14% of non-Southerners were childless. U.S. Bureau of the Census, *Sixteenth Census of the United States: 1940, Population: Differential Fertility 1940 and 1910* (Washington, D.C., 1945), Table 100, p. 314, Table 106, p. 338.

31. U.S. Census, 1900, Manuscript Census Schedules, Boston. Childlessness was very common as well among Minneapolis and Cleveland blacks in 1900. A rate was computed for those married women under 45 who had been married 10 to 19 years. In both cities, 19% of such women were childless. U.S. Senate Reports, Sixty-first Congress, 2nd Session, *Reports of the U.S. Immigration Commission* (Washington, D.C., 1911), Table 6, p. 784, Table 15, p. 762.

TABLE VI-6
Deaths per 100,000 Population from Venereal Disease
among Blacks in Six Cities, 1885–1890[a]

City	Deaths per 100,000 population
Boston	174
Philadelphia	198
New York City	186
Brooklyn	274
Baltimore	243
Washington, D.C.	335

Sources: U.S. Department of the Interior, *Vital Statistics of Boston and Philadelphia* (Washington, D.C., 1895), pp. 184–187, 216–219; U.S. Department of the Interior, *Vital Statistics of the District of Columbia and Baltimore* (Washington, D.C., 1895), pp. 174–181, 198–205; U.S. Department of the Interior, *Vital Statistics of New York City and Brooklyn* (Washington, D.C., 1894), pp. 488–495.

[a] Includes deaths from scrofula.

number of male sexual partners and thereby raising the risk of getting pregnant. Two infectious diseases, venereal disease and tuberculosis, may contribute to sterility and low fertility in women and men. In women, both diseases lead to infections in the lining of the uterus or in the Fallopian tubes, which tend to produce scarring and impede conception; in men, they lead to inflammation of the testicles, which may cause blockage of the passage from the testicles to the sperm-producing seminal vesicles. Venereal disease, often considered as the likely explanation for childlessness, was not especially common among blacks in northern cities during the late nineteenth century.[32] In fact, the incidence of deaths per 100,000 blacks from venereal disease in northern and southern cities, shown in Table VI-6, indicates a death rate almost twice as high in southern as in northern cities, and the lowest rate of all in Boston. Quite the contrary, the death rate from tuberculosis was much higher among blacks in northern than in southern cities, according to Table VI-7, and highest of all in Boston. This great romantic disease of the nineteenth century

32. Reynolds Farley, *The Growth of the Black Population: A Study of Demographic Trends* (Chicago, 1970), p. 12. Among black inductees during World War II, the incidence of venereal disease was highest among southern urban blacks, moderate for southern rural blacks, and lowest for northern urban blacks. Joseph A. McFalls, Jr., "Impact of VD on the Fertility of the U.S. Black Population, 1880–1950," *Social Biology*, v. 20, No. 1 (March 1973), pp. 2–20. See also Stanley L. Engerman, "Black Fertility and Family Structure in the United States, 1880–1940," *Journal of Family History*, v. 2, No. 2 (June 1977), pp. 117–138.

TABLE VI-7
Racial Differences in Mortality from Consumption
in Fourteen American Cities, 1890

	Rates per 100,000 population	
Locale	White	Black
Northern cities		
Boston	365.8	884.8
Philadelphia	269.4	532.5
New York City	379.6	845.2
Brooklyn	284.9	539.0
Cincinnati	239.1	633.3
St. Louis	159.9	605.9
Southern cities		
Baltimore	250.6	524.6
Washington, D.C.	245.0	591.8
Richmond	230.5	411.1
Savannah	371.1	544.0
Charleston	355.4	686.3
Atlanta	213.8	483.7
Mobile	304.1	608.2
New Orleans	250.3	587.7

Source: The U.S. Census, 1890, as quoted in Frederick L. Hoffman, *Race Traits and Tendencies in the American Negro* (Boston, 1898), p. 83.

that struck all classes and races fell with special force on blacks and recent migrants, who were fatigued, malnourished, and in poor health. In Boston the death rate from consumption among blacks was two and a half times greater than among whites. In Philadelphia's Seventh Ward, DuBois blamed bad ventilation, lack of outdoor light in home, poor protection against dampness and cold, and the custom left over from slavery of neglecting to change clothes "after becoming damp with rain."[33]

The likelihood of desertion and separation was as predictable as the chances of contracting tuberculosis in a West End black neighborhood. It derived from a long list of conditions (married women's employment, sickness, sterility), all of which were rooted in

33. W.E.B. DuBois, *The Philadelphia Negro* (Philadelphia, 1899; New York, 1967), pp. 152, 162.

poverty. These were the patterns of one black community, an admittedly unusual locale. It would take considerable effort to replicate these findings elsewhere, because the same kind of intensive tracing, based on census linkage, has not been performed elsewhere.[34] However, dozens of local studies, using the federal manuscript census schedules or special surveys of the black population, have reported a rate of female-headed households. While this measure is known to underestimate the extent of separation or desertion, it was probably as accurate in one city as in another. Another difficulty is that in the reported rates of black female-headed households, reproduced in Table VI-8, no consistent definition of household was used throughout. Most but not all studies excluded single-person households and some also omitted childless married couples. Although the absence of a single definition for a household poses serious problems for comparability, a range of percentages is still apparent, easily suggesting the outlines of distinct regional differences.

Between 1838 and 1920, the rate of female-headed households rose in a few cities, fell in others, and stayed about the same in even more. Black Boston fell within the middle range for northern cities, above Pittsburgh, Buffalo, and Troy, New York, but below St. Johns, New Brunswick, Cincinnati, Brooklyn, and New York City. Between emancipation and the turn of the century, female-headed households were uncommon among blacks in rural South Carolina, Virginia, or Mississippi, but quite common among blacks in southern cities, even prior to the Civil War. In fact, the female-headed household was more the product of the southern than the northern city. This conclusion can be reached by contrasting the rate of such households in northern and southern cities. Several northern cities exhibited the southern tendency toward high rates of female-headed households, but, on the average, the number of female-headed households in northern cities between 1838 and 1920 was about 25%, compared with 34% in southern cities. Even by the early twentieth century northern cities had failed to grow more "southern." It is true that three out of four of the twentieth century rates reported in Table VI-8 (for Buffalo and New York City blacks in 1905 and 1925) appear quite high: However, in Buffalo, the rate actually declined from 1905 to 1925 (when the full effects of the Great Migration should have been felt) while in New York City, it had always been high, even prior to the Civil War.

We still do not know why separation and desertion was less

34. An attempt to determine intercity variation in the rates of female-headed households can be found in Appendix D.

TABLE VI-8
Percentage of Black Mother-Headed Households, 1838–1925

Locale	Date	Percentage of mother-headed households	N
Northern cities			
Philadelphia	1838	18	1,447
	1847	23	2,459
	1850	23	1,739
	1880	26	2,886
Cleveland	1850	7[a]	72
	1860	17[a]	182
	1870	15[a]	338
	1880	16[a]	439
Boston	1850	25	368
	1860	16[b]	n.a.
	1870	26	670
	1880	24	763
Pittsburgh	1850	13[b]	n.a.
	1860	21[b]	n.a.
	1870	16[b]	n.a.
	1880	15[b]	n.a.
Cincinnati	1850	21[b]	n.a.
	1860	26[b]	n.a.
	1870	22[b]	n.a.
	1880	21[b]	n.a.
St. Johns, New Brunswick	1871	34	73
Oxford, Ohio	1880	16[a]	130
Evansville, Ind.	1880	31	403
Troy, New York	1880	15[b]	128
Buffalo	1885	10[b]	145
	1875	15[b]	159
	1905	39	105
	1925	14	73
Brooklyn	1860	33	138
New York City	1860	39	75
	1905	33	3,014
	1925	30	10,732
Southern cities			
Louisville	1850	34[b]	n.a.
	1860	33[b]	n.a.
	1870	20[b]	n.a.
	1880	23[b]	n.a.
Baltimore	1870	23[b]	385

(Cont.)

183

Table VI-8   (continued)

Locale	Date	Percentage of mother-headed households	N
Natchez	1880	40	661
Beaufort, S.C.	1880	36	419
Richmond	1880	34	4,612
	1900	38	456
Mobile	1860	44	125
	1880	34	2,791
New Orleans	1880	22[b]	12,452
Atlanta	1870	27[b]	639
	1880	32[b]	437
Savannah	1880	25[c]	n.a.
Southern rural			
York County, Va.	1865	15[b]	994
Montgomery County, Va.	1865	22[b]	994
Princess Anne County, Va.	1865	16[b]	500
Burnt Swamp Township, S.C.	1870	12	n.a.
Edgefield County, S.C.	1870	11	1,081
Louisa County, Va.	1880	13	1,506
St. Helena Island and Township, S.C.	1880	13	1,310
	1900	23	874
Rural Adams County, Miss.	1880	23	2,831
Mt. Alburn, Miss.	1880	17	504
Lane's Schoolhouse, Miss.	1880	24	411
Issaquena, Miss.	1900	23	957

Sources: Theodore Hershberg, "Free-Born and Slave-Born Blacks in Antebellum Philadelphia," in Stanley L. Engerman and Eugene D. Genovese, eds., *Race and Slavery in the Western Hemisphere: Quantitative Studies* (Princeton, 1975), pp. 395–426; Frank Furstenberg, Jr., Theodore Hershberg, and John Modell, "The Origins of the Female-Headed Black Family: The Impact of the Urban Experience," *Journal of Interdisciplinary History*, v. VI (Autumn 1975), pp. 211–233; Paul J. Lammermeier, "The Urban Black Family of the Nineteenth Century: A Study of Black Family Structure in the Ohio Valley, 1850–1880," *Journal of Marriage and the Family*, v. 35 (August 1973), pp. 440–456; Janet Riblett Wilkie, "Social Status, Acculturation and School Attendance in 1850 Boston," *Journal of Social History*, v. II, No. 2 (Winter 1977), pp. 179–192; James Oliver Horton and Lois Horton, *Black Bostonians: Family Life and Community Activism in an Antebellum City* (forthcoming, 1979); Canadian Census, 1871, Manuscript Census Schedules for St. Johns, New

common in northern than southern cities. We know that in black Boston a family system rooted in city life and in poverty was fundamental. However, most of the conclusions about black Bostonians depended on following married couples in the census, and this kind of information has not been available elsewhere. In Boston, one conclusion appeared from tracing couples in the census and from measures of household composition in a single year. Both kinds of evidence indicated that separation and desertion was far higher among city-bred blacks than among southern migrants. Two other studies, of Philadelphia and Evansville, Indiana, blacks in 1880 have also divided local blacks by their region of birth. Table VI-9 shows that in both cities, the incidence of female-headed households was much higher among native blacks than among southern migrants. As early as 1838, female-headed households were proportionately more frequent among the free born than the slave born in Philadelphia.[35] Hence, acculturation to the northern city, which so often involved declining regulation of community life by the church, neighbors, and kin and rising levels of material aspirations, had taken hold even before the Civil War.

The attitudes of black Bostonians toward stable married life

---

35. Theodore Hershberg, "Free-Born and Slave-Born Blacks in Antebellum Philadelphia," in Stanley L. Engerman and Eugene D. Genovese, eds., *Race and Slavery in the Western Hemisphere: Quantitative Studies* (Princeton, 1975), pp. 395–426.

Brunswick, 1871; William H. Newell, "The Origins of Social Pathology: Black School Enrollment and Attendance in Oxford, Ohio, 1877–1880," unpublished paper, 1978; Darrell Bingham, "The Black Family in Vanderburgh County, Indiana, in 1880," forthcoming, *Indiana Magazine of History;* Herbert G. Gutman, "Persistent Myths about the Afro-American Family," *Journal of Interdisciplinary History,* v. 6 (Autumn 1975), pp. 181–210; Herbert G. Gutman and Laurence A. Glasco, "The Negro Family, Household and Occupational Structure, 1855–1925, with Special Emphasis on Buffalo, New York, but including Comparative Data from New York, New York, Brooklyn, New York, Mobile, Alabama, and Adams County, Mississippi," unpublished paper presented at the Yale Conference on Nineteenth-Century Cities, November 1968; Joseph Garoznik, "Urbanization and the Black Population of Baltimore, 1850–1870," unpublished Ph.D. dissertation, SUNY–Stony Brook, 1974, p. 173; Thomas J. Goliber, "Cuyahoga Blacks: A Social and Demographic Study, 1850–1880," unpublished master's thesis, Kent State University, 1972, Table 12, p. 31; Herbert G. Gutman, *The Black Family in Slavery and Freedom, 1750–1925* (New York, 1976), pp. 485–530; John Blassingame, *Black New Orleans, 1860–1880* (Chicago, 1973), p. 236; William Harris, "Work and the Family in Black Atlanta, 1880," *Journal of Social History,* v. 9, No. 3 (Spring 1976), pp. 319–330; John W. Blassingame, "Before the Ghetto: The Making of the Black Community in Savannah, Georgia, 1865–1880," *Journal of Social History,* v. 6, No. 4 (Summer 1973), p. 475; Edward Magdol, "Against the Gentry: An Inquiry into a Southern Lower-Class Community and Culture, 1865–1870," *Journal of Social History,* v. 6, No. 3 (Spring 1973), p. 266; Vernon Burton, "Black Household Structure in Edgefield County, South Carolina," unpublished paper, 1976.

[a] Includes single member and childless households.

[b] Includes childless households, of at least two members.

[c] Method of computation unknown.

TABLE VI-9
Regional Origins and the Percentage of Female-Headed Households
in Philadelphia, Boston, and Evansville, Indiana, 1880

	Percentage of female-headed households					
Group	*Philadelphia*	*N*	*Boston*	*N*	*Evansville, Indiana*	*N*
Southern-born migrants	23	1739	21	92	27	407
Natives	29	941	36	520	34	41

Sources: Frank Furstenberg, Jr., Theodore Hershberg, and John Modell, "The Origins of the Female-Headed Black Family: The Impact of the Urban Experience," *Journal of Interdisciplinary History*, v. VI (Autumn 1975), pp. 211–233; U.S. Census, Manuscript Census Schedules, Boston, 1880; Darrell Bingham, "The Black Family in Vanderburgh County, Indiana, in 1880," forthcoming, *Indiana Magazine of History*.

matter as much as statistics like these. Unfortunately, it is more difficult to document the sentiments that accompanied separation than its incidence. But a careful reading of the testimony in Civil War pension applications suggests black Bostonians considered legal marriage the most desirable family arrangement. Certainly from the woman's point of view, a brief affair was the least desirable. Mary Harris said of her liaison with a man named Goodwin: "I was never living with Goodwin as his wife. This [the birth of her son] would never have happened but I was sick and poor and had to do something to help myself along and support my children."[36] Mary Williamson, describing her relationship with Rhodes Black, claimed, "We were together off and on but never kept house."[37] Housekeeping, which upgraded a relationship, involved co-residence, preparing meals for a man, and sexual relations, although the housekeeper kept her last name. A man and his kin were expected to acknowledge and help in the support of children from these unions. Housekeeping was still not as valued as legal marriage, as a casual remark of Anna Brown made clear: "He [her husband, John Brown] always told me that Rachel was his first wife, that he had a good many housekeepers but he was not married to any of them."[38] A more permanent arrangement than housekeeping was a consensual union, which performed most of the functions of legal marriage: an assured sexual

36. Civil War Pension of Lewis Harris, C.W. 3041409.
37. Civil War Pension of William Williamson, C.W. 1153203.
38. Affidavit of Anna L. Brown, May 19, 1915, Civil War Pension of John S. Brown, C.W. 895570.

partner and recognition of the offspring as the man's children, care in sickness, and provision of money. Even after Tom Cannon left his common-law wife Caroline for another woman, a neighbor reported that "he would come when he was sick or she was sick and when he got his pension he would come and give her some money."[39] In her affidavit to the pension bureau, Caroline Cannon also indicated that, after Tom left her, he still performed some of the functions of a husband: "He always got his mail where I live and gave me money from his pension and at times I gave him money from what I earned."[40] Still, women in these relationships did not use the man's name. Susan Jackson, who was the mistress of Elias Hall and the mother of his four children, explained the terms of their relationship: "He [Elias Hall] always acknowledged the children as his and supported them even before his wife died [but] I . . . always kept the name Jackson until I married Hall and I regarded myself as a widow.[41] Sometimes a "minister" performed a ceremony in the presence of friends and kin that specified a limited duration for the union ("a year and a day"). Susan Hall, who had undergone such a ceremony in her father's home, considered herself legally married: "I took his name, lived with him as his wife about nine months: he supported me: the neighbors looked upon us as man and wife: we treated each other as such."[42] Legal marriage, in function the same as a consensual union, was still preferable, in fact, the ideal, but it was often unrealizable, and so many blacks were willing to stretch their views to accommodate these less preferable alternatives.

PATTERNS OF MUTUAL AID

Among poor blacks some of the functions the family usually performs were met within the nuclear family, and others were met within the extended family. The extremely low fertility of northern blacks testified to the fact that the goal of reproducing the next generation was never adequately met. It is tempting to suggest that, function by function, northern-born blacks differed from Southerners, but proof of such diversity is lacking and the regional groups

39. Affidavit of Victoria Wallace, January 26, 1923, Civil War Pension of Thomas Cannon, File 1 of 2, C.W. 62799.
40. Affidavit of Caroline E. Cannon, October 4, 1922, Civil War Pension of Thomas Cannon, File 1 of 2, C.W. 62799.
41. Civil War Pension of Elias Hall, W.C. 634126.
42. Ibid.

were actually similar in many respects. Instead, it can be suggested that, all blacks, irrespective of their region of birth, had developed means of coping with poverty that placed great reliance on kin and friends.

These methods both resembled and departed from those of the white poor. A Boston social reformer, Alvan Sanborn, described Irish families on Turley street: wives were employed in "sadly irregular fashion" as washerwomen, the absent husbands were away from home harvesting crops, and the nomadic tenants "moved from house to house and street to street." He found families wasting money on installment purchases and large funerals, poor women who borrowed a lump of butter and a cup of sugar from their neighbors and relied on the streets' children to run errands, and friends who housed the invalids. Sanborn described the daily scene on the street with pathos: "Neighbors send in little treats to the sick, share with each other the good things they have humbugged out of charities, mind each other's children, give the use of their cooking stove, take in for a time evicted tenants of women and children when the father is on a dangerous spree, and shelter unfortunate women during confinement."[43] The lyrics of a popular song suggested a prevalent stereotype about *Irish* family life: "Mother takes in washing, so does Sister Ann, Everybody works in Our House but my old man."

An almost identical street scene could be found in black neighborhoods. Black families donated coal baskets to the needy, provided temporary shelter for strangers, and fed "the next door neighbor though they have little themselves.[44] Just as Alvan Sanborn was struck by the charitableness of Turley Street's Irish, so, too, Mary White Ovington, a settlement house worker in New York City, commented upon the extreme generosity of New York City black families in the early twentieth century: "Meals are furnished to the hungry, loans are provided for the penniless; garments are given to the shivering poor clad ones; remittance of money and boxes of clothing are sent to the home-friends of the South. . . . The M family of seven persons living in a basement took in and sheltered without charge for a whole winter a second family of five individuals."[45] In Philadelphia, DuBois listed charity applicants who had been relying on friends:

43. Alvan Francis Sanborn, *Moody's Lodging House and Other Tenement Sketches* (Boston, 1895), p. 116; Alvan F. Sanborn, "The Anatomy of a Tenement Street," *The Forum* (January 1895), pp. 554–572.

44. "Mission Sketches," *Charities*, v. XV, No. 1 (October 7, 1905), pp. 61–73.

45. Mary White Ovington, "The Negro Home in New York," *Charities*, v. XV, No. 1 (October 1905), p. 24.

laborer injured by falling off a derrick; five in the family. His fellow workmen have contributed to his support, but the employers have given nothing. . . . Man of twenty-three came from Virginia for work; was run over by cars at Forty-fifth street and Baltimore avenue, and lost both legs and right arm, is dependent on colored friends and wants something to do.[46]

For all of the similarities, the poor still differed in many respects, especially in their care of orphans, widows, and paupers. Some of these differences originated in slavery. In *The Black Family in Slavery and Freedom*, Herbert Gutman argued that slaves developed distinctive kinship patterns: a prohibition on cross-cousin marriage, the acceptance of illegitimate children albeit with strict attitudes toward adultery, a distinctive naming pattern.[47] They built upon these traditions in developing a pattern of kin and quasi-kin obligations. In his chapter on "Aunts and Uncles and Swap-Dog Kin," Gutman describes the importance of bonds between siblings (which some anthropologists have claimed is more important in black culture than that between husband and wives) and the practice of adopting orphans among families of the ex-slaves. A distinctive Afro-American kinship pattern of family obligation had taken root in Boston. But Boston blacks lived in a city where they had at one time been excluded from many city and state institutions. It seems unnecessary to show whether the tradition of self-help or the expectation of hostility was more important; each reinforced the other, helping to build a vital emphasis on mutual aid.

Care of orphans by black families was one part of this extended family system. Even in Reconstruction Virginia a Quaker relief official noted that "it is remarkable to witness how much these poor people do for orphan children." In Boston only a few black orphans could be found in state institutions; in 1880 16 blacks resided at the Industrial School for Girls and less than a dozen children that year were inmates at the Deer Island Truant Home, the largest Boston institution for homeless children. Published figures for the Massachusetts census in 1895 indicated that 3% of "homeless minors" in state institutions or children placed with foster parents were black, a representation no greater than that of blacks in the state's population. Given the greater proportion of blacks in poverty, a higher representation of blacks might have been expected. Instead, the rate

46. W.E.B. DuBois, *The Philadelphia Negro*, pp. 276–277.
47. Herbert G. Gutman, *The Black Family in Slavery and Freedom, 1750–1925* (New York, 1976).

was below that of Massachusetts Irish (14 per 1000 for blacks and for the Irish, 66 per 1000 in 1895).[48] It was quite common for black children to be raised by a natural parent and a stepparent. Most likely, the stepparent was regarded as the equivalent of a natural parent, and children were probably expected to provide a stepmother or stepfather with the same kind of assistance in old age that biological parents were due.[49]

Throughout the last three decades of the nineteenth century, few blacks entered the poorhouse. They were less than .05% of the inmates at Deer Island in 1870, 1% in 1880, and only 2% by 1900. Similarly, at the state institutions for paupers in 1895, black inmates were just 1% of the total.[50] This avoidance distinguished blacks from their nearest neighbors in poverty, the Irish. The Associated Charities of Boston was quite correct that "a larger proportion of Irish than of any other nationality come to downright pauperism."[51] An Irish immigrant was four times more likely than a southern black to be a pauper at a state almshouse in 1895 and five times more likely to be an inmate at a Boston workhouse in 1900. Observers at the time explained that "among the Irish there was a large proportion of single immigrant women who come to this country when young and for years probably gain fair employment but small savings. As time passes, employment becomes more difficult to obtain, and having no one to care for them, these women find their refuge in the almshouse."[52] This observation, while accurate, begs the question of why Irish women were unable to depend on friends, neighbors, or

48. Ibid., p. 228; Horace G. Wadlin, *Census of the Commonwealth of Massachusetts: 1895*, v. 11 (Boston, 1899), pp. 44–477.

49. Anthropologist Esther Goody contrasted fosterage in the West Indies and in West Africa. West Indians, much like black Bostonians, cared for orphans after the death of the child's mother. The foster parent, generally the female relative, was regarded as the permanent parent. Among West Indians, fostering occurred even with living parents and was designed to help further the child's education (through schooling in town or apprenticeship training). Male as well as female relatives acted as auxiliaries to the parents, and the natural parents, despite their physical absence, were still considered those to whom the grown child was obligated.

Esther Goody, "Delegation of Parental Roles in West Africa and the West Indies," in Demetri B. Shimkin, Edith Shimkin, and Dennis Frate, eds., *The Extended Family*, pp. 447–486.

50. Ibid.; U.S. Census, Manuscript Census Schedules, Boston, 1870, 1880, and 1900.

51. Frederick A. Bushee, *Ethnic Factors in the Population of Boston* (New York, 1903), p. 87.

52. Ibid., pp. 92–93.

relatives for care. The reason may have been that charity was often restricted to responsibility for the nuclear family and donations to the church, with a reduced commitment to distant friends and relatives.

In fact, such cultural differences probably explain the different housing arrangements of elderly black and Irish widows. According to the manuscript census schedules in 1870 and 1880, one half of Afro-American widows but only a quarter of Irish widows were living with children or relatives. Among black women over 65 in 1880, two out of every three lived with children or relatives. Although the Catholic church maintained its own homes for the elderly, the Irish elderly often entered state institutions, such as the almshouses, whereas among blacks, the elderly more often lived with sisters, children, and grandchildren. This residence could be temporary—moving away from a relative and then returning, as some life histories indicate. Soon after Anna Brown's first husband died, she moved in with her mother and remained with her for 10 years. She remarried, but when her second husband died (of alcoholism), she moved back with her mother. She left once—to spend 8 months at the Lakeville Sanitorium for consumptives—but after her recovery she returned to her mother's apartment.[53] Sons as well as daughters were responsible for the care of an elderly mother. Subsequent to her husband's death, Susan Jackson Hall supported herself as a laundress. She lived for 3 years with her daughter and son-in-law in Boston and then moved in with her son. She left Boston temporarily because, as she explained, "I was in the crazy house over death of my husband and son, Goodwin."[54] After her release from the insane asylum in Westboro, she lived with her son, who had moved to East Dedham. Applications for admission to the Home for Aged Colored Women also demonstrate the importance of family ties as well as some of the limits of family responsibility. Some of the applicants had no relatives, and others complained of abusive sons or nephews and alcoholic sons and daughters unable to provide assistance. Before entering the home, most of these elderly women had been living with relatives, and a few of the inmates who grew tired of the home returned to live with their relatives. Mrs. Major moved out after her unemployed son found a job. After Mary Jackson complained to her daughter that the overseers wanted to move her to the sick room,

53. Civil War Pension of John S. Brown, C.W. 895570.
54. Civil War Pension of Elias Hall, C.W. 634126.

her daughter immediately came for her.[55] Cases like these demonstrate that living with relatives was considered preferable to residence in a home.

In the midst of constant changes in jobs and residences, no form of mutual aid to orphans, paupers, or elderly women could be expected to last. All family arrangements were transitory. At much closer range, anthropologists have already reached these conclusions in studies of the black poor in the 1960s. In *Tally's Corner*, streetcorner men became more distant towards other men soon after they became involved with a woman or started a better-paying job. But if the affair ended or they lost the job, they reappeared on the streetcorner and resumed these friendships. In "The Flats," the black district of a small midwestern city, black women on welfare began to visit friends and kin more regularly when a marriage or love affair was about to end. Over a lifetime relocation near kin and aid from them were the most permanent features of black social life. The history of Lizzie Johnson illustrates the importance of kin at every phase of life. There is no way of knowing if Lizzie Johnson's story was "representative": Her pension application simply happened to supply more detail on this topic, but, at least it can be suggested that her story illustrates and amplifies some themes already mentioned.

After her mother, a widow, died, Lizzie went to live with her aunts. She recalled, "I was taken by mother's sister . . . as a member of her family and always made my home with her until my marriage."[56] These two aunts, Harriet Fessenden and Mary Dawson, who lived in Springfield, Massachusetts, raised her, along with Harriet's son. When Lizzie was 19, she married a young soldier, Charley Johnson. He and Lizzie moved in with his mother in nearby Warren, Massachusetts. After he went to war, Lizzie returned to her aunt's home. She soon learned that her husband had been killed in battle. Two years later (she was 22 at the time) Lizzie's cousin introduced her to one of the barbers at work, Lem Peters. They began to see each other, and Lizzie became pregnant. Peters left Springfield for Boston and Lizzie's aunts insisted that she go there and get Peters to marry her. Lizzie located him, but he refused to marry her. She then returned to Springfield and told her aunts that she had married Peters. Even after he failed to appear, Lizzie used his name. The pension bureau prohibited remarried women from drawing a widow's pen-

55. Applications for Admission, Home for Aged Colored Women, Records of the Home for Aged Colored Women, 1870–1900, Massachusetts Historical Society.

56. Affidavit of Lizzie L. Johnson, February 22, 1889, Civil War Pension of Charles H. Johnson, W.C. 50151.

sion. For several years Lizzie, claiming to have married Peters, refused to apply for her pension as Charley Johnson's widow.

Her daughter was born in her aunt's home and soon after that Lizzie began to call herself Mrs. Peters. She recalled, "After my said child was born I took the name of Peters to cover my disgrace for a while."[57] Soon after the birth, Lizzie began to take jobs in service, while her aunts cared for their niece, Ada. When Ada was about 5, Lizzie took a job as a live-in domestic in the home of a Springfield minister, where she and Ada lived for several years. During the summer of 1875, Lizzie became a waitress at a summer resort in Long Branch, New Jersey, and left Ada with her aunt, who had moved to Philadelphia. Lizzie went there at the end of the summer and stayed with her aunt for a week or two before she and Ada went to live with Lizzie's new employer. Lizzie and Ada remained in Philadelphia for about 5 years, but when Aunt Harriet returned to Springfield in 1880 they accompanied her and lived with her for a year. During the summer of 1881, Lizzie was a servant in a Newport, Rhode Island, boardinghouse, and Ada remained with her aunt. In the fall Lizzie and Ada moved to Boston. Soon after settling in Boston, Ada married a bookkeeper, Lizzie took a series of jobs in service, and saw her aunts occasionally. Aunt Harriet was living alone in Springfield, and Aunt Mary was living with her son in New York City.

In the categories of the census, Lizzie Johnson headed a "father-absent household," and she was the mother of an illegitimate child. Her history does not indicate ready acceptance of illegitimacy. In fact, she sacrificed her widow's pension for several years in order to maintain her deception. Although her aunts considered illegitimacy a stigma, they helped to raise Ada, just as they had cared for Lizzie.

In contrast to Lizzie Johnson's very small group of kin, anthropologists recently have described black extended families numbering about 100 members.[58] Because of death or migration, Lizzie Johnson may only have been able to get life-long assistance from her aunts and her daughter. Or she may have had not any reason to mention other relatives in her pension application. The black extended family of the past, even if reduced in size, was meeting some of the universal functions most families perform. At the same time, the demands from kin often conflicted with those from husbands or wives. The readiness to lend money to a relative or devote extra time

57. Ibid.
58. Demetri B. Shimkin, Gloria Jean Louie, and Dennis Frate, "The Black Extended Family," in Demetri B. Shimkin, Edith Shimkin, and Dennis Frate, eds., *The Extended Family*, pp. 25–148.

to them often came at the expense of a marriage. In so doing, they were redistributing their resources, but in such a way that the nuclear family became more impoverished. It is indeed ironic that responding to human misery should have helped perpetuate it, but that was precisely the fundamental moral dilemma so often confronting the black poor.

CONCLUSION

Previous work, including my own research, contributed to the view that the "two-parent household" was the dominant family form among blacks in the late nineteenth century. The desire to refute a view of family breakdown and pathology has been replaced by the perspective that black families were organized exactly like whites. This was not the case, and could not have been so, given racial differences in economic opportunities, and demographic possibilities, as well as the differential effects of urbanization.

The usual measure of the extent of marital breakup was the rate of female-headed households, as identified in the manuscript census schedules. Longitudinal data indicated that separation and desertion among Boston blacks were far higher than was suggested by a snapshot of female-headed households in any single year. Stable married couples were compared with deserting or separated couples to determine the correlates of marital dissolution. Other studies suggested these were the legacy of slavery, a surplus of women, or excess male mortality, but the factors found to be of significance here were instead sickness, poverty (menial jobs and unemployment for husbands, wage earning for wives), sterility, and urban birth. None of these contributory factors operated in isolation; they were connected in such a way that poverty led directly to higher rates of separation and desertion and took its toll indirectly through sickness, sterility, and the necessity for wives to work.

These patterns, so evident for blacks in one late nineteenth-century northern city, were even more prevalent in southern cities. By comparing the rates of female-headed households in different locales between 1838 and 1920, the following conclusions were reached:

1. The legacy of slavery did not appear to have contributed to marital stability.
2. The female-headed household was a product of the city, but especially the southern city.

3. Within the northern city, "long, close contact" with city life, rather than recent arrival, led to separation and desertion.

E. Franklin Frazier's classic *Negro Family in the United States* has fallen into disfavor, but his description of rural life among blacks (in the period between 1900 and 1920) forms a starting place in understanding these three observations. Rural black courtship practice, he believed, tolerated sexual intercourse if the engaged couple eventually married, and premarital pregnancy was common. The girl's family and the church exerted sufficient pressure to ensure marriage. In southern cities Frazier found "roving men and homeless women"[59] rather than the social controls so present in the rural South. Although he occasionally mentioned that these men were the products of the semifeudal state of southern agriculture, he too often slipped into references to "the migratory habits of the Negro." Still, many of his astute observations can be used to formulate a more dispassionate explanation. Between 1865 and 1900, the rural black population could not sustain its young: Many young men were forced to migrate, either permanently or temporarily, especially during the slack agricultural season. Many unmarried daughters also took temporary jobs as servants in southern cities. Young couples in southern cities engaged in the traditional courtship customs of the rural South— except that, in southern cities, the tight social controls of parental discipline and church were often lacking, and many of the prospective fathers had probably left town even before the pregnancy was known. Therefore, high rates of illegitimacy among blacks in southern cities helped to contribute to the growth of female-headed households.[60] However, the prevalence of illegitimacy was only one reason

59. E. Franklin Frazier, *The Negro Family in the United States* (Chicago, 1939; Chicago, 1966), pp. 209–224.

60. The rate of illegitimacy among blacks was quite high in southern cities, as the following figures demonstrate:

City and year	Percentage of illegitimate births
Boston, 1875–1880	7
Farmville, Virginia, 1896	15
Baltimore, 1884–1893	20
Washington, D.C., 1879–1894	22
Mobile, 1879–1894(?)	25
Knoxville, 1879–1894(?)	25

These rates were reported in Frederick L. Hoffman, *Race Traits and Tendencies of the American Negro* (Washington, D.C., 1896), pp. 95, 235–237; W.E.B. DuBois, "The Negroes of Farmville, Virginia: A Social Study," *Bulletin of the U.S. Department of Labor*, No. 14 (January 1898), p. 12; "Condition of the Negro in Various Cities," p. 276.

for the growth of female-headed households. In addition, black marriages were strained by the effects of poverty: low wages and a fluctuating income for husbands, and frequent employment for wives. To be sure, many of the absent husbands had taken temporary jobs as migrant laborers, lumberjacks, or railroad construction workers, but temporary absences had a way of becoming permanent.

In northern cities black marriages were also strained by a distinctive feature of northern life, tuberculosis, an apparent cause of sterility in many women and men. Childless couples were especially prone to separate or desert. Overall, black marriages had a better chance of survival in northern than in southern cities, except among city-bred blacks. Southern migrants, in forming their own little community based on allegiance to the church and family discipline, tended to recreate in the northern city some of the same conditions present in the rural South. All of these social controls were much weaker among city-bred blacks. The effect of black urbanization in the North was to diminish the powerful regulatory mechanisms in black life and substitute an extended family system based on obligations between foster parents, other kin, and friends.

The mistake of many observers has been to label such family arrangements "disorganized." In fact, kin and friends residing in several different households became the basis of family organization. The Irish poor tended much more often to rely on state institutions to aid their needy, whereas black orphans, paupers, and elderly were more often cared for within the family, a cultural difference that was no doubt related to hostility from Boston institutions as well as to the slave tradition of foster care. To be sure, many friendships were based on exploitation, countless relatives never honored their obligations to the family, and some intimate friendships endured less than a few weeks. It was personally trying to belong to a family system that made so many demands. But in a world where impermanence and insecurity in marriage and jobs were commonplace, the most abiding economic assets of the black poor were their friends and kin.

CHAPTER VII

CONCLUSION

But I don't like it when I hear a man say—be he colored or white—that we've never had anything, and we've always been so low. We've been without things, and we've been at the bottom! I agree. But we've been God-fearing. We've had God; and He's something to have—Someone. And I'll tell you: we've had each other to turn to.

Vanessa's grandmother, a migrant to Boston from rural South Carolina in Robert Coles, *The South Goes North*

After all, I was born in this city, and so were my parents. We're not the kind of Negroes that have come up here from the South in the last few years. There's nothing wrong with them. I'm not saying a word against them. It's just that they have one Hell of a time getting used to the city, whereas I'm onto things here.

Billy's bus driver, a Roxbury resident, in Robert Coles, *The South Goes North*

This study has been primarily concerned with the impact of the late nineteenth-century city on the community and family life of the black poor. The undertaking has been informed by an interest in the general and representative rather than the unique and specific, and the examination of Boston has served as a guide to pre-ghetto social conditions among urban blacks throughout the North. The results have derived from systematic comparisons at three levels: first, and most important, of blacks born in the North with those born in the South, of blacks and Irish in Boston, and of black Bostonians and blacks in other northern as well as southern cities. The conclusion has been that long-term residence in the northern city helped develop a commitment to mainstream values but failed to eliminate racial barriers in the acquisition of a middle-class income. The discrepancy between values and income often contributed to marital separations and desertions, and because marriages were often short-lived, obligations between kin and sharing between friends became the primary means of coping with poverty.

Whether it was Chicago or Cleveland, Boston or Philadelphia, the northern city in the late nineteenth century—a locale of limited but real opportunities for white unskilled labor—still failed to solve the problem of racial poverty. For those who claim that the handicaps of black workers could account for most of this failure, no confirming evidence has been uncovered, no unique deficiency of blacks in education or in their slave backgrounds. Instead, the handicaps of black workers arose from the operation of two distinct racial barriers to be found within Boston, exclusion and unsuccessful competition. Exclusion, the first of these, involved entry-level racial barriers in hiring and the recruitment of new black arrivals into service jobs. As a consequence, most black newcomers entered menial work and stayed in it, becoming drifters between low-wage jobs and moving incessantly from one city to the next. While a majority of the black work force were in a sense wanderers, about a quarter had permanently settled in the city. Even in this stable group, most were trapped in menial jobs, although some had established businesses, had entered better-paying jobs, or had been promoted out of menial labor. Nonetheless, aspiring entrepreneurs, professionals, clerks, and craftsmen confronted a second barrier, unsuccessful competition, not because of some unique cultural deficiency but because race was used as a means of firing them or forcing them out. Even in starting a small business, the traditional means of escape from prejudiced employers, blacks were handicapped, ultimately at a disadvantage because of their inability to generate sufficient capital or to regulate excessive competiton between black businesses. The visible result of these hidden processes of exclusion and unsuccessful competition was that 8 our of 10 black Boston workers held menial jobs, the lowest-paying jobs to be found. These dual racial barriers then slowly but inevitably helped create a class of working poor, of blacks with even lower incomes than Boston's white immigrants. Although inequality in jobs and incomes did not generally lead to starvation, disease and death were close by. Ironically, had the black population of the North been healthier, poverty would have been more widespread, for the number of mouths to feed was effectively limited by high rates of infant mortality and tuberculosis-induced sterility.

Racial poverty often had direct and predictable consequences for health, fertility, women's employment, and family life, but culture had as great an impact as simple economic exigencies. Unlike other Boston blacks, the Southerners were relatively protected from the effects of poverty because they were so insulated. Their social world, a trinity of strict religion, solidarity with kin and friends, and their strong drive for material success, left them socially separated and dependent on each other for aid and comfort.

It is tempting to find in these generalizations about southern blacks in Boston proof of the less than damaging effects of slavery on emancipated slaves. After all, the majority of Boston's Southerners were ex-slaves and their children who came to the city soon after the end of the Civil War. At first glance, their strong work ethic, interest in small business, and tightly knit community and family life tend to confirm a view of ex-slaves as family-oriented, business-minded, and upwardly mobile. But, the desire to reinterpret the world of slavery in the Upper South must be tempered by the realization that the limitations of the evidence are great. We know that Boston's Southerners were the cultural elite of the Upper South, more likely to be urban, light-skinned, and literate than blacks from the region and therefore unrepresentative of the mass of freed women and men. Even a more limited generalization about the lasting effects of slavery on this atypical group runs into difficulty. Southern migrants to Boston had not simply replicated their past; in the process of chain migration and in meeting the long-term needs of newcomers in the city, the life of southern migrants evolved into a halfway compromise between Boston and slave society, wherein the role of kin and friends was enormously enlarged. Thus, Southerners in Boston may have come closer to living out the ideals of slave community and family life than their kinfolk who had remained in the South.

It is more in keeping with the limitations of the evidence to offer generalizations about the effects of urbanization because, in that realm, some clear differences—attributable only to city life—have emerged. It is sometimes claimed that "the city" is at most an artificial construct and that most urbanites dwell in ethnic villages, where they have only perfunctory contact with the outside world. If that had been entirely true, then the children of southern parents— the second generation of urban blacks—should have held on to their heritage, instead of losing touch with it. Of course, African and Afro-American customs were only gradually replaced by white practices; but certainly a cultural change of enormous magnitude was all but complete by 1850. New traditions did not spontaneously come to life: They had to be consciously created and maintained. The "overassimilation" of black Yankees was continually reinforced by their more privileged economic, social, and educational status, and by two other fundamental trends—the diminished attachment to the black church (which had been the most important black community institution in the South, almost an adjunct of the family) and the tendency to mix with whites, at both the bottom and top layers of black society, found even in the most intimate of associations, interracial marriage.

Blacks born in the North were bourgeois in deed and in thought but not in economic assets. The time-honored reasons for remaining married—pressure from neighbors, the church, and kin and staying together for the sake of the children—were weakened. Community sanctions had been eroded and many couples were childless; alongside these changes, marriages were strained because of the standards of middle-class life to which many of these couples aspired. These patterns have to be considered as negative consequences of city residence because they were in fact experienced that way.

In coping with poverty, blacks often moved from one city to another and relied on lifelong obligations between kin (especially female kin) and short-term aid from friends and neighbors—patterns of survival fashioned not only out of the memories of slavery, but also from the urban necessities confronted by all poor people. Among blacks, kin ties were often more important than marital ones, whereas among the Irish the reverse was often the case. Unlike the home care of the dependent so common in black households, Irish families were more likely to send orphans or widows to state or religious institutions. In the evolution of these ways of survival in the city, even the mainstream values of northern-born blacks had to stretch to accommodate the realities of urban poverty.

It is easy to see that constant movement between cities and the redistribution of scarce resources actually helped perpetuate poverty. Most urban blacks were newcomers, continually moving about, who remained outside the competition for better jobs. A vicious cycle ensued, wherein blacks never remained long enough in any city to search for better-paying jobs or less prejudiced employers. Still, the existence of a vicious cycle of this kind does not demonstrate that the poor were unable to pursue those economic advantages that did appear. In fact, the history of black urbanization represents a continuous and active striving for economic gain—in the move from South to North during conditions of economic expansion, in the attempt to establish small businesses, and in the persistent efforts of city residents to enter better-paying jobs. When opportunities were made available, blacks pursued them, certainly often enough to suggest that it was less their culture than their race that was holding them back.

In sum, the black urban experience was a continuous process of interaction between racial barriers in employment, poverty and acculturation to mainstream values. Racism operated to confine black workers to low-wage jobs, and poverty placed heavy burdens on black health, childbearing, and marital life. The effects of poverty were moderated by the traditional slave-oriented culture of the southern migrants, but exacerbated by the middle-class values of northern-born blacks. Thus, the poverty cycle to be found was not one of limited aspirations and low economic status, but of high aspirations and low status.[1]

The features of central importance to black urban life—racial barriers in the economy, poverty, and acculturation—were shown as they unfolded in one northern city during the late nineteenth century. Any single instance is always in some respects unique: Boston was a

1. Gilbert Osofsky, "The Enduring Ghetto," *Journal of American History*, v. LV, No. 2 (September 1968), p. 254.

202 BLACK MIGRATION AND POVERTY

relatively segregated city, and a cosmopolitan and tolerant one, most evident in the unusual frequency of interracial marriage. Boston also contained a small black population and an atypical group of black newcomers willing to choose this out-of-the way location. But the notion that Boston was an unrepresentative case because of these unique features has not found support. Detailed studies of blacks in other northern cities (such as Philadelphia, with a community three times the size of black Boston) virtually duplicate the findings reported here. However, at this stage of research, it is unclear whether this was also the South's pattern. It has been common to view black life in Southern cities in terms of race relations, thereby neglecting the urban perspective. Systematic inquiry comparable to that in black Boston, distinguishing long-time residents from recent migrants, is required so as to separate the peculiar influence of southern race relations from the general effect of city life.

The classic work on the impact of black urbanization, E. Franklin Frazier's *The Negro Family in the United States*, was based on a study of Chicago migrants between 1915 and 1940. Despite the differences in locales and time periods, Frazier's conclusions bear a striking resemblance to those reported here. In the move from the South to the South Side, social controls of church, kin, and neighbors declined, just as secular and material values, racial consciousness, and personal ambition increased. The lack of a cohesive community life, the exposure to these new values, and the persistence of poverty and disease made "family desertion . . . the inevitable consequence of the urbanization of the Negro population,"[2] that is, the inevitable first phase, because, in the next one, Frazier found that "rebirth" strengthened family life, rates of juvenile delinquency declined, and so forth.

In Victorian Boston as well as in the twentieth-century city, desertion appears as a likely consequence of poverty and urbanization, while the traditional values of church, kin, and community were weakening and being replaced by middle-class, secular values, a pronounced racial pride, and a willingness to protest against discrimination. In contrast with Frazier's description, Boston urbanization resulted in the initial preservation of southern black culture but its subsequent destruction in the second generation, as new values emerged. These differences between black Boston and black Chicago reflect questions of composition rather than substance: My argument is that the impact of the city was delayed an entire generation,

2. E. Franklin Frazier, *The Negro Family in Chicago* (Chicago, 1932), p. 85.

making itself felt not on southern migrants, but on city-bred northern blacks. The move from South to North had actually strengthened and preserved slave culture, not so much because of the resiliency of that culture, although it was resilient, but because of the needs of the migrants, the pattern of chain migration, and the continued hostility from outsiders. Frazier constantly referred to the difference between old mulatto families and Southerners, but, he failed to systematically compare the socioeconomic or familial experience of Chicago-born blacks with that of Southerners. Had he done so, it seems likely that he would have reached conclusions like these. In fact, every systematic comparison of contemporary urban blacks, based on the census or national surveys of northern blacks, indicates a lower rate of separation and desertion among southern migrants than among city-bred blacks.[3] A virtual repetition of my conclusions about black Boston's Southerners has been reached by three anthropologists, Demtri Shimkin, Gloria Louie, and Dennis Frate, in their study of post-World War II migration from Holmes County, Mississippi, to Chicago. They interviewed five generations of the Bidwells. By 1969, when the study was conducted, about half of the Bidwells had permanently resettled in Chicago, although most of them visited Mississippi every summer. When the Bidwells first arrived in Chicago, they stayed with relatives who aided them in finding jobs. In the city the young men and women selected marriage partners from Holmes County and many of them belonged to the Holmes County Social Club, a neighborhood group of young people. The men worked on the railroad or in the steel mills and the women were maids or file clerks. Several of the married couples lived close to one another: Two brothers jointly bought a South Side home, which they shared, and rented a basement apartment to a nephew. Most of the people from Holmes County regularly attended neighborhood churches in Chicago, much like the ones they went to back home. The anthropologists concluded that the Bidwells, as an extended family, exhibit "considerable strivings toward stable employment, better education, and home ownership."[4]

3. Reynolds Farley, "Black Families in the U.S.: Demographic Trends and Consequences," as quoted in Heather L. Ross and Isabel V. Sawhill, *Time of Transition: The Growth of Families Headed by Women* (Washington, D.C., 1975), p. 77; Robert L. Crain and Carol Sachs Weisman, *Discrimination, Personality, and Achievement: A Survey of Northern Blacks* (New York, 1972), p. 735; Stanley Lieberson and Christy A. Wilkinson, "A Comparison between Northern and Southern Blacks Residing in the North," *Demography*, v. 13 (May 1976), p. 211.

4. Demetri B. Shimkin, Gloria Jean Louie, and Dennis A. Frate, "The Black Ex-

The black urban future belongs to the grandchildren of the Bidwells and others like them who constitute an increasingly large proportion of the black urban population. The percentage of black Bostonians born in the South has fallen from one half in 1900 to one quarter in 1970.[5] The number of third-generation blacks in late nineteenth-century Boston was too small to support any meaningful conclusions, but preliminary evidence from contemporary studies suggests that the third generation resembles the second. From an analysis of the 1960 census, sociologists examined differences in the rates of black youngsters being kept back one grade in school. Third-generation girls and boys were just as likely to fail a grade as second-generation youths.[6] Third-generation black Bostonians living in Roxbury were interviewed by psychiatrist Robert Coles and also by a team of social psychologists, headed by Robert Rosenthal, interested in the effect of ghetto education on the employment prospects of black youth. Coles talked with 10-year-old Billy, who was bused to a suburban school. Billy's father was a postal worker and his grandmother a migrant from South Carolina who had lived in Boston most of her life. Billy wanted to be a lawyer and Coles was struck by how he described his plans: to "do more, get further, go higher, climb up there," as Coles says, those familiar American ways of speaking.[7] Billy made clear, with a keen sense of irony, that his parents wanted exactly what his discontented suburban friends already had and that they wanted even more success for him. Billy's father told him to "learn how the white kids think because they're the bosses."[8] Still Billy wanted to learn from whites, not mimic them, to "keep our eyes on the white people, we can learn some of their tricks and then once we've learned them so that we can really use them, then they'll have a fight on their hands."

Another third-generation Roxbury youth, interviewed by the Rosenthal team, was not as ambitious as Billy. In junior high school, Andy Garrison was a truant and, on his sixteenth birthday, he had dropped out of school and entered a carpentry apprenticeship pro-

tended Family: Rural Institution/Urban Adaptation," in Demetri B. Shimkin, Edith Shimkin, and Dennis A. Frate, eds., *The Extended Family in U.S. Black Societies* (Urbana, 1978), p. 77.

5. U.S. Bureau of the Census, *1970 Census of the Population*, v. I, Part 23 (Washington, D.C., 1973), p. 375.

6. Lieberson and Wilkinson, "Comparison between Northern and Southern Blacks," pp. 199–224.

7. Robert Coles, M.D., *The South Goes North: Volume III of Children of Crisis* (Boston, 1967), p. 94.

8. Ibid., p. 95.

gram. The job required him to attend training classes in South Boston, but he stopped going soon after he started, and he eventually quit his job. At 20 Andy had been put on probation for shoplifting and had been out of work as much as he had been employed. He had taken several carpentry jobs off and on, but each time he stopped going to work when he saw no training was being offered or when the cold weather came. At 13 Andy had wanted to be a chemist and by 20 he wanted only a job that meant he could leave at "five-thirty, come home, eat, rest for about an hour, take a ride."[9]

Which of these two youths is most representative of third-generation black Bostonians, Billy—who is on the way to becoming a professional—or Andy—whose path leads only to less rewarding jobs? Billy still has the high aspirations of his father, and his record in the suburban school indicates no foreseeable blocks to future success, unlike Andy who has steadily lowered his horizons. Despite the optimism in one report and the pessimism in the other, it is still too early to tell what the future will bring these boys. The history of the third-generation in a sense completes the process of black assimilation up to the present today. It has already been established that the assimilation of the blacks was unlike that of white immigrants (Boston's Irish). Blacks were the only group where a generation of city residence gave them the American dream with so little of its economic reality. That unique result helped to mold a distinctive family and community life. Since the process of assimilation among urban blacks is without precedent in American ethnic history, the question is not whether to intervene, but where. Should policies of greater training and economic opportunities be offered to the second generation, to Billy's and Andy's parents, or directed toward the third generation? A more precise measure of the economic progress (or lack of progress) of the third generation can assist in choosing between these alternatives.

We have moved too quickly from the world of Peter Randolph and Walter J. Stevens to the employment prospects of these two youths, without pausing to consider all the intervening changes in the last 70 years. Has there been, as Gilbert Osofsky claimed, "an unending and tragic sameness" to the black urban condition, or are Andy and Billy operating in a different world than that of the late nineteenth century? One of the most far-reaching chances has been the emergence of a multi-block modern ghetto. Many ghetto residents

9. Robert Rosenthal, Bernard Bruce, Faith Dunne, and Florence Ladd, *Different Strokes: Pathways to Maturity in the Boston Ghetto* (Boulder, Colorado, 1976), p. 171.

without a car have difficulties in reaching suburban offices and factories. A modern ghetto youth can walk for blocks and never meet a
white person, so isolated has the ghetto become.

Despite changes like these, a strong case can be made that today's ghetto dwellers are just as trapped between their American
dreams and their poverty-level realities as the urban blacks of a
century ago. In *Tally's Corner*, Elliot Liebow furnished a portrait of
the streetcorner men in Washington, D.C.'s ghetto during the 1960s.
Tally and his friends moved between jobs, taking higher-paying work
in the summer pouring cement and during the winter falling back
into employment as dishwashers, bus boys, or parking lot attendants.
They moved as well into the neighborhood of the Carry-out shop and
quickly disappeared a few months later. The central feature of ghetto
life, as Liebow sees it, is transiency: "the instability of employment,
family and friend relationships, and the general transient quality of
daily life." The awareness of a trouble-filled future often "results in a
constant readiness to leave, to make it, to get out of town, and
discourages the man from sinking roots in the world he lives in."[10]
These menial workers viewed jobs as a source of prestige, pride, and
self-respect, and, by these standards, they perceived their own jobs as
lacking. As a response to failure, they devised "public fictions," accounts given to each other of the sources of their failure that thinly
papered over their pain. Liebow argues that economic circumstances—insecurity of employment, high job turnover, low wages—
had "important consequences for how the man sees himself, and is
seen by others; and these, in turn, importantly shape his relations
with family members, lovers, friends, and neighbors."[11] Although
the class of black poor is no longer as large as it once was, the same
circumstances of poverty life could be found a hundred years
earlier—before the ghetto had formed. The evidence of historical
continuity of this kind does not suggest, however, that some defeatist
culture was being passed on from parents to children, but rather that
the same sequence of urbanization and economic inequality kept
occurring, generation after generation.

The statistical observations of contemporary research back up

10. Elliot Liebow, *Tally's Corner: A Study of Negro Streetcorner Men* (Boston, 1967),
p. 70. Roger D. Abrahams observed the same process of instability in Philadelphia's
black ghetto: "One of the strangest feelings for someone moving into a ghetto from a
bourgeois background is the way in which friends will disappear for days, months,
even years, without saying good-bye, and will drift back with a minimum of comment
and explanation . . . [*Positively Black* (Englewood Cliffs, New Jersey, 1970), p. 121]."
11. Ibid., p. 21.

Liebow's streetcorner informants. Aspirations of city-bred blacks are high, far higher than those of southern blacks. A national survey of a representative sample of black workers in 1966 explored attitudes toward work. Northerners were more interested in "liking the job" than the wages it offered. Asked if they would quit work if offered enough money to live on, more northern-educated blacks than southern educated said yes. The surveyers interpreted these responses as evidence of "low work attachment,"[12] although it seems more likely that mainstream values are being elicited, a willingness to work but at a job with prestige and a chance for advance, an unwillingness to work at dead-end and demeaning jobs, the kind of jobs most of these men currently held. The other part of the black urban dilemma, inequality of income, is also as much a part of the urban present as of its past. In 1970 black median per capita income in Boston stood at 66% of that of whites, an 8 percentage point *decrease* from the previous decade,[13] despite a decade of social revolution. Of course, black urban life has changed in many ways. Rates of illegitimacy have soared, the ghetto has expanded, and the burden of large families, drug addiction and violent crime has increased in the last 70 years. At the same time, there are also more college graduates and members of the middle class, dramatic increases in life expectancy and in occupational attainment. It is not my intention to furnish a list of the gains and losses in the black urban past. My goal has been to understand the fundamental process that has contributed to the sameness in black urban life, and that process has been and remains the discrepancy between high aspirations and low incomes, and the effects of that discrepancy on the personal and family relations of the black poor.

It is abundantly clear that the pattern of contemporary black poverty derives not from the handicaps of slavery or of southern life, but from the disabilities that flow from the employment opportunities available to black men and women in northern cities. Contemporary programs necessary to uproot these inequalities also must be centered there, rather than in the rural South. Of course, one way to resolve the discrepancy between high aspirations and low incomes

12. Avril V. Adams and Gibert Nestel, "Interregional Migration, Education, and Poverty in the Urban Ghetto: Another Look at the Black–White Earnings Differential," *The Review of Economics and Statistics*, v. LVIII, No. 2 (May 1976), pp. 156–166.

13. Leon H. Mayhew, *Law and Equal Opportunity: A Study of the Massachusetts Commission against Discrimination* (Cambridge, 1968), p. 50; U.S. Bureau of the Census, *1970 Census of the Population*, v. I, Part 23 (Washington, D.C., 1973), pp. 363, 405, 420, 460.

is to lower aspirations, for the poverty-level class of blacks to become content with their lot. A more ready acceptance of poverty would also fit with the need for unskilled labor with "the values, the aspirations, and the psychic make-up that low-skill jobs required" to perform the kind of work that most Americans are willing to do.[14] Inflation in the 1970s tended to lower the real incomes of even middle-class whites. It may well come true that the American standard of living in the future will be far less lavish than it once was. But the question is not what the market basket of the future will contain, but where in the coming downward slide, one group will bear more than its fair share of the costs, and realize less than its fair share of the advantages.

The other means of resolving the problem of racial poverty is to raise incomes commensurate with aspirations—the offer of a decent wage, a secure job, and a promise for advancement—to continue in the direction of removing barriers in the way of equal access to education, job-related skills, employment, and promotion. In the 1960s jobs were plentiful and it appeared easy to achieve greater equity simply by increasing the number of new openings; in the 1970s levels of unemployment and inflation soared, and it was necessary to consider more equitable policies of scarcity rather than of plenty. It had also become clear by then that the creation of new opportunities was not going to eliminate the racial gap in income; that if blacks were to gain, some whites would have to lose. Without any changes in the skills or education of the black work force, integration in the job market would inevitably lower the income of the white working class and, if black educational attainment was increased, of the middle classes as well. In the 1970s a vocal segment of the Boston white working class fought the long overdue advent of court-ordered school desegregation, in part to prevent this black economic advance, and interest groups also lobbied against affirmative action programs being implemented by corporations and universities. Recent history also indicates that the initiative for advance comes from blacks themselves and from an interracial coalition, and while much of the momentum of the 1960s has slowed, it has not completely come to a halt. The road ahead will be difficult, and there are many who have become discouraged along the way, but others will continue the effort and new voices will be heard. The task remains what it has always been, to achieve the dual goals of economic and racial justice, and thereby realize the promise of the American city for blacks.

14. Elliot Liebow, *Tally's Corner*, p. 227.

APPENDIX A

SELECTED TABLES

TABLE A-1
Black Population of Boston, 1830–1970

Year	Black population	Decadal rate of increase	Blacks, as a percentage of all Bostonians
1830	1,875		3.1
1840	1,988	6	2.4
1850	1,999	1	1.5
1860	2,261	13	1.3
1870	3,496	55	1.4
1880	5,873	68	1.6
1890	8,125	38	1.8
1900	11,591	43	2.1
1910	13,564	17	2.0
1920	16,350	20	2.2
1930	20,574	26	2.6
1940	23,679	15	3.1
1950	40,457	70	5.0
1960	63,165	57	9.1
1970	104,596	66	16.3

Sources: U.S. Census, 1830–1970.

TABLE A-2
Number of Black Lifetime Migrants and Rank of Their City Destinations by State of Origin, 1870

	Origin											
	Virginia		Maryland		District of Columbia		Pennsylvania		New York		Nova Scotia and New Brunswick	
Destination	Rank[a]	N	Rank	N	Rank	N	Rank	N	Rank	N	Rank	N
Boston and Cambridge	9	971	7	289	6	74	5	147	5	169	1	287
New Haven	32	74	14	95	23	15	14	69	1	247	8	2
Providence	10	298	6	314	5	117	9	103	14	103	5	6
New York and Brooklyn	7	1,444	4	965	3	169	1	680	—	—	2	17
Philadelphia	4	2,055	2	2,622	2	178	—	—	3	192	3	9
Baltimore	3	2,485	—	—	4	101	4	162	6	162	—	0
Washington, D.C.	1	14,287	1	9,272	—	—	3	174	4	174	4	8
New Orleans	2	4,832	3	1,160	1	186	12	79	16	79	8	2
St. Louis	5	1,656	10	175	15	30	2	210	2	210	—	0
Memphis	6	1,464	13	113	18	21	26	12	27	12	—	0
Mobile	8	1,254	9	188	15	30	29	7	28	10	—	0
Cincinnati	10	794	15	92	13	36	10	101	15	101	—	0

Source: U.S. Bureau of the Census, *Population*, v. 1 (Washington, D.C., 1872), Table VIII, pp. 380–391.
[a] Based on 50 city destinations.

TABLE A-3
Racial Differences in Wage Distributions, Boston, 1900

weekly wages ca. 1900[a] (dollars)	Percentage of total employed workers		
	Blacks	Irish immigrants	Children of immigrants
MALES			
8–12	76	46	34
13–16	4	15	23
17–20	1	9	11
21+	1	2	2
Unknown	16	28	28
Total	4,510	58,122	47,732
FEMALES			
2–5	54	38	13
6–7	22	6	3
8–10	2	10	19
11–12	1	6	13
13–16	4	3	3
Unknown	27	37	45
Total	2,275	26,757	22,078

Sources: U.S. Bureau of the Census, Special Report, *Occupations at the Twelfth Census* (Washington, D.C., 1904), Table 43, pp. 494–499; Massachusetts Bureau of Statistics of Labor, *Thirty-fifth Annual Report* (Boston, 1905), p. 15; Massachusetts Bureau of Statistics of Labor, *Thirty-third Annual Report*, pp. 120–124.

[a] Males: jobs paying $8–$12 were clerk, copyist, drayman, locomotive engineer, fireman, hackman, janitor, laborer, packer, porter, printer, shipper, tailor, teamster, typist, waiter; those paying $13–$16 were baker, bartender, boilermaker, carpenter, confectioner, electrician, engineer, gas works employee, iron and steel worker, machinist, painter, paperhanger, pattern maker, policeman, salesman, stonecutter, surveyor, watchman; jobs paying $17–$20 included agent, blacksmith, bookkeeper, engraver, plasterer, plumber, and upholsterer; those paying $21 and more were commercial travelers and brick and stone masons.

[b] In women's jobs, messengers, errand girls, servants, and waitresses received $2–$5; laundresses, $6; clerks, janitresses, and saleswomen, $8–$10; bookkeepers, packers, and typists, $11–$12; carpet factory operatives, housekeepers, and stewards, $13–$16.

OCCUPATIONAL CLASSIFICATION

In this study I seek to explain why so many black workers entered menial jobs and remained confined to them. It is therefore useful to show how menial jobs were defined and to review some of their salient features.

Most students of American economic history have employed some variant on the occupational classification system devised by Alba M. Edwards, a census statistician in the 1930s. In *The Other Bostonians*, Stephan Thernstrom devised his own scheme, which was roughly similar to Edwards', and I have used his, with only minor changes.[1] I assigned apprentices to skilled rather than semi-skilled status based on the occupational group they planned to enter after completion of their training. Because of their meager wages, newsboys and messengers were considered menials rather than clerical or sales employees. Barbers, who served a brief apprenticeship, belonged as skilled rather than semiskilled workers. Barbering also represented a route to upward mobility for the man or woman who opened a small shop. Perhaps by the early twentieth century the trade had declined in status sufficiently to be moved down a notch, but, in this period, barbers were still regarded as craftsmen.

Each of the occupations held by Boston blacks was then assigned to one of six ranks, again roughly similar to Thernstrom's categories.

1. Stephan Thernstrom, *The Other Bostonians: Poverty and Progress in the American Metropolis, 1880–1970* (Cambridge, Massachusetts, 1973), pp. 289–292.

These ranks, from top to bottom, were professional and semiprofessional, business, clerical and sales, skilled, semiskilled, and menial. Thernstrom had another two (major proprietors, managers and professionals) and he separated semiprofessionals from true professionals. The small size of the black professional class made fine distinctions like these unnecessary. The one major difference between the two schemes was in Thernstrom's inclusion of service workers in his category "semiskilled and service," thus mixing factory jobs with menial work. For my purposes, it was far more important to consider menials as a single group, and the jobs that I assigned to this category are listed below:

Menial Jobs

beef carrier	*hod carrier*	*packer*
bootblack	*hostler*	*porter*
choreman	*janitor and janitress*	*sailor*
coachman	*laborer*	*stevedore*
cook	*laundress*	*steward*
domestic servant	*longshoreman*	*waiter and waitress*
drayman and hackman	*meat carver*	*watchman*
elevator operator	*messenger*	*whitewasher*
gardener	*newsboy*	

The assumption made throughout this book is that confinement to menial work was associated with poverty-level income and that movement out of menial work, even if only to become a factory operative, represented economic progress. This assumption seems warranted, based on what we know about the prestige and wages of menials. The disadvantages of menial jobs were legion: high job turnover, small chances for advance, limited on-the-job training, and, especially in service, close supervision by the employer. Menial work, as I have noted in Chapter VI, was the lowest in pay: The typical menial workingman earned $8 to $10 a week, whereas the skilled or clerical worker made about $10 to $18 a week. The average female domestic around the turn of the century could expect to receive a weekly wage of $5; it seems likely that the few black women employed as bookkeepers or schoolteachers made on the average about $3 or $4 a week more. Kelly Miller was fond of saying that the Negro rarely finds work above the cellar; in a figurative sense, he was correct because in pay and prestige these jobs were the bottom of Boston's occupational scale.

RELIABILITY OF THE CENSUS

Among all the sources of population data in this study, the greatest interpretative weight has been given to findings derived from the federal manuscript census schedules. Since results are only as good as the data from which they are derived, it is important to examine three topics concerning the "reliability" of the census: (a) the extent of underenumeration, (b) the accuracy of comparisons between blacks and whites, and (c) internal consistencies in the information about blacks.

UNDERENUMERATION

It is well known that, in recent censuses, blacks have been under-counted by as much as 10 or 12%.[1] How large was the underenumera-

1. Leon Pritzker and N. D. Rothwell, "Procedural Difficulties in Taking Past Censuses in Predominantly Negro, Puerto Rican and Mexican Areas," in David Heer, ed., *Social Statistics and the City: Report of a Conference Held in Washington, D.C., June 23, 1967* (Cambridge, 1968), pp. 71–73; Jacob S. Siegel, "Completeness of Coverage of the Nonwhite Population in the 1960 Census and Current Estimates and Some Implications," in Heer, *Statistics and the City*, pp. 13–54; Jacob S. Siegel and Melvin Zelnik, "An Evaluation of Coverage in the Census Population by Techniques of Demographic Analysis and by Composite Methods," *Proceedings of the Social Statistics Section, American Statistical Association* (1966), pp. 71–85; Ansley J. Coale and Norfleet W. Rives, Jr., "A Statistical Reconstruction of the Black Population of the United States, 1880–1970: Estimates of True Numbers by Age and Sex, Birth Rates, and Total Fertility," *Population Index*, v. 39 (1973), pp. 3–36.

TABLE C-1

**Enumeration of Boston Blacks in the Manuscript Census
Schedules, 1880, and the Boston City Directory, 1880**

		N
(a)	Present in Census and City Directory and Census	183
(b)	Present in City Directory but not in Census	108
(c)	Present in Census but not in City Directory	5690
	Likelihood of absence from both Census and City Directory, $(b \times c)/a$	3358
	Degree of Census underenumeration	33%

tion of Boston blacks in the census a century ago? One method of estimating census underenumeration, often employed by demographers, is to compare the completeness of underenumeration in the census with a second source. For the comparison, I used the Boston city directory, a yearly alphabetical listing of employed adult Bostonians, mostly males, which tended to include those who had lived in Boston for a year or two.[2] Because race was not designated in the directory, a cumbersome procedure had to be devised to locate listings of blacks. This involved tracing the names of blacks from the 1870 census to the 1880 city directory and attempting to locate this linked group in the census for the same year. Of the 291 blacks found in the 1880 Boston city directory, 183 were also in the federal manuscript census. The probability of being missed in both directory and census can be estimated with the procedure devised by two statisticians, C. Sekar and W. Deming. The steps involved, reproduced in Table C-1,[3] indicate that the 1880 census underenumerated Boston's black population by a third. This figure is much higher than similar estimates for whites. Peter Knights, using roughly similar methods, estimated that the census underenumerated Boston whites in 1860 and again in 1890 by 8%.[4] If his figures are correct, then the underenumeration of blacks was about one quarter more than for whites.

ACCURACY OF BLACK–WHITE COMPARISONS

In my research, Boston blacks and Irish are often compared, and the reliability of that comparison depends on the degree of accuracy

2. Peter R. Knights, "City Directories as Aids to Ante-Bellum Urban Studies: A Research Note," *Historical Methods Newsletter*, v. II (September 1969), pp. 1–10.

3. C. Changra Sekar and W. Edwards Deming, "On a Method of Estimating Birth and Death Rates and the Extent of Under-Registration," *Journal of the American Statistical Association*, v. 44 (March 1949), pp. 101–115.

4. Peter R. Knights, *The Plain People of Boston* (New York, 1971), p. 147.

in the information about each. Analyses of recent censuses indicate that blacks are more likely than whites to round off their ages to a digit ending in zero or five.[5] With relative ease, it is possible to detect a kind of similar internal inaccuracy in a single census, misreporting of age.[6] From year to year, ages fall in a normal distribution: There are about the same number of 18- as 19-year-olds. The method for detecting abnormal clumping by age is to consider each age bracket in relation to its neighbors. The "age heaping index," reported in Table C-2, is a summary of variations in each of the age brackets. It is computed by dividing the number of persons in each 5-year bracket by those on either side of it, summing each of these, and dividing by the total number of age brackets. If all was in order, the resulting mean should equal 1.0. This mean, divided by its standard deviation, gives a "coefficient of variance," a summary measure that can be used to compare the extent of variance in the means among blacks, natives, and immigrants.[7] Among Boston men, reported age was most accurate for blacks, followed closely by native whites, and somewhat farther back by foreign whites. For women, reported age was on a par for black and native white women, but way off the mark for immigrant women. Thus, comparisons of Boston black, native, and immigrant men are reasonably accurate but those of women are less so.

INCONSISTENCIES IN THE DATA ABOUT BLACKS

It is absolutely crucial for this study that someone with a Virginia birthplace was actually born in the South rather than in the

5. Reynolds Farley, "The Demographic Rates and Social Institutions of the Nineteenth-Century Negro Population: A Stable Population Analysis," *Demography*, v. 2 (1965), pp. 386–398.

6. Other researchers have used two other methods for detecting underenumeration, neither of which seems satisfactory for my purpose. One relies on demographic inferences about life expectancy to detect inaccuracy in the size of age cohorts from one census to the next and assumes an immigration-free population. That claim is reasonable for the country as a whole, but not for any single community. Another method, proposed by John Sharpless and Ray Shortridge, is to infer from the inaccuracy in age reporting the extent of underenumeration in the census. The idea is that detecting one kind of internal error, in age reports, suggests the existence of another. But it seems likely that the reasons for inaccuracy are different for each. In the former, the problem is the respondent's misreport and in the latter the census taker's laxity, due to lack of will or wariness to enter certain neighborhoods. It seems then that in the study of a single community, filled with migrants, the best method is to determine underenumeration based on comparison of two different sources. John Sharpless and Ray Shortridge, "Biased Underenumeration in Census Manuscripts: Methodological Implications," *Journal of Urban History*, v. 1, No. 4 (August 1975), pp. 409–439.

7. Ibid.

TABLE C-2
Summary Measures Derived from the Age Heaping Index
for Native Whites, Blacks, and Foreign Whites, 1880

	Males		
	(a) Mean	(b) Standard deviation	(a/b) Coefficient of variance
Native whites	1.01	.338	33.5
Blacks	1.03	.235	22.8
Foreign whites	1.11	.289	26.0
	Females		
	(a) Mean	(b) Standard deviation	(a/b) Coefficient of variance
Native whites	1.06	.314	29.6
Blacks	1.09	.325	29.8
Foreign whites	1.58	.927	58.7

Source: Carroll D. Wright, *The Social, Commercial and Manufacturing Statistics of Boston* (Boston, 1882), pp. 94–95.

North. Any population as poor, transient, and visible as blacks could be expected to be wary of the stranger who came to the door (even as in Boston, where one of the enumerators was black). One kind of error has already been suggested in Chapter VI: Black women, who were deserted or separated, sometimes claimed to be widowed. But there is still a substantial difference between healthy skepticism about some information and wholesale cynicism about all of it. One method for detecting the internal error in the census was to check the accuracy of the information given at two censuses: This method worked for the fixed parts of the individual's identity, color and date of birth (recorded in the census as age), but not the variant characteristics of occupation and address. The only difficulty—and it is a major one—is deciding whether inaccuracies could instead derive from errors in record linkage. A positive linkage depended on several factors considered together rather than any single one, and discrepancy in any single variable did not preclude making a positive identification. The positive linkage of Robert Lee from the 1880 to the 1900 census indicates a rather typical case of some misinformation; his age and his wife's age were discrepant. Nevertheless, it seems highly likely to me that Robert Lee in the 1900 census is the same individual enumerated two decades earlier (see tabulation below) and that information from census linkages between 1880 and 1900 can be used to determine internal inconsistencies in the data about blacks.

	1880	1900
Name	Robert Lee	Robert Lee
Age	32	50
Place of birth	South Carolina	South Carolina
Color	Mulatto	Black[a]
Occupation[b]	Waiter	Steward
Ward[b]	10	12
Address[b]	7 Shawmut Ave.	362 Northampton
Marital status	Married	Married
Wife's name	Catharine Lee	Catharine Lee
Number of years married	n.a.	22
Wife's birthplace	Massachusetts	Massachusetts
Wife's color	Mulatto	Black[a]
Wife's age	37	42
Wife's literacy	Literate	Literate
Wife's occupation[b]	Keeping house	No occupation

[a] All Afro-Americans in 1900 designated as "black."
[b] Not used as a means of making a positive linkage.

The comparison of the accuracy of information about age, color, literacy, and birthplace is reproduced in Table C-3. Boston census takers in 1900 designated all mulattoes as black, a kind of color blindness uncharacteristic of the age, although two and three decades earlier they had made this distinction. In the linkage of names between the 1870 and 1880 census, a chameleon-like color change had occurred; mulattoes were turning into blacks and blacks into mulattoes in one quarter of all cases. Since error in both directions was common, inaccuracies tend to cancel each other out, but the degree of variation here suggests extreme caution in making comparisons of mulattoes and blacks. Reports of age were reasonably accurate and only departed from a within-3-year age range in 14% of the cases. Birthplace, the most fundamental variable in this study, was off the mark only 3% of the time, and, when it was inaccurate, the mistakes were often minor: Maryland migrants became Virginians, for example, and there was little wholesale changing of regions. Literacy information was also quite consistent across censuses: only 3% of blacks went from literate to illiterate, or from illiterate to literate.

TABLE C-3
Discrepancies in Information from the Federal Manuscript
Census Schedules of Boston, 1880–1900[a]

(I) Color	
Mulatto in 1870, mulatto in 1880	209
Black in 1870, black in 1880	487
Mulatto in 1870, black in 1880	110
Black in 1870, mulatto in 1880	122
(II) Date of birth (reported age)	
Less than 3 years	923
3–5 years	83
6–10 years	47
11–15 years	14
16–20 years	5
21–25 years	2
(III) Literacy	
Literate in 1880, literate in 1900	792
Illiterate in 1880, illiterate in 1900	77
Literate in 1880, illiterate in 1900	17
Illiterate in 1880, literate in 1900	18
(IV) Place of birth	
Same birthplace	1165
Different birthplace, but same region	23
Different birthplace, different region	14

[a] Total number of observations differ for each variable because of missing information. The largest number of missing observations is found in the literacy category, because so many of the persisters in 1900 were children under 11 in 1880, with no designation of literacy in 1880.

IMPLICATIONS OF THE FINDINGS

A very large group of Boston blacks was missing from the census. Were they, as contemporary follow-up studies have shown, the transients, the poorest of the poor? There is no way of telling, but the sheer fact of their existence does not present any major challenge to the findings reported here. Many of my results derive from comparing blacks born in different regions. Only in the unlikely event that the rankings were reversed in the missing group would these findings stand in need of substantial revision. Another set of findings, about the higher status of Boston's Irish than blacks, is only strengthened by the degree of differential underenumeration. We know that blacks were much more underenumerated than whites, and its seems likely that, to a lesser degree, they were more underenumerated than the Irish. Still, it is clear that any contrast between the stable group of Boston's Irish and blacks tends to minimize the differences that could be found in a comparison of the true populations. Finally, the analysis of age heaping indices indicates that the census provided reasonably accurate information about Boston's blacks, probably somewhat more so than would be true in a census-based study of Boston's Irish or Italians. If data about the missing third, presumably the bottom third, could have been added, then the findings about the extent of racial poverty and inequality in Boston would only appear in more dramatic outline.

BLACK FEMALE-HEADED HOUSEHOLDS, 1850–1925

It seems likely that, if poverty, sickness, sterility, and urban life contributed to the growth of female-headed households in Boston, this should have been true as well in other cities. However, the kind of detailed evidence necessary to reach this conclusion, longitudinal data derived from tracing names from one census to the next, was unavailable elsewhere. A less detailed inquiry, similar in intent if not in the quality of the information, was designed using published information from the federal census and some unpublished data.

Rates of female-headed households in four southern and seven northern cities between 1850 and 1925 are presented in Table D-1. (The comparison was restricted to comparable studies that excluded single and childless households.) Far from a repetition of the conclusions reached about Boston blacks, it turned out that economic status had little or no impact on the rate of female-headed households. One economic indicator, the rate of black unemployment, was available only in Boston and Evansville, Indiana, a Midwest market town with a substantial black population. Despite the similarity in the level of black unemployment in both locales, the rate of female-headed households was 7 points higher in Evansville than in Boston. More complete evidence about the rate of black married women working reinforced the same noneconomic sequence, no direct relationship between the prevalence of black women employed and the proportion of female-headed households. Although some studies produced the expected result, the exceptions were numerous: St. Johns, New

TABLE D-1

Demographic and Economic Correlates of Black Female-Headed Households, 1850–1925

Locale and date	Percentage of female-headed households	Sex ratio	Percentage of black men employed in menial jobs	Rate of married women employed	Rate of unemployment among black workers	Child/ woman ratio
Philadelphia						
1850	23	68[a]	78			340
1880	26	66	79	22		290
Mobile						
1860	44		44			
1880	34	73	82	35[b]		262[b]
Brooklyn						
1860	33		71			
Boston						
1870	26	108	84	6		271
1880	24	108	84	16	8	281
St. Johns, N.B.						
1871	35	59	69	4		
Evansville, Ind.						
1880	31	106	91	11	10	175
Beaufort						
1880	36		60	20[c]		
Natchez						
1880	40		73	17[c]		

Richmond					
1880	34	70	80	35[b]	262[b]
1900	38	77			263
New York City					
1860	39	69			
1905	33	98	86	35[a]	197[d]
1925	30	98	72	46	205[e]
Buffalo					
1905	39	76	76		201
1925	14	48	48		206[e]

Sources: Theodore Hershberg, "Free-Born and Slave-Born Blacks in Antebellum Philadelphia," in Stanley L. Engerman and Eugene D. Genovese, eds., *Race and Slavery in the Western Hemisphere: Quantitative Studies* (Princeton, 1975), pp. 395–426; Frank Furstenberg, Jr., Theodore Hershberg, and John Modell, "The Origins of the Female-Headed Black Family: The Impact of the Urban Experience," *Journal of Interdisciplinary History*, v. VI (Autumn 1975), pp. 211–233; Herbert G. Gutman and Laurence A. Glasco, "The Negro Family, Household and Occupational Structure, 1855–1925, with Special Emphasis on Buffalo, New York, but including Comparative Data from New York, New York, Brooklyn, New York, Mobile, Alabama, and Adams County, Mississippi," unpublished paper presented at the Yale Conference on Nineteenth-Century Cities, November 1968; U.S. Manuscript Census Schedules, Boston, 1870 and 1880; Canadian Census, 1871, Manuscript Census Schedules for St. Johns, New Brunswick, 1871; Darrell Bingham, "The Black Family in Vanderburgh County, Indiana, in 1880," forthcoming, *Indiana Magazine of History.*

[a] For the population aged 15–44.

[b] A seven-city average (for Atlanta, Charleston, Mobile, New Orleans, Norfolk, Richmond, and Savannah) from Claudia Goldin, "Female Labor Force Participation: The Origin of Black and White Differences, 1870 and 1880," *Journal of Economic History*, v. 37 (March 1977), Table 4, p. 95.

[c] An estimate, based on dividing the number of married women employed as domestics or laundresses by the number of husband–wife households and correcting for the proportion of black women employed in these occupations. Data for the estimate were taken from Herbert G. Gutman, *The Black Family in Slavery and Freedom, 1750–1925* (New York, 1976), pp. 483, 487.

[d] For 1900.

[e] For 1920.

Brunswick, Evansville, Beaufort, and Natchez, where the rate of black married women employed was rather low, while the rate of female-headed households was high. The results for Boston blacks would lead to a third economic expectation, a higher proportion of female-headed households in conjunction with a higher percentage of black men employed in menial labor. But Table VI-8 reveals that the direct economic response to low wages for black men appeared only in some cities but not in others. A final contributory factor found to be of importance in Boston was childlessness. Outside of Boston, no city-based measures of the rate of childlessness were available, and so for the purposes of comparison a general indicator of fertility, the child/woman ratio, was substituted. It seemed likely that the lower the ratio, the higher the proportion of female-headed households, but every percentage in the expected direction was balanced by an exception. Relatively high fertility in Mobile or Richmond was accompanied by the common occurrence of male-absent households, and relatively low fertility among Buffalo blacks went along with a low proportion of such households. All that can be decided based on these results is that no clear intercity pattern has emerged, either to negate or to confirm the Boston findings.

A methodological problem may explain this failure to replicate. The results for Boston were based on a systematic comparison of individuals, while these intercity comparisons reported in Table D-1 relied on group characteristics. It may be impossible to detect from city to city the kind of correlates to be uncovered in a finely controlled comparison of individuals, so that, if the sources of desertion and separation in southern as well as other northern cities are to be known, longitudinal tracing, along the lines already performed in Boston, will be needed.

BIBLIOGRAPHIC ESSAY

Since most of the chapters in this book contain extensive biblio-graphic notations on primary and secondary sources, repetition here is unnecessary. I have compiled a selective guide to secondary work for general readers, centered on three topics: histories and contem-porary surveys of nineteenth-century Boston blacks, studies of nineteenth-century Boston, and works on black urbanization in the nineteenth and early twentieth centuries.

HISTORY OF BLACK BOSTONIANS

A general introduction to the history of Boston blacks is John Daniels's *In Freedom's Birthplace: A Study of the Boston Negroes* (Bos-ton, 1914). A valuable social investigation with useful historical ma-terial, it needs to be read as a guide to one Progressive reformer's attitudes about blacks, a mentality which combined beliefs in social ameliorism and racial inferiority. Published as part of a Bicentennial commemorative series, *Black Bostonia* (Boston, 1976) is a useful introductory pamphlet, which reprints some of the 1890's photo-graphs of Herbert Collins, a Boston black photographer. Another useful introductory volume, which also owes its origins to the Bicen-tennial, is William H. Robinson's *Black New England Letters: The Uses of Writings in Black New England* (Boston, 1977). A short pamphlet, emphasizing the changing residential pattern among Boston's blacks, is Rheable M. Edwards and Laura B. Morris, *The Negro in Boston* (Boston, 1964).

Two full-length biographies of black Bostonians are Stephen R. Fox, *The Guardian of Boston: William Monroe Trotter* (New York, 1970) and Edward Farrison, *William Wells Brown* (Chicago, 1969). Adelaide Hill's dissertation, "The Negro Upper Class in Boston: Its Development and Present Social Structure," Harvard University, 1952, is mostly concerned with the upper class in the late 1940s and early 1950s, although it contains interviews with a few community elders who recalled black social life in the late nineteenth century. Two of my previously published articles provide general background about late nineteenth-century black family life. In "The Two-Parent Household: Black Family Structure in Late Nineteenth-Century Boston," *Journal of Social History*, VI, no. 2 (Fall, 1972), pp. 1–31, I found the nuclear family to be the dominant form of black household organization. My study of black working women, "A Mother's Wages: Income Earning Among Married Italian and Black Women, 1896–1911," in Michael Gordon, ed., *The American Family in Social Historical Perspective* (New York, 1978), pp. 490–510, contains material on the history of Cambridge, Massachusetts black working women and their families.

Some of the best material on black social life can be found in the reports of Boston's social reformers. An exceptionally useful contemporary investigation of blacks in Boston and seven other Massachusetts cities in 1900 is "The Social and Industrial Condition of the Negro in Massachusetts," published as the thirty-fourth annual report of the Massachusetts Bureau of Labor (Boston, 1904). John Daniels's "Industrial Conditions Among Negro Men: Boston," *Charities*, XV, no. 1 (October 7, 1905), pp. 35–40, covers much the same ground as in his book, with emphasis on the occupational condition of black workingmen in 1900. All of the social investigations by Robert Woods offer useful remarks in passing about black Bostonians. These include *The City Wilderness: A Settlement House Study by Residents and Associates of the South End House* (Boston, 1899); *Americans in Process: A Settlement Study by the Residents and Associates of the South End House* (Boston, 1902); and a later work, with Albert J. Kennedy, *The Zone of Emergence: Observations of the Lower Middle and Upper Working Class Communities of Boston, 1905–1914* (Cambridge, Mass., 1962), especially useful for its material about Cambridge blacks. Albert Benedict Wolfe's *The Lodging House*

Problem in Boston (Cambridge, 1913) describes the social transformation of the South End in the early twentieth century. Most of the material collected in Frederick A. Bushee's *Ethnic Factors in the Population of Boston* (New York, 1903) was already available in the published volumes of the state census, but, like Daniels, it offers insights into turn-of-the-century attitudes about race and ethnicity.

The antebellum Boston black community has been singled out for special attention because of its important role in challenging northern discrimination and in lending support to Garrisonian abolitionism. A study of the social bases of community activism is provided by James and Lois Horton in *Black Bostonians: Family Life and Community Struggle in the Antebellum North* (New York, 1979). The transmission of activism from one generation to the next is considered in James Horton's "Generations of Protest: Black Families and Social Reform in Antebellum Boston," *New England Quarterly*, XLIX, no. 2 (June, 1976), pp. 242–256. Two dissertations concerning this period are Donald Jacobs, "A History of the Boston Negro from the Revolution to the Civil War," Boston University, 1968, and George A. Levesque, "Black Boston: Negro Life in Garrison's Boston, 1800–1860," State University of New York at Binghamton, 1976. Jacobs evaluated the crucial role of Boston's black community in aiding Garrison in "William Lloyd Garrison's *Liberator* and Boston's Blacks, 1830–1865," *New England Quarterly*, XLIV, no. 2 (June, 1971), pp. 259–277. Leon Litwack surveyed racial discrimination across the North in *North of Slavery: The Negro in the Free States, 1790–1860* (Chicago, 1961).

The struggle of antebellum black Bostonians in establishing their own schools and later in integrating the Boston schools is uncovered in Chapters 7 and 8 of Stanley K. Schultz's *The Culture Factory: Boston Public Schools, 1789–1860* (New York, 1972). Arthur White also analyzed these developments in his dissertation, "Blacks and Education in Antebellum Massachusetts. Strategies for Social Mobility," State University of New York at Buffalo, 1971, and in "The Black Leadership Class and Education in Antebellum Boston," *Journal of Negro Education*, XLII, no 4 (Fall, 1973), pp. 504–515. The lower rate of black than Irish children attending antebellum Boston's public schools is given special attention by Janet Riblett Wilkie in "Social Status, Acculturation and School Attendance in 1850 Boston," *Journal of Social History*, II, no. 2 (Winter, 1977), pp. 179–192. Leonard

Levy and Douglas L. Jones edited a collection of documents about the *Roberts* case of 1854, entitled *Jim Crow in Boston: The Origin of the Separate but Equal Doctrine* (New York, 1974).

In the nineteenth century Boston was one of the country's most segregated cities. The growth of residential segregation in pre-Civil War Boston is analyzed by Leo F. Schnore and Peter R. Knights, "Residence and Social Structure: Boston in the Antebellum Period," in Stephan Thernstrom and Richard Sennett, eds., *Nineteenth Century Cities: Essays in the New Urban History* (New Haven, 1969). Two overviews of the process of Boston ghettoization over more than a century are to be found in Stanley Lieberson, *Ethnic Patterns in American Cities* (New York, 1963) and in Nathan Kantrowitz, "Racial and Ethnic Residential Segregation in Boston, 1830–1970," *Annals of the American Academy of Political and Social Science*, 441 (January, 1979), pp. 41–54.

OTHER HISTORIES OF BOSTON

It has been said that no city's history since Medici Florence has been as much scrutinized as Boston's, and with some unusually excellent results. The classic community history remains Oscar Handlin's *Boston's Immigrants: A Study in Acculturation* (rev. ed. Cambridge, 1959), although his claims that antebellum blacks were far better off than the Irish need to be tempered by reading in the more recent studies by David Ward and James Horton. An overview of population growth and decentralization in antebellum Boston is provided in Peter R. Knight's *The Plain People of Boston, 1830–1860: A Study in City Growth* (New York, 1971). In *The Other Bostonians: Poverty and Progress in an American Metropolis, 1880–1970* (Cambridge, 1973), Stephan Thernstrom revealed the changing occupational and class structure of the city—and, by inference, the nation—and analyzed the history of black occupation segregation over 90 years of Boston's history in his chapter "Blacks and Whites." An earlier version of this chapter with data on the late nineteenth century was Stephan Thernstrom and Elizabeth H. Pleck, "The Last of the Immigrants? A Comparative Analysis of Immigrant and Black Social Mobility in Late Nineteenth-Century Boston," unpublished paper delivered at the annual meeting of the Organization of American Historians, April, 1970.

An important study of Boston's geographical expansion is David Ward's dissertation, "Nineteenth-Century Boston: A Study in the

Role of Antecedent and Adjacent Conditions in the Spatial Aspects of Urban Growth," University of Wisconsin, 1973, and some of this material is conveniently summarized in his article "The Emergence of Central Immigrant Ghettoes in American Cities, 1840–1920," *Annals of the Association of American Geographiers*, 58 (June, 1968), pp. 343–359. Sam Bass Warner, Jr. documented the physical enlargement of the compact seaport city through the development of its *Streetcar Suburbs. The Process of Growth in Boston, 1870–1900* (Cambridge, 1962). Roger Lane's *Policing the City—Boston, 1822–1885* (Cambridge, 1967) considered the growth of an urban and professional police department, as well as the nature of nineteenth-century urban crime. Nathan Huggins discussed upper-class attempts to aid the urban poor in *Protestants Against Poverty: Boston's Charities* (New York, 1970). Barbara Miller Solomon explored Brahmin attitudes toward the immigrants in *Ancestors and Immigrants: A Changing New England Tradition* (Chicago, 1956), and Arthur Mann examined liberal social reform in *Yankee Reformers in the Urban Age* (Cambridge, 1954). Geoffrey Blodgett's *The Gentle Reformers: Massachusetts Democrats in the Cleveland Era* (Cambridge, 1966) examined state and city reform movements. Marvin Lazerson studied the development of public schools from kindergartens to vocational programs in *The Origins of the Urban School: Public Education in Massachusetts, 1870–1915* (Cambridge, 1971).

THE HISTORY OF BLACK URBANIZATION

Books by W.E.B. DuBois, E. Franklin Frazier, St. Clair Drake and Horace Cayton led the way in the study of black urbanization, and remain the classics in the field. The major theme of W.E.B. DuBois's *The Philadelphia Negro: A Social Study* (Philadelphia, 1899; New York, 1967) was the impact of the color line on black opportunity. Having been trained at the University of Chicago's Department of Sociology, E. Franklin Frazier was drawn to consider black urbanization as a social process, which he did in his seminal work, *The Negro Family in the United States* (Chicago, 1939). St. Clair Drake and Horace Cayton changed Frazer's focus on migration, family life, and social problems, by subordinating these topics to the theme of the emergence of a separate city within a city in *Black Metropolis: A Study of Negro Life in a Northern City* (New York, 1945).

Subsequent to the publication of this book, the theme of the making of the ghetto has remained the preoccupation of black urban history. Indeed, the ghetto is considered to be one of the two major environments shaping the black experience, as in August Meier's and Elliot Rudwick's interpretative text, *From Plantation to Ghetto*, third rev. ed. (New York, 1976). A comparative and synthetic work on the growth of the ghetto is Kenneth L. Kusmer's *A Ghetto Takes Shape: Black Cleveland, 1870–1930* (Urbana, 1976). Other invaluable studies include Gilbert Osofsky, *Harlem: The Making of a Ghetto: Negro New York, 1890–1930* (New York, 1963); Allan Spear, *Black Chicago: The Making of a Negro Ghetto, 1880–1920* (Chicago, 1967); Thomas J. Philpott, *The Slum and the Ghetto: Neighborhood Deterioration and Middle-Class Reform, Chicago 1880–1930* (New York, 1978); Constance M. Green, *The Secret City* (Princeton, 1967); and Karl E. Taeuber and Alma F. Taeuber, *Negroes in Cities: Residential Segregation and Neighborhood Change* (Chicago, 1965). Osofsky argued that conditions of ghetto life have remained tragically the same over the last 150 years in "The Enduring Ghetto," *Journal of American History*, LV, no. 2 (September, 1968), pp. 243–255.

Black northward migration was first made a major topic of inquiry by Carter G. Woodson in *A Century of Negro Migration* (Washington, D. C., 1918). The impact of the migration on black community life is given prominence in Seth M. Scheiner's *Negro Mecca: A History of the Negro in New York City, 1865–1920* (New York, 1965). An overview of the Great Migration is offered in Florette Henri's *Black Migration the Movement North, 1900–1920: The Road from Myth to Man* (Garden City, New York, 1976). Nell Irvin Painter documented a dramatic instance of the move out of the South in *Exodusters: Black Migration to Kansas After Reconstruction* (New York, 1977). The effect of the migration on black political power is considered by Ira Katznelson in *Black Men, White Cities: Race, Politics, and Migration in the United States, 1900–1930, and Britain, 1948–1968* (Chicago, 1973).

August Meier noted that discrimination across the North began to increase in the late nineteenth century, affecting black political and economic fortunes. Meier was mainly concerned with the response of black intellectuals and politicians in *Negro Thought in America, 1880–1915: Racial Ideologies in the Age of Booker T. Washington* (Ann Arbor, 1963). David A. Gerber found Ohio race relations deteriorating statewide around the 1890s in *Black Ohio and the Color Line, 1860–1915* (Urbana, 1976), and Howard N. Rabinowitz traced a shift from "exclusion to segregation" in his study of six southern cities, *Race Relations in the Urban South, 1865–1900* (New York, 1977).

Until recently, the late nineteenth century was an unknown

period in black history, a hiatus following decades of abolitionist activism and preceding the Great Migration and the growth of the ghetto. New research in this period has documented a surge of community building amidst continuing inequality, with special emphasis in some books on the effects of Reconstruction. Studies of this period include David Manners Katzman, *Before the Ghetto: Black Detroit in the Nineteenth Century* (Urbana, 1973); John Blassingame, *Black New Orleans, 1860–1880* (Chicago, 1973); and Peter Kolchin, *First Freedom: The Responses of Alabama's Blacks to Emancipation and Reconstruction* (Westport, Conn., 1972). Theodore Hershberg and his associates at the Philadelphia Social History Project have mined the federal manuscript census schedules and excellent surveys of antebellum Philadelphia blacks in their social and demographic histories of blacks in that city. Hershberg and his associates have analyzed economic and residential differences between blacks and immigrants, the growth of female-headed households, the socioeconomic advantages of mulattoes over blacks, and the deteriorating position of blacks in antebellum Philadelphia. Four of these articles are among the selections reprinted in Theodore Hershberg, ed., *Toward the Interdisciplinary History of the City: Work, Space, Family and Group Experience in Nineteenth-Century Philadelphia* (New York, 1979).

SUBJECT INDEX

STUDIES IN SOCIAL DISCONTINUITY

Under the Consulting Editorship of:

CHARLES TILLY   EDWARD SHORTER
University of Michigan   *University of Toronto*

William A. Christian, Jr. Person and God in a Spanish Valley

Joel Samaha. Law and Order in Historical Perspective: The Case of Elizabethan Essex

John W. Cole and Eric R. Wolf. The Hidden Frontier: Ecology and Ethnicity in an Alpine Valley

Immanuel Wallerstein. The Modern World-System: Capitalist Agriculture and the Origins of the European World-Economy in the Sixteenth Century

John R. Gillis. Youth and History: Tradition and Change in European Age Relations 1770 – Present

D. E. H. Russell. Rebellion, Revolution, and Armed Force: A Comparative Study of Fifteen Countries with Special Emphasis on Cuba and South Africa

Kristian Hvidt. Flight to America: The Social Background of 300,000 Danish Emigrants

James Lang. Conquest and Commerce: Spain and England in the Americas

Stanley H. Brandes. Migration, Kinship, and Community: Tradition and Transition in a Spanish Village

Daniel Chirot. Social Change in a Peripheral Society: The Creation of a Balkan Colony

Jane Schneider and Peter Schneider. Culture and Political Economy in Western Sicily

Michael Schwartz. Radical Protest and Social Structure: The Southern Farmers' Alliance and Cotton Tenancy, 1880-1890

Ronald Demos Lee (Ed.). Population Patterns in the Past

David Levine. Family Formations in an Age of Nascent Capitalism

Dirk Hoerder. Crowd Action in Revolutionary Massachusetts, 1765-1780